Athene Series

Feminist Scholarship on Culture and Education

(continued)

FEMICIDE
IN
GLOBAL
PERSPECTIVE

Diana E. H. Russell
Roberta A. Harmes

EDITORS

Teachers College, Columbia University
New York and London

Published by Teachers College Press, 1234 Amsterdam Avenue, New York, NY 10027

The authors gratefully acknowledge permission to reprint the following materials:

Chrystos, There is a Man Without Fingerprints and No More Metaphors. Reprinted from: *Not Vanishing* by Chrystos (Press Gang Publishers, Vancouver, Canada, 1988).

Karen Stout, Intimate Femicide: A National Demographic Overview, *Journal of Interpersonal Violence*, 6(4), pp. 476–485, © 1991 by Sage Publications, Inc. Reprinted by Permission of Sage Publications, Inc.

Rod Skilbeck, The Shroud Over Algeria: Femicide, Islamism and the *Hijab*, *Journal of Arabic Islamic & Middle Eastern Studies*, 2(2), pp. 43–54, © 1995 by Journal of Arabic, Islamic & Middle Eastern Studies. Permission obtained from *Journal of Arabic Islamic & Middle Eastern Studies*.

Shereen W. Mills, Intimate Femicide and Abused Women Who Kill: A Feminist Legal Perspective. Reprinted by Permission of Author.

Charlotte Watts, Susanna Osam, and Everjoice Win, *The Private Is Public: A Study of Violence Against Women in Southern Africa*, pp. 1–66, © 1995 by WiLDAF. Permission obtained from WiLDAF.

European Journal on Criminal Policy and Research, 6, 1998, pp. 75–90, Intimate Femicide in Israel: Temporal, Social, and Motivational Patterns, Simha F. Landau and Susan Hattis Rolef, © Kluwer Academic Publishers. Permission obtained from Kluwer Academic Publishers.

Permission obtained from *Columbia Human Rights Law Review*. Originally published by Sharon K. Hom as Female Infanticide In China: The Human Rights Specter and Thoughts Towards An(other) Vision. 23 *Columbia Human Rights Law Review*, 249 (1992).

Rosemary Gartner, Myrna Dawson, and Maria Crawford, Woman Killing: Intimate Femicide in Ontario, 1974–1994, *Resources for Feminist Research/Documentation sur la Recherche Feministe*, 26(3–4), pp. 151–174, © 1998 by Resources for Feminist Research/Documentation sur la Recherche Feministe. Permission obtained from Resources for Feminist Research/Documentation sur la Recherche Feministe.

Jenny Mouzos, Femicide: An Overview of Major Findings, *Trends & Issues in Crime and Criminal Justice*, No. 124, pp. 1–6, © Australian Institute of Criminology 1999. Permission obtained from the Australian Institute of Criminology.

Library of Congress Cataloging-in-Publication Data
Femicide in global perspective / Diana E. H. Russell and Roberta A. Harmes, editors.
    p. cm.—(Athene series)
  ISBN 0-8077-4048-9 (cloth : alk. paper)—ISBN 0-8077-4047-0 (pbk. : alk. paper)
    1. Women—Crimes against—Cross-cultural studies. 2. Homicide—Cross-cultural studies. 3. Uxoricide—Cross cultural studies. I. Russell, Diana E. H. II. Harmes, Roberta A. III. Series.
  HV6250.4.W65 F464 2001
  364.15'23'082—dc21   00-053271

ISBN 0-8077-4047-0 (paper)
ISBN 0-8077-4048-9 (cloth)

Printed on acid-free paper

Manufactured in the United States of America

08 07 06 05 04 03 02 01   8 7 6 5 4 3 2 1

This book is dedicated to all the victims of femicide and those who have suffered for their loss. It is also dedicated to all the organizations and individuals who are willing to face the reality of femicide, take an active role in raising awareness about it, and engage in actions to combat this most extreme form of violence against women.—*Diana E. H. Russell*

I would like to dedicate this book to the memories of all femicide victims; to my global sisters who fight to create a world free from male violence; to feminist scholar Diana Russell for her dedicated research on femicide; and to Laura X, Director of the National Clearinghouse on Marital and Date Rape, who gave me the opportunity to work with Diana Russell.—*Roberta Harmes*

Contents

Acknowledgments

My greatest debt of gratitude goes to Roberta Harmes for the amount and quality of the work she has done for our book. Although Roberta has helped me with many previous books and numerous articles, this is the first time that we are co-editors. It was her responsibility to locate the articles on femicide by doing exhaustive and continuous searches on and off the Internet. The results of these endeavors can be found in the bibliography at the end of the book, which includes only those works that use the term *femicide*.

In addition, Roberta did most of the work entailed in obtaining permissions to publish or reprint our contributors' works. She also did her usual miraculous job of finding whatever information I needed for the chapters I authored. And she scanned, then edited, all the contributions that had been published before.

Besides the chapters I wrote, I edited some of the contributors' chapters, made the decisions about which articles to include, and had final responsibility for the manuscript.

I am also tremendously indebted to Tammy Gordon for the fabulous editing she did on all my chapters as well as several of the contributors' chapters. She also gave me her assessment of the strengths and weaknesses of many of the articles from which we had to make our selection. Besides Tammy's roles as my editor and adviser, she also located some new articles on femicide that had not materialized in Roberta's searchers. Like Roberta, she always got her work back to me with incredible promptness. I also greatly valued her interest and enthusiasm for the project as well as her emotional support.

I am grateful to Gayle Pitman for her excellent editing assistance on early drafts of some of my chapters, as well as for her very helpful evaluations of some of the articles on femicide we had collected. I was very distressed to lose her valuable assistance when she obtained her Ph.D. and teaching employment.

I would also like to thank Teachers College Press for agreeing to publish this work. I feel particularly lucky to have had acquisitions editor Susan Liddicoat to oversee the publication of this book. She has been wonderful to work with and, like Tammy and Roberta, she has also been unbelievably prompt with all her communications.

I also appreciate the personal support I have received during the preparation of this manuscript from Esther Rothblum and Jeanne Quint. In addition, I am grateful to Jan Dennie for her excellent coding job on the database for Chapter 3 and Marie Schwaim for her assistance with the quantitative analysis for that chapter.

—Diana E. H. Russell

I would like to thank Diana Russell for inviting me to co-edit this volume with her. I am also grateful to Susan Liddicoat for her guidance, patience, and understanding. I particularly want to acknowledge my colleagues at Colorado College: Diane Brodersen, the interlibrary loan coordinator; Robin Satterwhite, the social science librarian; and Leroy Smith, the humanities librarian. Finally, I would like to thank my sister, Sheri Harmes, for her valuable assistance with technical computer problems.

—Roberta Harmes

Preface

It has been exceedingly difficult to decide which articles to exclude in this volume. Following are the criteria we used to select the materials included.

1. The term *femicide* had to be used in more than a token fashion. (A surprising number of articles used the term *femicide* only once, often in the title.) The inclusion of two poems is the only exception to this criterion.
2. The substantive and stylistic quality of the article had to be good or excellent.
3. Preference was given to contributions from non–North American countries.
4. Preference was given to atypical types of femicide. This explains why some excellent articles on intimate partner femicide were excluded.

At first we planned to require that my definition of *femicide* be used, but we reneged on this idea because so many researchers on intimate partner femicides use the term more broadly. Nevertheless, as will become evident shortly, these femicides typically meet my definition of femicide as well.

The bibliography on femicide lists most of the materials in which the term *femicide* was used. Harmes located many of them on the Internet as well as from other reference works. We excluded from our bibliography a few articles that we judged to be worthless, as well as newspaper articles and some brief pieces obtained from the Internet.

Between the time that I submitted the proposal for this anthology to Teachers College Press and the completion of the manuscript, we located several more articles on femicide. Consequently, articles that we had intended to include were sometimes discarded in favor of new ones that we had discovered. Roberta and I want to thank the many authors who kindly gave us permission to publish their articles, including those that we haven't been able to include in this volume. We regret that our page limit necessitated our having to eliminate several excellent articles—sometimes merely because they were too long and/or difficult to excerpt.

We are especially grateful to the contributors who gave us permission to delete sections of their articles and/or to edit them in order to try to accommodate our space limit. I feel particularly embarrassed because my authorship of seven chapters has certainly contributed greatly to the lack of space for the work of other authors. I thought many times of excluding some of my contributions, particularly my chapter on femicidal pornography. However, I decided against it because it is an important subject and so different from the subject matter in the rest of the book.

We also regret having to exclude a chapter entitled "Honor Femicides Among Palestinian Arabs," based on a transcript of a presentation by two Palestinian women at the International Conference on Violence, Abuse, & Citizenship, in Brighton, the United Kingdom, in 1996. We were unable to locate the presenters to request their permission to publish in *Femicide in Global Perspective*. We are distressed about this, because we thought it especially important that a chapter on honor femicides be included in our anthology.

We are hopeful that this anthology will demonstrate to researchers, theoreticians, and activists all over the world the vital importance of using the term *femicide* instead of *homicide*—a term that erases the significance of gender to this most extreme form of violence against women.

Femicide graffiti. (Photograph by Chris Domingo)

There Is a Man Without Fingerprints

Chrystos

who tortures   rapes   murders
Three of us have grown cold under him in six months
The police are testing his semen scraped out
    of our dead vaginas   They have no clues
He attacks with a nylon stocking right inside the door
Those keys dangling from our locks don't speak his name
in the morning   He uses our kitchen knives   wearing gloves
to keep his hands clean
He tortured one of us for eight hours before her death
The coroner knows these things with the precision of our terror
    We show signs of defending ourselves
cut palms   bruised knuckles   He thinks the barrio
is his territory   All of the women lived alone
I live alone   holding a knife of murder in my stomach ready for
    him
I watch the street as I come home with razor eyes ready for him
I kick open my door ready for him
He attacks between 8 and 10 at night   Knew the habits
of the women he's killed   Watching us
from coffee shop windows in cool sips
The police   who don't like to be called pigs
are keeping him under wraps   They say
they don't want us to panic
I only know about him   because a woman police dispatcher
announced him in my History Of Women class
Her words a morgue
This is not a poem   it's a newspaper a   warning written quickly
Always be on guard   ready to kill   to survive
He has no face   He could be   any man
watching you

1

CHAPTER 1

Introduction:
The Politics of Femicide

Diana E. H. Russell

"*How much of this truth can I bear to see and still live unblinded?*"
—Audre Lorde, 1981

"*All instances of sexual terror serve as lessons for* all *women.*"
—Jane Caputi, 1987, p. 47

Public awareness about violence against women has increased dramatically over the last three decades in the United States and many other countries as a result of women's protests. However, despite the extensive newspaper coverage on murders of women by men in the United States—including what appear to be increasing numbers of serial killers who target women and girls—few people seem to register that many of these murders are extreme manifestations of male dominance and sexism. In contrast, many individuals recognize that some of the murders of African Americans, Latinos, Asian Americans, Native Americans, and other people of color are racist, that some of the murders of Jews are anti-Semitic, and that some of the murders of gay men and lesbians are homophobic.

I have chosen the term *femicide*—the killing of females by males *because* they are female—in the hope that naming these crimes will facilitate this recognition. By locating the killing of women within the arena of sexual politics, I reject the popular conception of woman killing as a private and/or a pathological matter. When men murder women or girls, the power dynamics of misogyny and/or sexism are almost always involved (as will be demonstrated in Chapter 3).

Femicides are lethal hate crimes. Although 20 states in the United States have passed legislation that criminalizes hate crimes based on gender and/or sexual orientation, not a single misogynist murder of a woman has been prosecuted as a hate crime, to my knowledge. This failure to utilize gender-based hate crime laws does not apply to other bias-based murders.

Femicide is on the extreme end of a continuum of the sexist terrorization of women and girls. Rape, torture, mutilation, sexual slavery, incestuous and extrafamilial child sexual abuse, physical and emotional battery, and serious cases of sexual harassment are also on this continuum. Whenever these forms of sexist terrorism result in death, they become femicides.

GOALS OF THIS BOOK

One of the major goals of this anthology is to demonstrate the value of conceptualizing *femicide* as the killing of females by males *because* they are female. This is why we include in this volume only those articles in which the term *femicide* is used. We hope that these articles will demonstrate the usefulness of the concept as well as the prevalence and severity of femicide, its global dimensions, and the urgent need to put it on the action agenda. We also hope that it will facilitate a greater acceptance and more widespread usage of this term, especially by feminists. Our more ambitious aspiration is that the term *femicide* will soon be incorporated into the language of all wo/men working in the area of violence against women and that it will subsequently become part of every wo/man's vocabulary.

Because femicide is such a serious and widespread problem throughout the world, bringing the international scope of femicide to readers' attention is another important goal of this volume.

Our concern about femicide does not mean that more women are murdered than men in the United States. On the contrary, many more men are murdered than women in this country, and men are mostly murdered by other men. However, just as white people who murder other white people rarely do so out of hatred for white people, it seems safe to assume that men who murder other men rarely, if ever, do so out of hatred or contempt, or a sense of entitlement, possessiveness, and/or superiority toward other men as a gender. Nor are women who murder men typically motivated by these feelings and attitudes toward men. Most women who kill men are motivated by self-defense.

OBSCURING THE RELEVANCE OF GENDER

Rarely have I encountered such ardent efforts by male researchers and writers to use gender-neutral terminology as when they discuss the subject of women's murder—despite the fact that the vast majority of murders of women are by men. For example, FBI agents Robert Ressler and John Douglas and academician Ann Burgess (1988) state that "*individuals* may kill to engage in sexual activity, dismemberment, mutilation, evisceration, or other activities that have sexual meaning only for the offenders" (p. 141; emphasis added). This formulation erases the fact that these activities are overwhelmingly practiced by males. Similarly, Canadian anthropologist Elliott Leyton (1986) writes in *Hunting Humans*, "In our own society, an increasing number of *people* kill for the pleasure it appears to give them" (p. 63; emphasis added). Leyton would probably find it difficult to name a single woman to whom his statement would apply.

Many writers (particularly males) outside of academia obfuscate gender issues in a similar manner. Following is a police official's description of the projected profile of Seattle, Washington's Green River Killer, who is believed to have murdered about 50 women, most of them prostitutes: "We're looking for an intelligent person [*sic*], a person [*sic*] that might have animosity against women in some way or perhaps has a biblical interpretation toward cleansing women such as baptizing them in the river or whatever" (quoted in Caputi, 1987, p. 112).

The Columbine High School massacre, perpetrated by Eric Harris and Dylan Klebold in Littleton, Colorado, on April 20, 1999 (Hitler's birthday), offers a more recent example. In response to this tragedy, President Bill Clinton, among others, repeatedly described it in gender-neutral terms as reflecting a problem among American "youth" or "kids" or "children" (see, for example, Braun, 1999; Broder, 1999; Federal News Service, 1999; Scottish Media Newspapers Limited, 1999). It would have been more appropriate to refer to *male* youth or young American males. After President Clinton called a summit on "youth violence," this term was then frequently reiterated in the media coverage of this meeting.

Speaking at the summit meeting about the "200,000 dramatized acts of violence and 40,000 dramatized murders that the typical American child had seen by the age of 18," Clinton went on to say: "Kids [*sic*] become attracted to it and more numb to its consequences. As the exposure to violence grows, so in some deeply troubling cases of particularly vulnerable children [*sic*], does the taste for it. We should not be surprised that half the video games a typical seven-grader [*sic*] plays are violent" (Federal News Service, 1999).

President Clinton was not the only one who couched male violence in gender-neutral terms. Many male journalists also used other gender-neutral terms to describe Harris's and Klebold's shootings. For example, one journalist referred to Harris and Klebold as "the teenagers responsible" (Scottish Media Newspapers Limited, 1999), and another referred to what occurred at the school as "violence by teenagers" (Broder, 1999). John Broder also wrote about the "homicidal rage in 'young people'" and "the violent outbursts of adolescents."

Clearly, the fact that is repeatedly erased by these gender-neutral statements is that it is almost always males, not females, who act out in violent ways. Similar gender-neutral statements were made in the media coverage of another mass femicide that took place in Jonesboro, Arkansas, on March 24, 1998, in which four 11- and 12-year-old girls and one woman were killed by two boys. In contrast to the previous examples, freelance writer Trish Wilson (1999) observed that,

> Not one reporter made the connection between two boys brandishing pistols and assault rifles to the wholesale slaughter and injury of girls. Even after it became known that the older boy's girlfriend had recently broken up with him, that he had threatened her, and that she was one of the shooting victims who had survived, the media continued to refuse to make the connection.

Wilson points out that "the most important topic of all has been absent from discussion—femicide, the outright murder of girls." She also emphasizes that two *boys* had engaged in the slaughter of four girls and one woman—"not 'students,' 'people,' or 'classmates,'" or "a teacher."

As the Jonesboro case illustrates, gender-erasing language seems to co-occur with denial that the murders are a manifestation of lethal misogyny. Even in the blatant case of mass femicide in Montreal in December 1989 in which Marc Lépine yelled "You're just a bunch of fucking feminists!" as he fatally shot 14 women students, most journalists and male commentators denied Lépine's misogynist motivation.

Several women contributors to a book on the Montreal mass femicide noted that the mainstream media in Quebec "scrambled to ignore or downplay the significance of the victims being women" and also ignored, ridiculed, or rejected with hostility feminists' assertions that the massacre "was not the isolated act of a madman but a horrifying reflection of misogyny" in Quebecian society (Publisher's note, 1991, p. 9). As soon as it became known that all the victims were women, this mass femicide was "immediately labelled 'inexplicable,' 'incomprehensible'" by the media when "the murderer himself furnished all the evidence necessary to understand what he'd done," according to Armande Saint-Jean (1991, pp. 61–62).

Many male commentators like Yves Lamontagne also tried to depoliticize this mass femicide by maintaining that "This is not a social phenomenon, but an individual gesture carried out by someone who was sick" (cited by Côté, 1991, p. 67). Note the extreme minimization of this devastating crime revealed by the word "gesture," and the gender neutrality reflected in choosing the word "someone" to refer to Marc Lépine.

FEMINIST REACTIONS TO FEMICIDE

Unfortunately, many feminists, including activists against violence against women, also fail to recognize the sexual politics of femicide. Of the many demonstrations and marches against violence against women in which I have participated, only two or three have included femicide or the murder of women in their signs and chants. Given the erasure of femicide by many feminists, we can hardly be too surprised that nonfeminists fail to recognize the political nature of most woman killing.

This serious lapse in feminist consciousness is particularly ironic since femicides are the most extreme form of misogynist violence against women. In addition, the media provide extensive coverage of femicides—albeit often in an exploitive, titillating manner. Furthermore, murder is the fate of some rape victims and battered women—issues about which there has been massive feminist mobilization for many years. Although only relatively small percentages of female rape and battery victims are actually killed, the fear of being killed is a major aspect of the trauma of these crimes. Indeed, the fear of being murdered by a man is probably felt by most women at some time in their lives, including those women who have never been abused.

I consider the infrequent use of the term *femicide* by feminists to be the major reason that femicide remains the most neglected form of violence against women. Many feminist's unfamiliarity with this term may also explain why the many disparate feminist campaigns organized to combat femicides in the United States and elsewhere have not succeeded in getting the different strands of the movement against violence against women to routinely include woman killing on their agendas.

The naming and definition of newly recognized forms of women's oppression can play a critical role in mobilizing feminists to try to combat and prevent the problem. Before the term *sexual harassment* was invented by feminists to name the exploitative advances toward women made by millions of men in the workplace, this problem with no name was ignored by almost everyone—including feminists. Until feminists realize that there is a term that applies to the killing of females *because* they are females, they will likely not recognize the link between different kinds of femicide nor engage in a concerted campaign to protest and try to prevent femicides. As Betty Friedan discovered in the 1950s, naming a problem is vital for both consciousness raising and action.

Scholarly neglect of femicide by feminists is revealed by the fact that only a small fraction of the feminist authors of books and articles on violence against women ever mention the problem of woman slaughter, and fewer still use the term *femicide* to describe these murders. Ironically, feminists have written more books on women who kill men (for example, Browne, 1987;

Gillespie, 1989; Jones, 1980; Walker, 1989) than books on men who kill women. Jane Caputi (1987) was the first feminist to publish a book in the United States with a feminist analysis of one of the most frightening types of misogynist murder—serial femicides. That same year (1987) British feminist scholars Deborah Cameron and Elizabeth Frazer's book on sexual murder was published. Jill Radford's and my co-edited anthology, *Femicide: The Politics of Woman Killing* (1992), followed five years later. However, these books have proved insufficient to break through the wall of feminist resistance to recognizing the ubiquitous problem of femicide.

What other factors may account for feminists' failure to tackle the problem of femicide?

• There are no survivors of femicide for whom feminists can be advocates. This may discourage feminists from dealing with this issue—let alone focusing on it or creating organizations to combat it. However survivors of *attempted* femicide as well as the families and other intimates of completed and attempted femicides (we must avoid describing them as "successful"!) need supportive advocates, particularly in dealing with the legal system.

A national organization for parents of murdered children in the United States that lobbies politicians and serves as a support group for grieving parents is an excellent model for this kind of advocacy. However, it is important that feminist organizations catering to grieving parents include a political analysis of murder that recognizes the role of sexism and misogyny in most cases of murdered girls.

• The finality and the extremity of femicide may be another reason for the lack of feminist organizations dealing with this crime. These characteristics may make it more depressing and difficult to work on than rape and woman battering. Feminist writers on this subject have also had to be mindful of the effect of their writings on the families of the dead women and wary of accusations that writers are exploiting their grief.

• Perhaps the most significant reason for many feminists' continuing silence on this issue is that this ultimate form of male violence, like the threat of a nuclear holocaust, is simply too terrifying to think about. Perhaps denial and numbing enable women to avoid having to face their vulnerability to becoming a victim of femicide—particularly active heterosexual women who are at much greater risk of being killed by a male partner or ex-partner than lesbians are.

Whatever the explanations are for most feminists' failure to deal with femicide, this volume shows that increasing numbers of gender-sensitive researchers and journalists (see the Bibliography) in many different countries are finally using this terminology when writing about this widespread form of male terrorization of girls and women.

THE VALUE OF NAMING FEMICIDE: AN EXAMPLE

Natalie Nenadic (1996) credits feminist activist Asja Armanda as the first person to name as femicide the widespread fatal sexual atrocities that were perpetrated by Serbian men against Croatian women in Bosnia-Herzegovina during the civil war in that region (p. 456, fn. 1). Nenadic notes that the addition of the word *femicide* to our feminist vocabulary made it possible for Armanda and other women to recognize that the large numbers of misogynist rape-murders of women occurring in this region of the world, which were a deliberate and systematic part of the Serbs' war strategy, constituted a uniquely horrendous mass crime against women.

Some of the women survivors of this mass femicide sought out Catharine MacKinnon to be their attorney in international legal proceedings (see MacKinnon, 1993; MacKinnon, 1994). MacKinnon decided to charge the perpetrators in a New York court. In a groundbreaking move, she charged them with both genocidal *and* femicidal practices. Including femicide as a distinct and separate crime from genocide made it possible for MacKinnon to include crimes that were specific to the women victims in Croatia and Bosnia-Herzegovina.

Nenadic (1996) notes that the charge of genocide as a separate category of crime at the Nuremberg War Crimes Tribunal established an international precedent that changed the way genocide was perceived and handled by the international community. She suggests that

> Charging the crime of Femicide . . . as a separate category of crime within the rest of the Hague War Crimes Tribunal can do for women what Nuremberg did for subordinated racial, national, ethnic, and religious groups. (p. 462)

Nenadic reports that "indigenous women's and survivor groups are pushing for this recognition" (1996, p. 462).

MacKinnon's distinction between femicidal and genocidal practices provides a dramatic example of how the naming of femicide can assist women's efforts to draw attention to lethal atrocities against women, whether they occur in wartime or peacetime,[1] as well as facilitating our work to combat these very serious and widespread—but neglected—crimes.

The next chapter discusses various definitions of *femicide* and related concepts, as well as providing two typologies of femicide.

NOTE

1. Having mentioned the term *peacetime*, it is also important to recognize that peace between men does not mean that the war against women—including the per-

petration of thousands of femicidal acts—has ended or even diminished. When people talk about peacetime, we should always ask, "Peacetime for *whom?*"

REFERENCES

Braun, Stephen. (1999, May 1). Real mayhem renews cry against video game kind. *Los Angeles Times*, p. A1.
Broder, John M. (1999, May 19). Searching for answers after school violence. *New York Times*, p. A16.
Browne, Angela. (1987). *When battered women kill*. New York: Free Press.
Cameron, Deborah, & Elizabeth Frazer. (1987). *The lust to kill: A feminist investigation of sexual murder*. New York: New York University Press.
Caputi, Jane. (1987). *The age of sex crime*. Bowling Green, IN: Bowling Green State University Popular Press.
Côté, Andrée. (1991). The art of making it work for you. In Louise Malette & Marie Chalouh (Eds.), *The Montreal massacre*, translated by Marlene Wildeman (pp. 67–70). Charlottetown, Prince Edward Island, Canada: Gynergy Books.
Federal News Service. (1999, June 1). Remarks by President Bill Clinton, First Lady Hillary Rodham Clinton, Attorney General Janet Reno, and Robert Pitofsky . . . White House briefing on youth violence. [On-line]. *Federal News Service*. Available DIALOG File: 660.
Gillespie, Cynthia K. (1989). *Justifiable homicide: Battered women, self-defense, and the law*. Columbus: Ohio State University Press.
Jones, Ann. (1980). *Women who kill*. New York: Holt, Rinehart & Winston.
Leyton, Elliott. (1986). *Hunting humans*. New York: Pocket Books.
Lorde, Audre. (1981). Need: A choral of black women's voices. In Frederique Delacoste & Felice Newman (Eds.), *Fight back! Feminist resistance to male violence* (pp. 63–67). Minneapolis, MN: Cleis Press.
MacKinnon, Catharine A. (1993). Crimes of war, crimes of peace. In Stephen Shute & Susan Hurley (Eds.), *On human rights: The Oxford amnesty lectures* (pp. 83–109). New York: Basic Books.
MacKinnon, Catharine A. (1994, Spring). Rape, genocide, and women's human rights. *Harvard Women's Law Journal*, 17, 5–16.
Nenadic, Natalie. (1996). Femicide: A framework for understanding genocide. In Diana Bell & Renate Klein (Eds.), *Radically speaking: Feminism reclaimed* (pp. 456–464). Melbourne, Australia: Spinifex Press.
Publisher's note. (1991). In Louise Malette & Marie Chalouh (Eds.), *The Montreal massacre*, translated by Marlene Wildeman (pp. 9–10). Charlottetown, Prince Edward Island, Canada: Gynergy Books.
Radford, Jill, & Diana E. H. Russell. (Eds.). (1992). *Femicide: The politics of woman killing*. New York: Twayne/Gale Group.
Ressler, Robert, Ann Burgess, & John Douglas. (1988). *Sexual homicide: Patterns and motives*. Lexington, MA: Lexington Books.

Saint-Jean, Armande. (1991). Burying women's words: An analysis of media atti-
    tudes. In Louise Malette & Marie Chalouh (Eds.), *The Montreal massacre*, trans-
    lated by Marlene Wildeman (pp. 61–65). Charlottetown, Prince Edward Island,
    Canada: Gynergy Books.
Scottish Media Newspapers Limited. (1999, May 1). Clinton calls summit on youth
    violence. *The Herald*, p. 16.
Walker, Lenore E. (1989). *Terrifying love: Why battered women kill and how society
    responds*. New York: Harper & Row.
Wilson, Trish. (1999). The Columbine shootings: Thoughts from teenagers. *Feminista!*
    [On-line serial periodical] 3(1). [Available on-line: http:www.feminista.com/v3n1/
    wilson.html]

CHAPTER 2

Defining Femicide
and Related Concepts

Diana E. H. Russell

The term *homicide* is derived from the Latin word *hom*, meaning "man."
Like the words *mankind* and the generic use of *man*, *homicide* applies to
women, too. Feminists have long objected to using the words *mankind* instead of *humankind* and *man* instead of *people* because of their inherent
sexism, but the words *homicide* and *manslaughter* have not attracted the same
feminist criticism as many other words sometimes humorously referred to
as "Manglish." As one of the few feminist critics of the term *homicide* (see
Radford & Russell, 1992), I will endeavor to avoid using it for male-on-female
murders in my contributions to this volume. When I use the term *murder*
instead of *homicide*, then, I do not intend to honor the legal distinction between murder and manslaughter.

According to the three dictionaries I consulted, *homicide* is not only
defined as "the killing of one human being by another" but also as "a person who kills another," that is, the murderer (*Random House Webster's
College Dictionary*, 1996[1]). Hence, it seems reasonable to infer that the term
female homicide refers to female murderers and *male homicide* to male
murderers. However, there are no comparable criminological terms for the
murder of females and the murder of males. The lack of such terms reveals
the paucity of attention to gender analyses in the male-dominated field of
criminology. Furthermore, in an informal survey of the meaning of *female
homicide*, I discovered that many people think this term refers to the killing
of women. In the interests of encouraging more gender-focused research on
murder, which I use as synonymous with *killing*, I offer the terminology
below. Although these generic terms do not take intent into account the way

the term *femicide* does, the following terminology is suggested in place of the ambiguous terms *female homicide* and *male homicide*.

Genderizing Murder-Related Terminology

1. Genderizing the killing of a woman/girl and a man/boy
   Since feminists have created the term *woman-killing*, I suggest we continue to use this term. The terms *girl-killing* for the killing of a girl and *female-killing* for the killing of a woman and/or a girl are consistent with *woman-killing*.
   The comparable terms for the killing of a male would therefore be *man-killing*, *boy-killing*, and *male-killing*.
2. Genderizing the killer of a woman/girl and/or a man/boy
   Male-perpetrated murder and *female-perpetrated murder*
3. Genderizing the killer and the killed
   The four possible types of genderized murders are:
   a. Male-on-male killing
   b. Male-on-female killing
      i. femicide (to be defined below)
      ii. nonfemicidal murder
   c. Female-on-female killing
   d. Female-on-male killing

THE HISTORY OF THE TERM *FEMICIDE*

The term *femicide* has been in use for almost two centuries. It was first used in *A Satirical View of London at the Commencement of the Nineteenth Century* (Corry) in 1801 to signify "the killing of a woman."[2] In 1827, the third edition of *The Confessions of an Unexecuted Femicide* was published. This short manuscript was written by femicide perpetrator William MacNish about his murder of a young woman. And, according to the 1989 edition of *The Oxford English Dictionary*, *femicide* appeared in Wharton's *Law Lexicon* in 1848, suggesting that it had become a prosecutable offense (p. 825).[3] However, even after my recent discovery of the history of the term *femicide*, I was not inclined to substitute the dictionary definition for my own because I was, and still am, convinced that the sexist aspect of most murders of women by men needs to be incorporated into the definition of femicide. My definition of femicide is *the killing of females by males because they are females*.

When I heard the word *femicide* for the first time in 1974, I immediately thought it would be a fitting new term for the misogynist killing of women. I believed that use of such a term would help to remove the obscuring veil of the male-biased terms *homicide* and *manslaughter*. If one imagines referring to the killing of males as femicide and the unlawful killing of males "without malice aforethought" as *womanslaughter* (as in *Webster's College Dictionary*, 1996), the sexism inherent in the terms *homicide* and *manslaughter* becomes even more obvious.

I used the term *femicide* for the first time when I testified about this crime at the International Tribunal on Crimes Against Women in Brussels in 1976 (Russell & Van de Ven, 1976, pp. 144–146). However, I did not provide an explicit definition of this concept at that time. In 1990, Jane Caputi and I defined femicide as "the murder of women by men motivated by hatred, contempt, pleasure, or a sense of ownership of women" (1990, p. 34), whereas in 1992, Radford and I defined it simply as "the misogynist killing of women by men" (Radford & Russell, 1992, pp. xi, 3).

Although *The Oxford English Dictionary*'s definition of *femicide* as "the killing of a woman" does not connote sexist murder, it seems rather doubtful that the term was intended to cover gender-irrelevant murders, for example, a man accidentally shooting and killing a female bystander. The femicide victim of MacNish, for example, was a young woman he had seduced, impregnated, abandoned, and then murdered (1827).

On being reminded subsequently that mothers-in-law of some newly married women in India sometimes participate with their sons in murdering their daughters-in-law by setting them on fire because of their insufficient dowries (*dowry femicides*), I decided to refer to such acts by mothers-in-law as *female-on-female murder* rather than to expand my definition of *femicide* to include female perpetrators.

I substituted the word *females* for *women* in my definition of *femicide* for this book in recognition of the fact that many girls and female babies are victims of femicide. Similarly, because many boys and male youth are perpetrators of femicide, my definition refers to "males" instead of "men."

In addition, my definition extends the term *femicide* beyond misogynistic killings to apply to *all forms of sexist killing*. Misogynistic murders are limited to those motivated by the hatred of females, whereas sexist murders include killings by males motivated by a sense of entitlement to and/or superiority over females, by pleasure or sadistic desires toward them, and/or by an assumption of ownership of women.

Other Researchers' Definitions of *Femicide*

Desmond Ellis and Walter DeKeseredy (1996) contend that "feminist sociologists differentiate between the intentional killing of males (homicides) and the intentional killing of females by males (femicides)" (p. 68). Elsewhere, these authors state that this is also how North American feminists define femicide. However, their use of the term *intentional* is problematic since nonintentional killings of women can also be instances of femicide. For example, a battering husband may not have intended to kill his wife when he attacked her, but this unintentional act would certainly qualify as femicide by my definition.

Jacquelyn Campbell and Carol Runyan (1998), among others, have redefined femicide as "all killings of women, regardless of motive or perpetrator status" (p. 348). Their rationale for this redefinition is that they want to avoid having to make inferences about the motives of the killers. This does not explain, however, why they do not use a term like *woman-killing* instead of changing the meaning of *femicide* in such a drastic way. Their redefinition is almost certain to create confusion in this new area of research, as when they were guest editors of a special issue on femicide for *Homicide Studies* and they *required* the contributors to use their new definition of this term without ever making this explicit. I, for one, was a casualty of this requirement. Although inferring motives can be difficult or even impossible at times, all hate crimes require the assessment of the criminals' motives. However, it seems doubtful that any politically progressive individual would endorse forgoing the concept of *racist murder* because of the difficulty of establishing motive.

According to my definition, just as murders targeting African Americans can be differentiated into those that are racist and those that are not, and murders targeting lesbians can be differentiated into those that are lesbiphobic and those that are not, so can murders targeting women be differentiated into those that are femicides and those that are not. When the female gender of a victim is immaterial to the perpetrator, we are dealing with a nonfemicidal murder. For example, an armed male robber who shoots and kills the male and female owners of a grocery store in the course of his crime has not committed a femicide. The same applies to a man who accidently kills a female bystander when attempting to target a man.

For Campbell and Runyan, on the other hand, the latter examples do qualify as a femicide. Several other researchers likewise use the term *femicide* to refer to all murders of women regardless of the motivation for these fatal acts. By omitting the final clause of our definition of femicide ("*because they are female*"), these researchers have removed the political component in my definition.

Fortunately, most if not all the researchers who use Campbell and Runyan's redefinition of *femicide* focus on intimate partner femicide. Hence, their studies probably include only a few cases that do not qualify as femicidal by my definition. Because many men who kill their partners do so *because* they are women, the differences in our definitions are far less salient than is the case for many other types of murder. Nevertheless, I hope that those who write or conduct research on nonpartner femicides will adopt my definition rather than using the depoliticized definition used by several other researchers.

Ellis and DeKeseredy (1996) report that Indian (South Asian) feminists use the term *femicide* to refer to "the intentional killing of females by men and of females by other females in the interests of men" (p. 70). According to Ellis and DeKeseredy, Indian feminists differentiate between three types of femicidal female-killings: "parental killings-by-neglect, killings following discovery of sex status [of parents' children], and husband/mother/father-in-law killings for consumption" (p. 70).[4]

It appears that Indian feminists have adapted my and Radford's original definition of *femicide*—to fit the reality of female-killing in their country. Indian girls and women face a reality in which female fetuses are frequently aborted because of the wide-spread preference for male children, female babies and children often die from deliberate neglect by their mothers, and a married woman's husband, mother-in-law, and father-in-law not infrequently participate in her murder because of dissatisfaction with the amount of dowry received for her from her parents.

The clause that the Indian women include in their definition of femicide ("in the interests of men") is unique and thought-provoking. Most female-perpetrated killings of women *because* they are women probably *are* done in the interests of a man or of men. The Indian feminists' definition of femicide prompted me to develop the typology of female-on-female murders shown in Table 2.1 below.

Ethnicity and Femicide

Campbell and colleagues Karen Soeken, Judith McFarlane, and Barbara Parker (1998) provide a few statistics on ethnicity and femicide. One major advantage of their limited use of the term *femicide* is that considerable data are available on the murder of women, whereas this is not the case on the killing of females by males *because* they are females. These researchers report that

> Femicide is the leading cause of death in the United States for African American women aged 15–34 (Farley, 1986) and the seventh leading cause of premature death for women overall. . . . Although rates of homicide within intimate heterosexual relationships is higher for African American than European

Table 2.1. Typology of Female-perpetrated Femicides

Females Acting as Agents of Patriarchy	Females Acting as Agents of Male Perpetrators	Females Acting on Own Behalf
Dowry-related murders, e.g., mothers-in-law who murder their daughters-in-law or assist male relatives with such murders	Accessories to femicides, e.g., sex slavery in which wife/ partner assists husband/ partner to commit femicide; Battered wife participants in husband-initiated daughter-femicides, or femicides involving other female relatives	Jealousy-motivated murders e.g.; jealous mother kills daughter-in-law; Jealous woman kills husband's female lover; Jealous lesbian kills Female lover
Male child preference-related murders, e.g., mothers who kill their girl babies (infanticide), or engineer their deaths by abandonment, neglect, starvation, or similar measures		Financial/greed-related murders, e.g., woman kills mother, rich female relation, rich female employer, or Other female for financial gain
Genital mutilation-related deaths, e.g., deaths caused by primitive and/or unhygenic methods used by female operators; deaths of genitally mutilated females when giving birth because of mutilation-related complications	Gang-related femicides, e.g., accessories to gang members who participate or assist male members in femicides of female gang members and/or others females	Suicides by females who kill themselves because of abusive actions by other females, e.g., female lovers, violent mothers, female sexual perpetrators, mothers who collude with male perpetrators
Female accessories to some murders e.g., fatal cases of genital mutilation operations in which mothers force daughters to undergo, and/or cases in which female relatives forcibly restrain victims during operations and/or witness and sanction them; mothers and other female relatives who assist in forcing widowed daughters to burn to death in the funeral pyre of their husbands	"Honor" femicides, e.g., females who are accessories to or assist male relatives in "honor" femicides Suicides by females driven to kill themselves, e.g., by abusive husbands, fathers, sons, pimps, male harassers, male incest perpetrators, i.e., females who, because of male abuse, destroy themselves (femicidal suicides)	Anger-motivated murders by females, e.g., female incest survivors who murder colluding or abusive mothers Drug-related murders, e.g., angry females who kill other females to feed their habits Ideologically motivated murders e.g., radical political women who feel entitled or obliged to kill female ideological enemies

American couples, they become comparable when socioeconomic status is controlled (Centerwall, 1984).

Other female causes of death have been reduced since 1940, but death by femicide has increased for both European American and African American women (Farley, 1986). Femicide happens far less frequently to Hispanic women and has only been measured separately in the past few years, so that national rates over time are unavailable. (p. 90)

TYPES OF FEMICIDE

Most of the research to date has been done on *intimate partner femicide*, which most researchers refer to as "intimate femicide"—a predominance that is reflected in the contributions to this book. Karen Stout (1991) defines *intimate femicide* (her term) as "the killing of women by male intimate partners" (p. 476). Maria Crawford and Rosemary Gartner (1992) did not originally limit their definition of intimate femicide to male killers ("the killing of women by their current or former intimate partners" [cited in DeKeseredy & MacLeod, 1997, p. 70]). However, in 1998, Myrna Dawson and Gartner defined intimate femicide "as the killing of women by intimate male partners, that is, current or former legal spouses, common-law partners, and boyfriends" (p. 383).

Campbell and Runyan (1998) use the term *intimate partner femicide* instead of just *intimate femicide*. I prefer this term over *intimate femicide* because the latter term might be assumed to apply to femicide by parents and other family members. However, no researcher who uses the term *intimate femicide* includes these kinds of relatives. In addition, those who are not familiar with the meaning of the term *intimate femicide* are unlikely to be able to figure out what it means. In contrast, the term *intimate partner femicide* speaks for itself.

Dawson and Gartner (1998) note that intimate femicides have "a number of characteristics in common that distinguish them from other primary group killings" (p. 379). This, they maintain, has encouraged researchers to move away from using concepts such as *family violence* "which imply commonalities among killings across very different types of intimate relationships" (p. 379).

There are many other kinds of femicides that can be identified, for example, serial femicides, rape femicide, racist femicide, wife femicide, acquaintance femicide, lover femicide, date femicide, prostituted woman femicide, drug-related femicide, "honor" femicide, lesbiphobic femicide, child sexual abuse–related femicide, and mass femicide. These are not discrete categories since a particular case of femicide may fall into two or even three categories, for example, a racist, drug-related rape femicide.

Covert or Social Femicide

The concept of femicide includes covert forms of woman-killing such as women being permitted to die because of misogynistic attitudes and/or social institutions. For example, wherever women's right to choose to be mothers is not recognized, thousands of women die every year from botched abortions. Hence, these deaths qualify as femicides. As I testified in the International Tribunal on Crimes Against Women in 1976:

> The number of women who actually die every year as a consequence [of bungled abortions] is not known, but it is probably as high as the number of casualties in the most lethal, patriarchal, geopolitical wars. (Russell & Van de Ven, p. 26)

Similarly, writing about the United States in 1970—a period in which the death penalty had been ruled unconstitutional by the U.S. Supreme Court—Kate Millett (1970) pointed out that

> Indirectly, one form of "death penalty" still obtains even in America today. Patriarchal legal systems in depriving women of control over their own bodies drive them to illegal abortions; it is estimated that between two and five thousand women die each year from this cause. (pp. 43–44)

Millett's estimate of 5,000 femicides as a result of illegal abortions is far too low—even for 1970. According to the witness from Portugal who testified at the International Tribunal on Crimes Against Women, "about 2,000 women die every year as a consequence of abortion practices" in her country alone (Russell & Van de Ven, 1976, p. 9). As for recent statistics: A World Health Organization report published in 2001 indicated that "30 million illegal abortions resulted in 200,000, to 400,000 deaths each year" ("Bush rolls back," 2001, p. A20).

Other examples of covert femicides include: deaths from unnecessary surgeries such as hysterectomies; genital mutilation (particularly excision and infibulation); experimentation on women's bodies, including the use of insufficiently tested methods of birth control, some of which have turned out to be carcinogenic; dangerous marriage practices such as those in which extremely young females are married to much older men, some of whom die as a result of forced sexual intercourse; and the deliberate preference given to boy children in many cultures, resulting in countless female deaths from neglect, illness, and starvation in numerous impoverished nations, such as China and India.

Instead of *covert femicide*, Sharon Hom (1991-92) uses the concept *social femicide* "to suggest the implication of the role of an existing social order in practices which result in death and devaluation of female lives" (p. 260, fn. 38). The lethal consequences of son preference is one example of social femicide that Hom analyzes in Chapter 12 of this volume, citing a United Nations estimate that "about one million female children per year die as the result of neglect" (Hom, 1991-92, p. 260, fn. 38). She concludes that "female infanticide reflects the deadly impact for female children of the value systems and 'preferences' of patriarchal societies, and thus is a form of social femicide" (p. 260, fn. 38).

Hom's inclusion of the "devaluation of female lives" in her definition of social femicide does not qualify it as femicide by my definition (the killing of females by males *because* they are females). Since the devaluation of female lives is characteristic of all patriarchies—i.e., every known society on the planet—Hom's definition is too inclusive, in my opinion. If we exclude the "devaluation of female lives" from the definition of *social femicide*, I think the term is an excellent addition to the study of femicide and preferable to the concept *covert femicide* because it connotes a more macro and political dimension.

A Typology of Femicide

Different femicide typologies can be developed depending on the research and/or analysis to be undertaken. Dawson and Gartner (1998) suggest that

> *The relationship between a victim and an offender* is critical to understanding the context and dynamics of homicide. . . . Recognizing the explanatory power of the victim-offender relationship in lethal violence, homicide researchers now commonly analyze homicides by disaggregating the relationship between the victim and offender. (pp. 378–379, emphasis in original)

These observations also presumably apply to femicide.

Desmond Ellis and Walter DeKeseredy (1996) identified a continuum of femicides based on the relationship between victims and perpetrators, with intimate femicide at one end and stranger femicide at the other. They then developed a typology based on this continuum, differentiating among intimate femicides, relational femicides, acquaintance femicides, and stranger femicides (p. 71).

My typology, which builds on Ellis and DeKeseredy's, differentiates between femicidal killers and nonfemicidal killers. It also distinguishes four types of femicides: (1) intimate partner femicides, (2) familial femicides, (3) femicides by other known perpetrators, and (4) stranger femicides. Table 2.2 provides examples of perpetrators in three of the four mutually exclusive categories of femicide.

My typology uses the term *familial femicide* instead of the term *relational femicide* used by Ellis and DeKeseredy (1996) in their typology because I consider all four of the categories of femicide to be relational. I also find the term *other known perpetrator of femicide* preferable to *acquaintance femicide* because the latter term does not seem appropriate for relationships such as dates[5] and/or friends.

GENOCIDE, GYNOCIDE, AND FEMICIDE: SIMILARITIES AND DIFFERENCES

Genocide is defined very differently by different sources. For example, *Webster's New World Dictionary* (1958) defines *genocide* as "the systematic killing or extermination of a whole people or nation." *The American Heritage Dictionary* (1992) defines it in similar fashion as "the systematic

Table 2.2. Typology of Femicides Based on Relationship Between Killers and Their Victims

Partner Femicides	Familial Femicides	Other Known Perpetrators of Femicides	Stranger Femicides
Male lovers/ sex partners	Fathers/ stepfathers	Male friends of family	Male strangers
Husbands	Adoptive brothers/	Male friends of victim	
Ex-husbands	stepbrothers/		
Common-law husbands	half-brothers	Male co-workers/ colleagues	
Ex-common-law husbands	Uncles/ stepuncles	Male authority figures, e.g.,	
Ex-male lovers/ sex partners	Grandfathers/ stepgrandfathers	teachers, priests, employers	
Boyfriends (committed)	Sons/stepsons	Male acquaintances	
Ex-boyfriends (committed)	Fathers-in-law	Male dates (not sexual)	
Other male intimate partners	Brothers-in-law Other male relatives	Other known male perpetrators	

and planned extermination of an entire national, racial, political, or ethnic group." However, the Convention on Genocide's definition, which was approved by the General Assembly of the United Nations on December 9, 1948, defined it in a far more inclusive way:

> Genocide means any of the following acts committed with intent to destroy, in whole or in part, a national, ethnical [sic], racial or religious group, as such:
> (a) Killing members of the group;
> (b) Causing serious bodily or mental harm to members of the group;
> (c) Deliberately inflicting on the group conditions of life calculated to bring about its physical destruction in whole or in part;
> (d) Imposing measures intended to prevent births within the group;
> (e) Forcibly transferring children of the group to another group (quoted in Kuper, 1981, p. 11; and p. 210 for the complete text of the Genocide Convention).

Feminist theologian Mary Daly and Jane Caputi (1987) use the word *gynocide* to apply to intentional measures of effecting the destruction of women in a specific population. They define *gynocide* as

> The fundamental intent of global patriarchy: planned, institutionalized spiritual and bodily destruction of women; the use of deliberate systematic measures (such as killing, *bodily or mental injury, unlivable conditions, prevention of births*), *which are calculated to bring about the destruction of women as a political and cultural force, the eradication of Female/Biological religion and language*, and ultimately the extermination of the Race of Women and all Elemental being. (p. 77; emphasis added)

Hence, like the definition used by the Convention on Genocide, Daly and Caputi's definition includes other forms of oppression besides physical annihilation. Andrea Dworkin (1976) also subsequently defined gynocide as "the systematic *crippling, raping*, and/or killing of women by men . . . the relentless violence perpetrated by the gender class men on the gender class women" (p. 16; emphasis added).

In keeping with Daly and Caputi's and Dworkin's broad definitions of *gynocide*, I propose adopting the Convention on Genocide's broad definition of *genocide*. However, I consider it preferable to define *gynocide* in like manner as any of the following acts committed with intent to destroy females as a gender, in whole or in part:

1. By killing, that is, femicide
2. By causing serious bodily or mental harm to females, by widespread rape, child sexual abuse, sexual harassment, physical violence, verbal abuse, restrictions of freedom, and so on
3. By deliberately inflicting on females conditions of life calculated to bring about their partial physical destruction, for example, by discriminating against them economically so that they remain dependent on men, by socializing them to believe that it is their duty to spend significant portions of their lives and energies raising children and keeping house rather than competing with men in the paid work force, and so on
4. By imposing measures to prevent births for racist and/or other inappropriate reason(s).
5. By forcibly transferring to men (including men who sexually or physically abuse their children) the children of divorcing couples involved in custody battles (despite women's typically having had the major responsibility for raising them), particularly if the mother is less well-off economically than the father or if she is considered unfit merely for racist, lesbophobic, or other inappropriate reason(s).

While at least four of the five criteria of gynocide apply to what is happening to females in the United States today, I do not believe that these acts are *intended* to destroy significant numbers of women *because* they are female—as our definition requires. Hence I do not consider females in the contemporary United States to be experiencing a period of gynocide.

While genocide and gynocide include femicidal acts, these terms are not confined to these acts. Nor do these terms apply to lethal acts that occur on an individual level. Femicide is reserved for the ultimate act of male sexism—the literal destruction of the lives of women and girls on an individual, non-institutionalized level as well as on a large-scale institutionalized level. Unlike the terms *genocide* and *gynocide*, *femicide* is not limited to intentional efforts to exterminate females as a gender.

In summary: Although the terms *gynocide* and *femicide* both include acts of female-killing by males, they are complementary rather than competitive.

CONCLUSION

Unfortunately, the terms and definitions used in the chapters by other contributors to this volume may not be in accordance with those proposed here. Nevertheless, I hope this essay will serve as a useful guide in the new field of femicide research. I also hope that it will challenge what British feminists call "malestream" criminology researchers and that some of the terminology and definitions will be incorporated into that field.

NOTES

1. *The American Heritage Dictionary* (1992) and *The Pocket Oxford Dictionary* (1992) are the other two dictionaries consulted.

2. *A Satirical View of London* (1801). Prior to this, I believed that Carol Orlock was the first to use this term as the title of her manuscript that was never published.

3. The following dictionaries define *femicide* in the same way as the *Oxford English Dictionary* (2nd edition), 1989, that is, as "the killing of a woman": *New English Dictionary on Historical Principles*, 1901; *Black's Law Dictionary* (6th edition), 1990; *Bouvier's Law Dictionary and Concise Encyclopedia* (3rd edition), 1914; *The Random House Dictionary of the English Language* (2nd edition), 1987; *A Satirical View of London*, 1801; and *Wharton Law Lexicon* (the London edition), 1848.

4. The source cited by Ellis and DeKeseredy for the Indian women's definition of femicide is inaccurate. Personal communications to Ellis about this fact (February 7 and March 16, 2000) were unanswered, and Harmes' efforts to locate the definition were unsuccessful.

5. Some researchers include date femicides as a form of intimate partner femicide. Since the concept of date can apply to the first time out with a stranger (a blind

date), whereas the terms *boyfriend* and *lover* are used for more committed and longer-term relationships, I have categorized date femicides as a form of "other known perpetrator" femicides.

REFERENCES

American heritage dictionary (3rd ed.). (1992). Boston: Houghton Mifflin.

Black, Henry Campbell. (1990). *Black's law dictionary: Definitions of the terms and phrases of American and English jurisprudence, ancient and modern.* St. Paul, MN: West Publishing Company.

Bouvier, John. (1914). *Bouvier's law dictionary and concise encyclopedia.* Kansas City, MO: Vernon Law Book Company.

Bush rolls back family planning (2001, January 23). *San Francisco Chronicle,* p. A20.

Campbell, Jacquelyn, & Carol W. Runyan. (1998, November). Femicide: Guest editors' introduction. *Homicide Studies, 2*(4), 347–352.

Campbell, Jacquelyn, Karen Soeken, Judith McFarlane, & Barbara Parker. (1998). Risk factors for femicide among pregnant and nonpregnant battered women. In Jacquelyn Campbell (Ed.), *Empowering survivors of abuse* (pp. 90–97). Thousand Oaks, CA: Sage Publications.

Caputi, Jane, & Diana E. H. Russell. (1990). Femicide: Speaking the unspeakable. *Ms.: The World of Women, 1*(2), 34–37.

Centerwall, Brandon S. (1984). Race, socioeconomic status, and domestic homicide: Atlanta, 1971–1972. *American Journal of Public Health, 74,* 813–815.

Crawford, Maria, Rosemary Gartner, & Women We Honour Action Committee. (1992). *Women killing: Intimate femicide in Ontario, 1974–1990.* Toronto: Women We Honour Action Committee.

Corry, John. (1801). *A satirical view of London at the commencement of the nineteenth century.* London: G. Kearsley.

Daly, Mary, & Jane Caputi. (1987). *Websters' first new intergalactic wickedary of the English language.* Boston: Beacon Press.

Dawson, Myrna, & Rosemary Gartner. (1998). Differences in the characteristics of intimate femicides: The role of relationship status and relationship state. *Homicide Studies, 2,* 378–400.

DeKeseredy, Walter S., & Linda MacLeod. (1997). Counting the pain and suffering: The incidence and prevalence of woman abuse in Canada—Intimate femicide. In Walter DeKeseredy & Linda MacLeod (Eds.), *Woman abuse: A sociological story* (pp. 70–71). Toronto, Canada: Harcourt Brace.

Dworkin, Andrea. (1976). *Our blood: Prophecies and discourses on sexual politics.* New York: Harper & Row.

Ellis, Desmond, & Walter DeKeseredy. (1996). *The wrong stuff: An introduction to the sociological study of deviance.* Scarborough, Ontario: Allyn & Bacon.

Farley, Reynolds. (1986). Homicide trends in the United States. In Darnel F. Hawkins (Ed.), *Homicide among Black Americans* (pp.13–27). New York: University Press of America.

Hom, Sharon K. (1991-92). Female infanticide in China: The human rights specter and thoughts towards (an)other vision. *Columbia Human Rights Law Reporter*, 23(2), 249–314.

Kuper, Leo. (1981). *Genocide: Its political use in the twentieth century.* New Haven, CT: Yale University Press.

MacNish, William. (1827). *The confessions of an unexecuted femicide* (3rd edition). Glasgow: W. R. M'Phun, Trongate.

Millett, Kate. (1970). *Sexual politics.* Garden City, NY: Doubleday.

New English dictionary on historical principles. (1901). Oxford, UK: Oxford University Press.

Oxford English dictionary. (2nd ed., vol. 5). (1989). Oxford, UK: Clarendon Press.

Pocket Oxford dictionary. (8th ed.). (1992). Oxford, UK: Oxford University Press.

Radford, Jill, & Diana E. H. Russell. (Eds.). (1992). *Femicide: The politics of woman killing.* New York: Twayne/Gale Group.

Random House Webster's college dictionary. (1996). New York: Random House.

Rosenfeld, Richard. (1997). Changing relationships between men and women: A note on the decline of intimate partner homicide. *Homicide Studies, 1*(1), 72–83.

Russell, Diana E. H., & Nicole Van de Ven. (Eds.). (1976). *The proceedings of the International Tribunal on Crimes Against Women.* San Francisco, CA: Frog in the Well.

Stout, Karen D. (1991). Intimate femicide: A national demographic overview. *Journal of Interpersonal Violence, 6,* 476–485.

U.S. Department of Health and Human Services. (1991). *Healthy People 2000.* Washington, DC: U.S. Department of Health and Human Services.

Webster's college dictionary. (1996). New York: Random House.

Webster's new world dictionary. (1958). New York: World Publishing Company.

Wharton, John, & Jane Smith. (1987). *The law lexicon, or, dictionary of jurisprudence* (London edition). Littleton, CO: F. B. Rothman. (original work published 1848)

Femicide in
the United States

Protest rally and march to commemorate the lives and mourn the deaths of two prostituted femicide victims in San Francisco, California. (Photograph by Scott Braley)

No More Metaphors

Chrystos

For the Green River Victims

To be a prostitute is to walk cold wet streets
in a dangerous night dependent
on the hunger of strangers   vulnerable to their hatred
fists   perverse desires   diseases
To use one's face & body   literally
to pay the rent   the pimp   utilities   nylons   lipstick
to wear a bruise where the heart beats
to be a tunnel for the spit of men
to be a hole for the hatred of women
to sell one's body nightly
you could say it's
the only honest work a woman gets

To be a murderer of prostitutes
is to be free
to do it
as many times as you want
or to be warm   fed regularly
in a cell for which one pays no rent
have free tobacco   library   arts & crafts   sports programs
rehabilitation
To live to an old age
secure in tight walls
radio playing with wet dreams at night
of their bodies
breasts slashed open
their faces no longer flowers
memories of the way
it really is

29

CHAPTER 3

Femicide by Gunfire: A Year of Lethal Hate Crimes in the United States

Diana E. H. Russell

Time magazine published brief summary data with accompanying photographs (where obtainable) of all known victims of lethal gunshots that occurred in the United States during the first week in May 1989 (Magnuson, 1989). This chapter provides a gender analysis of these data that author Ed Magnuson omitted. More specifically, my goal here is to determine what percentage of the gunshot murders of women that occurred that week were femicides.

Because I define *femicide* as the killing of females by males *because* they are female, pursuing my objective was not a simple matter of counting the number of females who were fatally shot. (The section on methodology to follow will explain how I ascertained whether a woman was a victim of femicide or nonfemicidal murder.) For those who define *femicide* merely as the killing of women, no such problem exists. However, their definition also precludes them from being able to find out the percentage of murders that qualify as gender hate crimes. This question is increasingly important now that gender has finally been recognized as a basis for hate crimes in some states.

Although the *Time* data are more than a decade old, the information provided in this article affords us a unique opportunity to determine the ratio between femicides and nonfemicidal murders in one particular year. The quantitative data on murder reported by other studies and compendia of statistics typically lack any qualitative data about each case. Where such qualitative data *are* available, including in random-sample surveys, information about each case in the sample is generally lacking. Therefore, despite the age of the *Time* data and the meager amount of qualitative data provided about each murder, this article is worthy of our analytical efforts.

There were 464 deaths for both murder and suicide by guns during the first week in May 1989. Males were the victims in 83% ($N = 387$) of these deaths, and females in 17% of them ($N = 77$). Fifty-three percent ($N = 248$) of the 464 deaths were murders and 47% were suicides. With regard to murder, Magnuson (1989), the author and data analyst of the *Time* article, noted that the victims "were frequently those most vulnerable in society: the poor, the young, the abandoned, the ill and the elderly" (p. 31). Note that Magnuson completely overlooked females as a vulnerable group.

The information provided in the 28 pages of thumbnail sketches of the 464 deaths by gunshot during what Magnuson (1989) refers to as "the seven deadly days" (p. 30) makes it possible to do the gender analysis that he failed to do. The data are particularly valuable because they include *all* murders of women by gunshot—not just a sample of them—and because the official FBI statistics on murder are known to be far more accurate than the statistics on any of the other violent crimes on which it keeps records. Furthermore, guns are used in most murders. According to Ann Goetting (1988), "Firearms are the most common means of inflicting death in this country [United States]. Between 1968 and 1978 the proportion of killing committed with firearms varied between 63% and 65.7%" (pp. 10–11).

With regard to *intimate partner femicide*, Karen Stout (1991) found in her study of U.S. murder statistics published in the FBI's *Uniform Crime Reports* that "victims were killed by a type of firearm (handgun, shotgun, rifle, and so on) in 67.9% of the cases" (pp. 482–483). This percentage constitutes more than two-thirds of the murders and is only very slightly higher than the range from 63% to 65.7% reported by Goetting (1988) for all murders by firearms in the United States.

On analyzing the homicides committed nationwide in 1992, the Bureau of Justice Statistics concluded that "firearms were used to kill 69 percent of wives and ex-wives . . . [and] 60 percent of girlfriends" (Ewing, 1997, p. 154). These figures are very similar to Stout's 67.9%.

These studies reveal that firearms are used in about two-thirds of the murders and intimate partner femicides in the United States. Given Ewing's (1997) observation that "intrafamilial killings" are "most often committed with firearms that have been present in the home long before they were used to kill" (p. 159), it is also evident that the high percentage of gun ownership in the United States is a major factor in the high rates of femicide and homicide. It is all the more alarming, then, that, according to Ewing, "gun ownership and access have reached all-time highs over the past decade" (p. 161).

METHODOLOGY

Research analyst Karen Trocki and I developed a code sheet for all cases of woman-killing to be completed by two independent coders. It included the following information: the age of the victim and the murderer; the victim's relationship with the murderer; the ethnicity of the victim; the presumed motive for the murder; and any other information in the brief descriptions about the case that was relevant to judging whether or not the male murderers were motivated by sexism.[1] Although all the suicides by gunshot were also coded, these will receive little attention in this chapter because it is impossible to determine which ones were provoked by men and/or patriarchal institutions.

The coders had to decide how each case best fit into the following six categories: (1) definite femicide, (2) possible femicide, (3) murder but not femicide, (4) suicide, (5) female-on-female murder, and (6) not ascertainable. I then checked the coders' decisions, noting wherever they had disagreed, and used my own judgment in such cases, as well as collapsing the first two categories. Most of the following analysis will focus on a comparison of the femicides and the nonfemicidal murders described in *Time*.

RESULTS AND DISCUSSION

The first point to note about the data on gender and death by gunshot is that of the 464 deaths by firearms during the first week in May 1989, 91% ($N = 387$) of the victims were male compared to only 9% ($N = 77$) who were female (these figures include suicides). Of the female deaths by firearms, the percentage of suicides was higher than the percentage of femicides (45% vs. 34%). As several participants emphasized at the speakout on femicide at the International Conference on Violence, Abuse, and Women's Citizenship held in Britain in 1996, some women who commit suicide have been driven to do so by their male partner's misogyny (see Chapter 11 and Table 2.1 in Chapter 2). It is well known that women, particularly women who feel powerless, tend to turn their anger on themselves. Hence some (or many) of the female suicides are probably covert cases of femicide. *Femicidal suicides* is the term I propose for this phenomenon.

We recommend that future research examine the significance of sexism and misogyny as causes of female suicide, particularly by exceptionally vulnerable women such as the victims of male abuse and violence in the home (wives and daughters). We already know that battered women who are also raped by their husbands are more likely to be murdered by these men, as well as to murder them (Campbell & Alford, 1989). Are they also more likely to become victims of femicidal suicide?

The Prevalence of Femicides

Of the 36 women murdered by men (excluding the cases that were not ascertainable and those perpetrated by women), 72% (N = 26) were judged to be femicides and 28% (N = 10) as nonfemicidal murders. In the analysis to follow, comparisons will be made between these two types of murders of females. However, the small numbers involved make it difficult to be confident about some of the results of these comparisons. For this reason, statistical analyses were not performed on these data.

The Gender of the Murderers

Of the 39 women murdered by gunshot (excluding the suicides and the cases that were not ascertainable), 92% (N = 36) were murdered by one or more men while only 8% (N = 3) were murdered by women. This percentage of female-on-female murder is very close to the 4% figure found in a study conducted by the National Commission on the Causes and Prevention of Violence in the late 1960s (Mulvihill, Tumin, & Curtis, 1969). These low percentages for female-on-female murders indicate how atypical it is for women to murder when they are not fighting for their lives.

The Number of Victims and Perpetrators of Woman-Killing

In no case was there more than one female victim. In three cases, a male was murdered at the same time as a woman, and in nine cases there were two victims because the male perpetrators also killed themselves.

The Age of Female Murder Victims

The ages of the femicide victims range from 16 to 61 years, with the mean age being 34.6 years. The age range for the nonfemicidal victims was almost identical: from 15 years old to 60. However the mean age was a few years younger for the nonfemicidal victims (30.5 years).

The Ethnicity of Female Murder Victims

Ethnicity was only ascertainable from the black-and-white photographs (when available) and the names (in the case of Latinas and Native American women) that accompanied the descriptions of all those murdered in the first week of May, 1989. These indicators of ethnicity are very problematic. Since some individuals who identify as Black look White, the errors are likely to be more in the direction of mislabeling victims as White rather than as African American. Despite this probable bias, over half (52%) of all the female murder victims were African American, just over a third (35%) were White, and 13% were Latina. These figures are virtually identical for the femicides.

When the percentages are recalculated to take account of the numbers of White, African American, and Latina women in the United States population in 1989 (the year the data were collected), the overrepresentation of African American women among the femicides and the nonfemicidal murders is even greater. More specifically, when the total number of White females in 1989 (106,738,000) is added to the total number of African Americans (16,115,000) and Latinas (10,188,000; total: 133,041,000), we see that approximately half of the femicide victims were African American women, although they made up only 12% of the women in these three ethnic groups that year (U.S. Bureau of the Census, 1991, pp. 17–18). In contrast, only a third of the femicide victims were White women, although they constituted 80% of the women in these three ethnic groups in 1989.

It is noteworthy that during the first week of May 1989, not a single Asian American woman was murdered by gunshot in the United States. The same applies to Native American women, assuming that the murders of these women came to the attention of law enforcement personnel.

In her statistical study of intimate partner femicide in the United States, Stout (1991) reported that:

> Although White women (including Hispanic) comprise the majority of victims (60.4%), African-American women are disproportionately represented at 37.1% of all intimate femicide victims. Forty-one Native American women (.9%) and 41 Asian women (.9%) were victims of intimate femicide. (p. 481)

These findings about the enormous overrepresentation of African American women as victims of femicide *and* nonfemicidal murder, along with Campbell's (1992) disturbing observation that "homicide is the leading cause of death for African-American women, aged 15–34" (p. 99), highlight the importance of putting African American women at the top of the agenda for those engaged in research, policy making, and activism to combat lethal violence against women.

The Relationships Between Female Murder Victims and Their Male Perpetrators

Husbands and ex-husbands were the perpetrators in exactly half of the femicides in the *Time* study, while just over 25% of the perpetrators were boyfriends and ex-boyfriends. Hence, over 75% of the femicides qualify as intimate partner femicides. This comes as no surprise, since study after study has shown that women are most likely to be killed by a member of their families (e.g., Ewing, 1997; Kellerman & Mercy, 1992; Smith & Brewer, 1992; Wilson & Daly, 1992). In addition, 100% of the murders by intimate partners were cases of femicide.

A study conducted by murder expert James Fox together with a team headed by Lawrence Greenfeld of the Bureau of Justice Statistics, found that by 1996, "Murders by intimates [had] dropped dramatically over the past 20 years" (Lardner, 1998, p. A10). However, George Lardner (1998) noted that this finding only applied to the murder of men: "The percentage of women killed by intimates has remained steady, at about 30 percent of all female homicide victims" (p. A10).

Whether or not the huge discrepancy between Fox and Greenfeld's study and the *Time* data is due to the fact that their statistics were not limited to murders by firearms is unknown.

When intimate partner femicides are broken down and the numbers of different kinds of partners are calculated as a percentage of the total number of such femicides, we find that

- 35% were perpetrated by legal or common-law husbands.
- 30% were perpetrated by estranged husbands or ex-husbands.
- 30% were perpetrated by boyfriends/lovers and/or cohabiters.
- 5% were perpetrated by ex-boyfriends and ex-lovers.

Since there are obviously more married women at any one time than those who have left their marriages, this breakdown shows that women are at greater risk of becoming femicide victims of their ex-husbands or the husbands from whom they are estranged or separated than they are by the men to whom they are still married. Based on the data set provided by Statistics Canada's Homicide Survey, Margo Wilson and Martin Daly (1994) noted that "compared to coresiding couples, separation entails a sixfold increase in risk [of femicide] to wives" (quoted in Ellis & DeKeseredy, 1997, p. 591). After completing comprehensive reviews of this issue, Desmond Ellis and Walter DeKeseredy (1997) conclude that marital "estrangement is a significant predictor of intimate femicide" (p. 591, n. 1, p. 607).[2]

"Men's effort to reassert power and control was the underlying issue in the estranged-partner homicides," Campbell (1992) notes (p. 106). Referring specifically to battered women, Ewing (1997) concurs with Campbell's emphasis on these men's desire to control women:

> Most battered women killed by their batterers are those who . . . not only tried but succeeded in leaving their batterers. Their mates . . . could not accept the loss of control they experienced when "their" women left them. Unable to regain that control by any other means, they resorted to the ultimate form of control: murder. (pp. 23–24)

However, this finding does not apply to the *Time* data on femicide by ex-boyfriends and boyfriends (5% versus 30%, respectively).

Femicidal Suicides

Many researchers on male violence toward partners have noted that "the coupling of homicide with suicide is a frequent occurrence with men who kill family members" (Hart, 1988, p. 241; see also Campbell, 1992; Browne, 1987). *Time*'s nine cases of suicide–murder all qualified as femicides because of the misogyny evident in the descriptions of these crimes. Following are five examples:

> Sylvia Contreras, 26: After nine years of violence and abuse from her *common-law husband*, Sylvia Contreras had fled their house after yet another beating. Juan Valencia, a farmworker, *begged for a reconciliation* when she returned to fetch their three children. *After she refused*, he was heard to say, "If you're not going to live with me, you're not going to live at all." She ran out of the house. He chased her into the yard, his .22 rifle in hand. Neighbors watched helplessly as he shot her repeatedly in the chest. Then he turned the weapon on himself, ending his rage, his remorse and his life. (Magnuson, 1989, p. 35; emphasis added)

> Elisia Cruz Saavedra, 32: On Elisia's birthday, Odilon [Saavedra] broke the bedroom window where his *estranged wife*, the mother of three daughters, was with her four-year old. The mother fled. He caught her as she frantically knocked on a neighbor's door. He shot her three times with a pistol, then shot himself. (Magnuson, 1989, p. 36; emphasis added)

> Mary E. Brown, 58: He [Jones] and Brown had a five-year *on-and-off relationship that she had tried to end*. He shot her three times with a revolver, poured gasoline on her and set her afire. Then he shot himself, and was caught in the flames. (Magnuson, 1989, p. 41; emphasis added)

> Diana Bird, 38: A cocktail waitress, she was coming off her shift at a hotel casino when her unemployed *ex-husband*, ejected earlier for harassing her, returned and shot her with a pistol in front of other casino employees. He then turned the gun on himself. (Magnuson, 1989, p. 45; emphasis added)

> Marian Andino, 34: *Formerly married to each other*, they [she and her ex-husband] were still living together, but *Andino was planning to move* to Puerto Rico at the end of the month. Distraught, Montes shot her with a handgun, then shot himself. (Magnuson, 1989, p. 58; emphasis added)

This subset of femicidal suicides constitutes just over a third (35%) of all the femicides, indicating how frequently men—mostly husbands and significant others—kill themselves after murdering their partners. For example, the femicidal suicides described above all involved estranged or ex-husbands/ boyfriends. In three of the cases it seems clear that the men killed their female partners because their partners planned to leave or refused to reconcile. In contrast, there is no case among the 464 deaths in which a woman committed suicide after murdering a man. Hence, the suicide–murder phenomenon is clearly a male syndrome.

CONCLUSION

Magnuson's descriptions of the deaths by gunshot that occurred during a week in May 1989 are far from satisfactory for inferring whether or not they qualify as femicides. The only rationale for using them is the lack of more satisfactory data sets. For example, it is impossible to obtain data on femicide from national and state statistics on murder gathered by the FBI and published annually in the *Uniform Crimes Reports*. This may be why all the other empirical analyses of femicide in this book use the revised definition of this concept, that is, woman-killing, not the killing of females by men *because* they are female.

One of the major findings to come out of this analysis of the *Time* data is that almost three-quarters (72%) of the male-perpetrated murders of women by gunshot during a week in 1989 were femicides (excluding the cases that were not ascertainable and those perpetrated by women). Another is the finding that of the female deaths by firearms, the percentage of suicides was even higher than the percentage of femicides (45% vs. 34%). On the basis of this finding, I recommend that future research examine the significance of sexism and misogyny as causes of female suicide, particularly by exceptionally vulnerable women such as the victims of male abuse and violence in the home (wives and daughters).

Many other important questions need to be addressed in research on femicide. Important examples (two of which I mentioned previously) include: Are wife rape victims more likely to become victims of femicidal suicide? Are men who rape their wives also more likely to die at their own hands? And why are African American women at far higher risk of becoming victims of femicide than White, Latina, Asian, and Native American women?

Magnuson's total neglect of the relevance of gender to his analysis of the 464 murders by gunshot in the United States during a week in 1989 is typical in both scholarly and popular writing. I hope that my critique of this practice in this chapter and others in this volume will serve to discourage this serious oversight by showing the value of undertaking gender-based analyses.

Acknowledgments. I would like to thank Karen Trocki for her assistance with the development of codes for the analysis of the data in *Time* magazine, Jan Dennie and Gretchen Lieb for coding the data, and Marie Schwaim for her contribution to the analysis of the data.

NOTES

1. Examples of sexist motivations that would qualify murders of females by males as femicides:

a. Most cases of the murder of women by their husbands, lovers, and boyfriends are sexist—and therefore instances of femicide. These femicides are motivated by men's perception of "their" woman as their possession and/or as their inferior and/or as having no right to initiate the termination of their relationship. Many of these men believe they are entitled to use violence toward their female partners as a means of controlling them or punishing them or as an expression of jealousy toward them—including lethal violence.

b. Sex-related or sexual murders are sexist—and therefore instances of femicide. For example, when johns (customers of prostituted women) kill their female victims because they see them as "bad women" or when other males kill prostitutes for the same reason; or when males kill females because they are necrophiliacs; or because they become enraged when a female rejects their sexual overtures (e.g., some stalkers); or when males are sexually excited by acting out sexual murders (serial killers, rapists/murderers, etc.); or when males so devalue females that they feel entitled to express their sadistic misogyny by killing them; or when males are motivated to act out sexual torture and murder for monetary gain (e.g., to make snuff movies).

c. Male mass murderers (almost all mass murders *are* male) who target females are motivated by sexism. Many want to kill a specific woman among those they target—typically a girl friend, lover, or wife, or "crush" who has rejected them or with whom they have quarrelled, and/or a woman they want to impress. Other male mass murderers who do not specifically target females, may nevertheless be motivated by rage and revenge toward a particular woman.

d. Male-perpetrated familicides are also usually motivated by a man's anger, desire for revenge, and/or sense of ownership—thereby qualifying as a form of femicide; for example, when a man murders his wife, children, and/or other female relatives or friends to punish his wife for actual or perceived infidelity.

2. In contrast, Stout (1991) found in one of her studies that the majority of women killed by intimate partners were married. However, in another of her studies, she reports finding that "persons who are separated are the most frequent perpetrator of intimate femicide" (1993, p. 81).

REFERENCES

Browne, Angela. (1987). *When battered women kill*. New York: Free Press.

Campbell, Jacquelyn C. (1992). If I can't have you, no one can: Power and control in homicide of female partners. In Jill Radford & Diana E. H. Russell (Eds.), *Femicide: The politics of woman killing* (pp. 99–113). New York: Twayne/Gale Group.

Campbell, Jacquelyn C., & Peggy Alford. (1989). The dark consequences of marital rape. *American Journal of Nursing, 89*, 946–949.

Ellis, Desmond, & Walter S. DeKeseredy. (1997, December). Rethinking estrangement, interventions, and intimate femicide. *Violence Against Women, 3*(6), 590–609.

Ewing, Charles Patrick. (1997). *Fatal families*. Thousand Oaks, CA: Sage Publications.

Goetting, Ann. (1988). Patterns of homicide among women. *Journal of Interpersonal Violence, 3*(1), 3–20.

Hart, Barbara. (1988). Beyond the "duty to warn": A therapist's "duty to protect" battered women and children. In Kersti Yllo & Michele Bograd (Eds.), *Feminist perspectives on wife abuse* (pp. 234–248). Newbury Park, CA: Sage Publications.

Kellerman, Arthur L., & James A. Mercy. (1992). Gender-specific differences in rates of fatal violence and victimization. *Journal of Trauma, 33*(1), 1–5.

Lardner, George, Jr. (1998, March 18). Murder by intimates have declined. *Washington Post*, p. A10.

Magnuson, Ed. (1989, July 17). Seven deadly days. *Time, 134*(3), 30–61.

Mulvihill, Donald J., Melvin M. Tumin, & Lynn A. Curtis. (1969). Task force on individual acts of violence. *Crimes of violence* (Vol. 11). Washington, D.C.: U.S. Government Printing Office.

Smith, Dwayne M., & Victoria E. Brewer. (1992, Winter). Sex-specific analysis of correlates of homicide victimization in United States cities. *Violence and Victims, 7*(4), 279–286.

Stout, Karen D. (1991). Intimate femicide: A national demographic overview. *Journal of Interpersonal Violence, 6*(4), 476–485.

Stout, Karen D. (1993). Intimate femicide: A study of men who have killed their mates. *Journal of Offender Rehabilitation, 19*(3–4), 81–94.

U.S. Bureau of the Census. (1991). *Census of United States, 1990*. Washington, D.C.: U.S. Government Printing Office.

Wilson, Margo, & Martin Daly. (1992). Till death us do part. In Jill Radford & Diana E. H. Russell (Eds.), *Femicide: The politics of woman killing* (pp. 83–93). New York: Twayne/Gayle Group.

Wilson, Margo, & Martin Daly. (1994, March). Spousal homicide. *Juristat Service Bulletin, 14*(8), 1–15. Ottawa: Canadian Centre for Justice Statistics.

CHAPTER 4

Intimate Femicide:
A National Demographic Overview

Karen D. Stout

The killing of women by male intimate partners is a problem that has received negligible attention within the social sciences and within scholarship
focusing on violence against women. Many explanations are given for the
scarcity of literature on intimate femicide victims. However, despite the lack
of focused research in this area, the literature suggests that when women are
killed, they are most frequently killed by husbands and boyfriends. This research focuses on the problem of intimate femicide. The topic of femicide,
along with the subtopic of intimate femicide, is a necessary link in the research to date on violence against women.

Intimate femicide is the word choice for the present research in order to
clearly focus attention on a subgroup of homicide victims: women killed by
their intimate male partners. This subgroup has received very little attention
from sociologists, criminologists, social workers, and other professional and
academic groups. Victims of intimate femicide have also received little attention from scholars researching topics related to violence against women.
The word choice of *intimate femicide* does not mask the intent of the research
and most readily identifies the problem of females being killed by current
and former male partners. The word choice of *intimate femicide* will link
this research, by name and by intent, with other studies that examine violence against women.

The most consistent information regarding the killing of women by male
intimate partners is the notation of the lack of research in this area (Campbell,
1981; Chimbos, 1978; McClain, 1982; Wilbanks, 1982). Yet the evidence
of women killed by husbands and male intimates is not new information

discovered in the 1970s by feminists, behavioral scientists, or the public at large. As early as 1911, MacDonald noted, "There are thousands of innocent persons murdered in the United States each year. Most of these are helpless women" (p. 91). In 1948, von Hentig cautioned that "when a man is found murdered we should look first for his acquaintances; when a woman is killed, for her relatives, mainly her husband and after that her paramour, present or past" (p. 393). A decade later, in a city study of Philadelphia, Wolfgang (1958) found that 41% of female homicide victims were killed by their husbands.

More recent studies continue to confirm the problem of females killed by male intimate partners. Dobash and Dobash (1979) chronicled the history of wife beating and wife murder from as early as 753 B.C. through the mid-1970s. Okun (1986) noted, "Since the founding of America's first battered women's shelter in 1974 through the end of 1983, well over 19,000 Americans have died in incidents of woman abuse or other forms of conjugal violence" (p. xiv).

Intimate femicide by male partners takes place in the context of close relationships. That the violence occurs between people who know each other well, who may have a bond of love between them, and who may share children seems unbelievable to many people, including the victims who end up involved in a violent relationship. Peplau (1979) brought to attention some of the components of close relationships that may not often be in the forefront of our minds when considering intimate relationships. She stated:

> Americans are sentimental about love. In thinking about romance, we emphasize intimacy and caring; we like to view our lover and the relationship as unique. We de-emphasize the part that culture values and social roles play in determining whom we love and how we conduct ourselves with them. In particular, we neglect a crucial aspect of love relationships—power. (p. 106)

Unfortunately, violence has been a means through which many intimate partners have chosen to exercise power and to channel frustrations and anger. Levinson (1981) has presented data suggesting that, worldwide, women are the most preferred victims of family violence. In the United States, females are disproportionately represented as victims of incestuous assault, sexual harassment, rape, and battering.

Gelles and Cornell (1985) noted that "we do not commonly think of the family as society's most violent social institution. Typically, family life is thought to be warm, intimate, stress-reducing, and the place that people *flee* to for safety" (p. 12; emphasis in original). As a result of the reluctance of research and practitioners to expose and/or see violence in families and close partnerships, research on child abuse, wife abuse, and wife rape have only recently become a focus of scholarly inquiry.

Wilbanks (1982) addressed an apparent bias by researchers that may prevent research on women killed by men:

> Apparently, female murderers are much more interesting to researchers than female murder victims. The female killer seems to be an anomaly; men are expected to be aggressive and violent but women are not. On the other hand, the female victim is not an anomaly; because women are viewed as vulnerable and passive, we are not surprised when women are victimized. Gender stereotypes about women, then, appear to have affected researchers' approach to the subject of women and homicide. (p. 160)

McClain (1982), concerned about the lack of research on African American female victims of homicide, suggested that the "triple legitimate" victim status of Black females—poor, Black, and female—may also account for the absence of research on their role as victims of lethal violence (p. 205).

Other scholars suggest that women's view of the world and the meanings that women attach to violence against them have been obscured and/or negated (Spender, 1980; Stanko, 1985). This perceived negation prompted Stanko (1985) to advocate a woman-defined struggle against male oppression and to interject into public and professional consciousness the meaning that violence has to women in their lives.

Each of these overlapping perspectives is important in the process of piecing together the historical void of research on violence against women and the present absence of in-depth research on intimate femicide. It is important to note that few people wish to think that men and women who are in a "love" relationship would have the capability to kill their partner—male or female. However, researchers and practitioners need to question why women may be viewed as "appropriate" victims and as such have not been deemed worthy of study.

This research identifies the problem of intimate femicide and suggests that it is a societal problem that is worthy of study and serious discussion. Intimate femicide is, in fact, the final act of violence against females by male partners. This research inquiry will address some basic questions needed to clearly identify the problem. Information will be presented on U.S. intimate femicide rates, the relationship of the victim to the offender, age of victims and offenders, race and ethnicity of victims and offenders, weapon choice, and other situational information.

METHOD

This research addresses intimate femicide in the United States. The focus of this research is on females, age 16 and over, who were killed by male intimate partners during 1980, 1981, and 1982. All females, 16 and older, killed by male intimate partners whose deaths were classified as "murder or non-negligent manslaughter" are included in the data analyzed. Male intimate partners include husbands, common-law husbands, ex-husbands, friends, and boyfriends, aged 16 and over. The homicide cases in which the relationship of the victim to the offender was unknown were disqualified because this relationship is the integral classification criterion in this research project.

The data for this descriptive, exploratory study are derived from the *Uniform Crime Reports: Supplemental Homicide Report, 1980–1982*.[1]

O'Brien (1985) criticized the validity of the *UCR* data, particularly when comparing jurisdictions across the country. The critique is related to the political issues confronting law enforcement agencies, differing laws, number of police per capita, and other related political factors, such as the political need to show decreases in crime rates. However, O'Brien (1985) suggested that

> It is important to emphasize that the homicide rate is an exception. Trends in homicides within the United States and differences in homicide rates between jurisdictions (given a large base population so that rates are not unstable) are probably valid. (p. 36)

Block (1981) brought to our attention that while the homicide data may be more valid than data on other types of violent crimes, it is important to recognize that the victim of the crime is dead and cannot convey his or her perspective. The death of the victim leaves the crime to be reconstructed by the police or by the offender. This is important in this study when assessing the relationship of the victim to the offender and the circumstances surrounding the death of the woman. The coding of these variables is done by the FBI (versus assigned personnel in each *UCR* state program) to enhance coding consistency. However, it is important to bear in mind that these classifications may not reflect the circumstances or relationship as might have been defined by the victim.

RESULTS

National Overview or Intimate Femicide Rate

Figure 4.1 depicts the rate of femicide in the 50 U.S. states. Rates of femicide range from 2.3 per million in the state of Iowa to 16.2 per million in the state of Alabama. This pictorial illustration of intimate femicide shows clearly

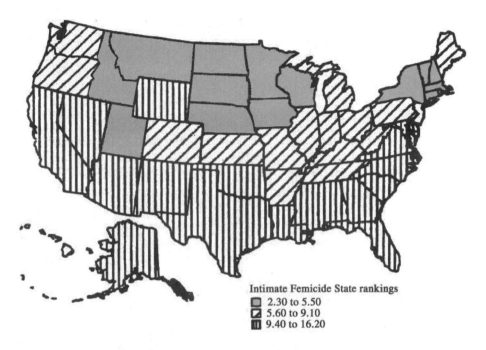

Intimate Femicide State rankings
▨ 2.30 to 5.50
▨ 5.60 to 9.10
▥ 9.40 to 16.20

FIGURE 4.1. U.S. Intimate Femicide Rates

that the rate of intimate femicide is highest in the southeast and southwest regions of the country.

Relationship of Victim to Offender

The majority of women killed by intimate partners were married, with 2,415 (57.7%) women classified as wives. Girlfriends (n = 1,041, 24.9%) have the next highest frequency of lethal victimization, followed in frequency by common-law wives (n = 332, 7.9%), ex-wives (n = 205, 4.9%), and friends (n = 196, 4.7%).

Age of Victims and Offenders

Reviewing national data from 1980 to 1982, the age of victims ranged from 16 to 91. The modal age or most frequent age of the victim was 26. The mean victim age was 35. The age group of 25 to 29 was the modal grouped age category. The number of killings by male intimate partners declines with each subsequent age category. The age group of 30 to 34 was the modal group age for the male offender. As in the grouped age data for victims, the number of killings declined for each subsequent age group after the modal age group of 30 to 34.

Race and Ethnicity

Although White women (including Hispanic) comprise the majority of victims (60.4%), African American women are disproportionately represented at 37.1% of all intimate femicide victims. Forty-one Native American women (0.9%) and 41 Asian women (0.9%) were victims of intimate femicide. Race data were missing on 20 victims. The ethnicity of victims is classified separately from race in the *UCR*. The majority of victims (n = 2,764, 66%) were of non-Hispanic origin. Three hundred and nine (7.4%) were Hispanic, and the remaining 1,116 (26.6%) were classified as "unknown."

This research indicates that, most frequently, intimate femicides are intraracial. Of 2,528 femicides where the race of the victim and offender was known to be White, 2,413 White females were killed by White male partners. Of Black female intimate victims killed, 1,530, or 98.5%, were killed by Black male intimate partners. Of 41 female Native Americans, 25 (61%) were killed by Native American male intimate partners. Forty-one Asian females were killed by a male intimate, with 24 (58.5%) of these killings being intraracial. In 27 of the 4,189 cases of intimate femicide, the race of the victim or offender was unknown.

Situation and Circumstance

The situation surrounding the incident of intimate femicide is described by the *UCR* as the number of offenders involved in the killing and the number of victims involved in the killing. As might be expected in intimate killings, the vast majority (96.8%) of intimate femicide killings involved a single offender and a single victim. The second most frequent situation was that of multiple victims killed by a single offender.

The next exploratory analysis on intimate femicide centers on the circumstance in which the killing took place. Was the killing the result of a robbery? An argument? A brawl under the influence of alcohol? The *UCR* lists five types of circumstances:

1. "Felony type," which includes killings that occurred during the commission of rape, robbery, burglary, arson, other sex offense, narcotic drugs laws, and other felony-type crimes
2. "Other than felony type," which includes lovers' triangle, brawl–alcohol influence, brawl–narcotic influence, argument over money or property, other arguments, and gangland killings

3. "Manslaughter by negligent circumstances" or "Other nonfelony type"
4. "Justifiable homicide–civilian," and
5. "Facts do not permit determination."

The majority of intimate femicide cases fell into the "Other than felony type" of circumstance in the "other arguments" category. This would be consistent with the lay and police terminology of "domestic quarrel." These 2,426 "domestic quarrels" ended in the death of the female partner. The second most frequent category ($N = 203$) was that of "lovers' triangle." This is the category often described in lay and academic literature as "crimes of passion." Ninety deaths were attributed to alcohol or drug use on the part of the offender. The terms *domestic quarrel, lovers' triangle,* and *crimes of passion* diminish the seriousness of the killing of more than 2,600 women and mask the reality that these are crimes of violence and control.

Weapon Choice

Intimate femicide victims were killed by a type of firearm (handgun, shotgun, rifle, and so on) in 67.9% of the cases. The second leading weapon for intimate femicides was a knife (14.4%), followed by personal weapons (beatings with hands, feet) in 8% of cases.

DISCUSSION

Each day in this country, approximately four women are killed by a male intimate partner. The rates of intimate femicide are highest in the Southeast and Southwest. Prior research by Stout (1989) suggests that a negative correlation exists between intimate femicide rates and services available to address violence against women, such as shelters and rape crisis centers. Perhaps helping professionals need to evaluate the need for shelter services in those states where intimate femicide rates are high.

This demographic analysis of intimate femicide suggests that victims of intimate femicide are most often in the age group of 25 to 29, with the offender most often in the age group of 30 to 34. These killings are intraracial and within the same ethnic groups. Women are most often killed by a gun and by a single offender. Killings are precipitated by an argument. Wives are the most frequent victims of intimate femicide, followed by girlfriends. Common-law wives are killed more often than ex-wives.

This analysis of demographic factors describes the prevalence of intimate femicide and presents information on the nature of the event and the nature of victim/offender relationships. While women age 25 to 29 appear to be at highest risk for lethal victimization by male partners, it is important to note that women of all ages fall prey to intimate femicide—the final act of violence against women. No one should negate the possibility of lethal danger in the lives of clients. It appears relevant to note that most intimate femicides are recorded as the end result of an argument. This implies that educational and clinical intervention strategies should continue toward the goal of nonviolence in the family home and lends evidence to debunk the myth that these deaths are attributable to unfaithfulness on the part of the victim.

The first step in any research endeavor is to identify the problem. Hopefully, the data presented here are an initial step toward identifying intimate femicide as a social problem meriting attention and action. It is hoped that professionals working with victims and perpetrators of battering will take seriously the issues of intimate femicide and women's fear of lethal victimization. In addition, it is hoped that this research will encourage others to examine the problem of femicide. Possibilities for fruitful research include a focused analysis on battered women who are killed by their male batterers and research on rape/femicides. Further, future research should focus on the outcome of these cases to determine whether the prosecution rate is lower and sentencing in cases of femicide is milder than with other homicide cases. Such research would be a valuable contribution to the emerging literature on violence against women.

NOTES

This is an edited version of an article that was previously published by Karen Stout under the same title in the *Journal of Interpersonal Violence*, 6(4), 476–485, 1991.

1. The data used to analyze the 1980–1982 incidence of intimate femicide and the subsequent demographic information were made available by the Inter-University Consortium for Political and Social Research. The data for the *Uniform Crime Reports, 1980–1982: Supplemental Homicide Report* were originally collected by the Federal Bureau of Investigation. Neither the collector of the original data nor the consortium bear any responsibility for the analysis and interpretations presented in this research.

REFERENCES

Block, Richard. (1981). Victim–offender relationships in violent crime. *Journal of Criminal Law and Criminology, 72*, 743–761.

Campbell, Jacquelyn. (1981). Misogyny and homicide of women. *Advances in Nursing Science, 3*, 67–85.

Chimbos, Peter C. (1978). *Marital violence: A study of interpersonal homicide*. San Francisco: R & E Associates.

Dobash, R. Emerson, & Russell Dobash. (1979). *Violence against wives: A case against patriarchy*. New York: Free Press.

Gelles, Richard J., & Claire P. Cornell. (1985). *Intimate violence in families*. Beverly Hills, CA: Sage Publications.

Levinson, David. (1981). Physical punishment of children and wifebeating in cross-cultural perspective. *Child Abuse & Neglect*, *5*, 193–196.

MacDonald, Arthur. (1911). Death penalty and homicide. *American Journal of Sociology*, *16*, 88–115.

McClain, Paula D. (1982). Cause of death—homicide: A research note on Black females as homicide victims. *Victimology: An International Journal*, *7*, 204–212.

O'Brien, Robert M. (1985). *Crime and victimization data*. Beverly Hills, CA: Sage Publications.

Okun, Lewis. (1986). *Woman abuse: Facts replacing myths*. Albany: State University of New York Press.

Peplau, Letitia Anne. (1979). Power in dating relationships. In Jo Freeman (Ed.), *Women: A feminist perspective* (pp. 106–121). Palo Alto, CA: Mayfield.

Spender, Dale. (1980). *Man made language*. London: Routledge & Kegan Paul.

Stanko, Elizabeth A. (1985). *Intimate intrusions: Women's experience of mate violence*. London: Routledge & Kegan Paul.

Stout, Karen. (1989). Intimate femicide: Effect of legislation and social services. *Affilia*, *4*(2), 21–30.

von Hentig, Hans. (1948). *The criminal and his victim*. New Haven CT: Yale University Press.

Wilbanks, William. (1982). Murdered women and women who murder: A critique of the literature. In Nicole Rafter & Elizabeth Stanko (Eds.), *Judge, lawyer, victim and thief* (pp. 151–180). Boston: Northeastern University Press.

Wolfgang, Marvin. (1958). *Patterns of criminal homicide*. New York: Wiley.

CHAPTER 5

Femicidal Pornography

Diana E. H. Russell

INTRODUCTION

The normalization of lethal violence against women is manifested in the ubiquitous, often eroticized portrayals of males slaughtering females in slasher films, mainstream movies, TV programs, and video games. The normalization of misogynist murder is also evident in femicidal depictions of women in pornography. Humor is also used for this purpose, particularly in pornographic cartoons.

Ironically, it tends to be the better-educated Americans who typically believe that endless images of brutal males engaged in gory femicides are harmless when depicted in pornography (see the public opinion data in Russell, 1998) even while many of these same individuals express concern about the negative effects of portrayals of nonsexualized forms of violence on TV, in video games, in music, and in mainstream movies. After the Columbine high school massacre perpetrated by Eric Harris and Dylan Klebold in Littleton, Colorado, on Hitler's birthday (April 20) in 1999, President Clinton (June 1, 1999) made the following statement at a White House briefing in response to the "daily dose of violence" that the entertainment industry feeds children:

> Now, 30 years of studies have shown that this desensitizes our children to violence and to the consequences of it. We now know that by the time the typical American child reaches the age of 18, he or she has seen 200,000 dramatized acts of violence and 40,000 dramatized murders. Kids [sic][1] become attracted to it and more numb to its consequences. As the exposure to violence grows, so, in some deeply troubling cases of particularly vulnerable children [sic], does the taste for it. We should not be surprised that half the video games a typical

seventh-grader [sic] plays are violent. Anyone who doubts the impact of the cultural assault can look at what now, over 30 years, amounts to somewhere over 300 studies, all of whom [sic] show that there is a link between sustained exposure ... to violent entertainment and violent behavior. (Federal News Service, June 1, 1999; no page numbers provided)

However, when feminists point out that pornography, which is also a part of the entertainment industry, desensitizes male viewers to degrading behavior toward females, promotes sexual callousness toward females, perpetuates rape myths, and undermines males' internal and social inhibitions against acting out degrading and violent behavior toward females, most educated Americans claim that there is no scientific evidence to justify these conclusions. This claim is false and illogical. It makes no sense to maintain that nonpornographic violence promotes violence but pornographic violence does not.

This illogical double standard is frequently defended with the additional illogical argument that any critique of pornography is an attack on free speech. Meanwhile, there is substantial evidence to show that such depictions *do* play a significant role in fostering viewers' negative attitudes toward women, in eroticizing violence perpetrated by males against women, and in promoting the acting out of misogynist porn-induced and/or porn-sanctioned behaviors (see, for example, Check & Guloien, 1989; Russell, 1993, 1994). It is impossible to know how many women and girls are annually sacrificed by men who have been conditioned to normalize and eroticize femicide by watching common, everyday, American-style entertainment.

EXAMPLES OF FEMICIDAL PORNOGRAPHY

The following descriptions of photographs provide examples of pornography that depicts *sexual femicide* (the killing of females by males for sexual gratification).[2] Of all the kinds of power one person can wield over another, the ultimate is the power of life and death.

Picture 1

This is a poster advertising the notorious 1979 film called *Snuff* in which a woman was tortured, mutilated, and killed. In the final scene, a man rips out her uterus and holds it up in the air while he ejaculates. Some people claim that the violent scenes were simulated, while others believe they were real.

The poster features a picture of a beautiful young naked woman, her head lolling backward. The picture has been cut into four pieces with a gigantic pair of bloody scissors displayed alongside the woman's body. Large quantities of blood are shown flowing from her neck, breasts, and upper pelvic region because these parts of her body were cut by the scissors. Three blurbs add the final touch to this movie advertisement promising audiences an orgy of woman-hating sexual violence:

The picture they said could NEVER be shown. . . .

The film that could only be made in South America . . . where life is CHEAP!

The *bloodiest* thing that *ever* happened in front of a camera!!

Comment 1. Even if we assume that the femicide and mutilation portrayed in the movie *Snuff* were simulated by trick photography, whether it was indeed simulated is difficult to ascertain. The protests by feminists that greeted the opening of this 1979 movie caused the word *snuff* to become the generic term for pornographic films of sexual femicides. In order for snuff movies to have become a marketable underground genre in the pornography industry, a significant number of men must find it sexually arousing to watch sexualized femicides. This is a terrifying and macabre reality for women, many of whom have been killed or threatened by woman-hating strangers, acquaintances, dates, boyfriends, lovers, husbands, johns, members of the nuclear family, and more distant relatives.

Picture 2

A photo of a naked woman in *Cheri* magazine shows her standing in a Christ-like position with her arms outstretched and her head slumped to one side. Blood is splattered all over her body. Someone outside the picture frame is pulling the woman's left nipple with a pair of heavy pliers. The caption below the heading SNUFF LIB reads: "The incredible and mysterious saga of a film none of us will ever see. By *Cheri*'s resident master of gore."

Comment 2. The term *snuff lib* suggests that aspiring perpetrators of femicide have been oppressed by having to remain in the closet. It is also a call to men who would like to commit femicide to come out of the closet and act out their femicidal desires. Given all the serial killers of women that this culture has produced in the last 30 years, distributing pornography like this picture represents the height of irresponsibility. And how repulsive it is that *Cheri* magazine would have, or even pretend to have, a "resident master of gore."

Picture 3

The June 1978 *Hustler* magazine cover shows a woman who has been placed head first into the opening of a manual meat grinder and is coming out the other end looking like ground beef. Her buttocks and legs, which have been doused with sleek body oil, protrude gracefully from the top of the grinder. A mound of ground woman (head and upper body) has accumulated on a plate on a table under the meat grinder. A sign that resembles a meat packaging stamp proclaims, "Last all meat issue—Grade 'A' Pink." The following quote from Larry Flynt also graces the cover: "We will no longer hang women up like pieces of meat."

Comment 3. Feminists have frequently protested that women in pornography are treated like pieces of meat. Larry Flynt used this charge as a pretext to escalate his assault on women. Although his taunt—"We will no longer hang women up like pieces of meat"—sounds like an unexpected concession to feminists, the picture is announcing that he will grind women up—that is, kill them—instead. There is an obvious cannibalistic element in this piece of sexualized femicidal *Hustler* porn.

Picture 4

Inside *Hustler*'s June 1978 woman-in-a-meat-grinder issue are two photos of naked women being served as meat dishes. The first photo shows a naked woman lying on her back between two hamburger buns. She is the meat patty, surrounded by onion, tomato, and lettuce. Ketchup that looks like blood has been poured on her stomach and legs, as well as between her large breasts. She is holding her legs apart to display her vulva and pubic hair. An excerpt from the accompanying text reads, "Grilled indoors or out, this pink patty takes two hands to handle."

The adjoining photo depicts a headless, squatting woman—with her back and buttocks facing the viewer—as the meat in a plate of spaghetti noodles. The viewer can see the woman's genitals because she has reached her hands underneath her torso between her severed legs to hold her labia apart. Once again, she is covered by sauce that looks like blood.

Comment 4. Here Flynt carries the woman-as-meat "joke" further: He will no longer hang women up like pieces of meat—he will make meals out of them. Once again, sexualized cannibalism is implicit in these two pictures. These pictures and the cover picture are graphic evidence of Flynt's crudity, misogyny, and violent sentiments toward women.

Picture 5

A photograph published in a 1979 *Hustler* issue entitled "The Best of *Hustler*," shows a naked woman, head shaved and hands in cuffs, sitting on a chair with her legs straddled over the armrests, exposing her vulva. A uniformed male officer on her right has one hand under her right leg while he holds her head with the other, turning her face toward him as he gazes intently into her blank face. A uniformed woman on the woman's left is shaving off the naked woman's pubic hair with a razor and shaving cream.

Comment 5. This photograph is from a photo-story entitled "The Naked and the Dead" about the fate of the woman in the picture just described. The woman is already naked in the first picture as she is led from a cell by fully clothed guards. In the second scene she is shown having her head shaved—an act reminiscent of the shaving of inmates' heads in Nazi concentration camps. The picture described above comes next, followed by one in which the woman is raped by a male guard. The final picture is blank except for the word POOF! in large letters, suggesting that the woman was a victim of femicide.

Once again, we have to think about what it means for the humiliation, rape, and femicidal attack on a woman to be considered entertaining for men, to be used by men as masturbation material, and to be judged by Larry Flynt or one of his staff as an example of "The Best of *Hustler*."

Pictures 6 and 7

Eleven photographs were published in a photo-essay entitled "Sakura" in the December 1984 issue of *Penthouse* magazine. A haiku, a classic Japanese poetry form, accompanies the photos in an attempt to provide them with artistic credibility and to render their appeal to necrophilia more acceptable to middle-class consumers. Photographer Akira Ishigaki describes the meaning of the title as follows:

> *Sakura* is the word for the cherry blossom. From my childhood . . . I recall the resemblance between the petals of the cherry blossom and a woman's body. In the spring of my twelve years, I caressed the petals with my fingers, kissed them gently with my lips.

Ishigaki's sensitive and subtle verbiage contrasts dramatically with the brutal, femicidal photographs that eroticize the torture, bondage, hanging, and death of young Japanese women or girls (several look like teenagers). The implicit message of this series is that the portrayal of extreme brutality toward women and girls can be published in a soft-core pornography magazine when it meets society's artistic standards.

Picture 6. The main focus of one of the pictures in "Sakura" is on the naked buttocks and legs of a girl/woman who is lying face down, hands tied behind her back, her legs close together with the bare soles of her feet toward the viewer and her genitals partially exposed. Her inert body, lying on a barren rocky cliff by the sea, looks like a corpse.

Comment 6. There is an eerie lifelessness about this photograph. Ishigaki has used his skills to glamorize and eroticize the buttocks of a female corpse. The effect is chilling and macabre; the frozen posture conveys the impression of rigor mortis. Pictures like this and the previous series of photographs (described in Comment 5) eroticize necrophilia and can also intensify the erotic response to it in those males who are already sexually excited by this idea or practice.

Picture 7. Another "Sakura" photograph shows a girl/woman in a harness, her arms bound behind her back, suspended from a tall tree by a rope that is tied to the harness. She is dressed in a long Japanese-looking outfit and short white socks, one leg exposed to her thigh. She is apparently dead or unconscious, her body limp, her head slumped forward. Around her are many tall trees with leafless branches. The photo's ambience is bleak and menacing.

Comment 7. This picture evokes recollections of the lynching of African Americans who, after being tortured and murdered, were typically left hanging from trees. Two months after this issue of *Penthouse* magazine appeared on the stands, Jean Kar-Har Fewel, an 8-year-old Chinese girl living in North Carolina, was found raped and murdered and tied to a tree with ropes around her neck. Many feminists believe that *Penthouse* magazine owner Bob Guccione is partly responsible for her horrifying death.

Ishigaki's delicate prose and technically beautiful photography contribute to making the vicious content of these pictures more acceptable, thereby serving to legitimize the violence against women and girls implied in these scenes.

Picture 8

An old Japanese print from the late fourteenth century entitled "Disembowelment" was republished in a Japanese magazine on sadomasochism entitled *A Garden of Pain.* At the center of the picture is a very old woman draped in traditional attire, one breast exposed, seated on the floor. Her left hand is plunged into the vagina of a young woman who is standing beside her doubled over at the waist. The young woman is naked but for a flimsy cloth around her waist; her mouth is gagged, her torso is bound, and her overall appearance is one of extreme discomfort.

A second young nude woman in the foreground is lying on her back, her feet tied to a horizontal pole on the ground to keep her legs apart. Her arms and shoulders are bound, and her bloody innards are piled on top of her stomach and cascading to the floor beside her. Sitting cross-legged on a low table behind the old woman is a fully clothed, smiling young man who is masturbating his oversized penis as he watches her at work.

This intricate picture illustrates an ancient Japanese folk tale. According to the text, the print depicts:

> a celebrated occurrence of the time—rather similar to certain so-called "ritualistic" murders . . . of modern times. . . . According to the legend, a wealthy young reprobate, Shangi Kuto, . . . grew increasingly to have tastes which we would now call "de Sadian!" The story relates how he conferred a substantial amount of gold on one Hessuto Mofini, a withered old crone with a fervent hatred of young women, with the stipulation that she arrange some extravagant "entertainment" for him. The aged women . . . drugs two young girls, trusses them up in her house and, while the young "playboy" watches (and masturbates) she disembowels them with a large, sharp knife . . . having earlier subjected them to various tortures, including the insertion of lighted candles into their respective vaginas.
>   . . . The old woman and young Shangi Kuto suffer beheading and mutilation at the hands of starving dogs, after being tried before a celebrated judge. . . .
> (All quotations marks in the original; no page numbers available.)

Comment 8. I cannot recollect ever reading about a woman who mutilated and murdered other women for money in my research on murder over the years. I have come across a few cases of women who have murdered and mutilated their abusive husbands. But these kinds of female perpetrators are very rare compared with the numbers of men who have engaged in mutilation murders—of both males and females. Jack the Ripper is perhaps the most notorious (or celebrated) example of such a serial killer (see the photograph of a portrayal of one of his victims on display as a tourist attraction in Figure 5.1).

It is worth noting that at least the Japanese folk tale makes it clear that the old woman does not represent women in general (she is described as having "a fervent hatred of young women"). The painful fate of the old woman and young playboy described in the folk tale sets it apart from most Western pornography, in which the rapists and other perpetrators typically go unpunished. The failure of pornography to portray negative consequences

FIGURE 5.1. This realistic sculpture of one of Jack the Ripper's femicide victims is part of a popular tourist exhibit devoted to this notorious femicide perpetrator at the London Dungeon in London, England. Costumed tourist guides shepherd groups of visitors through the exhibit while trying to engender anxiety and fear of a live Ripper in female visitors. (Photograph by Diana E. H. Russell)

to men who hurt women contributes to its destructive impact on men and women.

Picture 9

A line drawing of a gory femicidal torture scene in what appears to be an outdoor setting is another fourteenth-century Japanese print that was re-printed in *A Garden of Pain*. With his left hand, a balding, middle-aged man has shoved a long curved sword so far up a naked woman's vagina that it has exited through her stomach. With his right hand, this man, wearing a robe and a smile on his face, is using a plier-type instrument to tear off the woman's right nipple. The woman's body is arched backward, her neck is circled by a rope, and her arms and a foot are tied to a pipe a few feet below her head, forcing her legs wide apart. Long needles protrude from her neck. The tube of a small enema-like syringe has been stuck up her anus. Her right leg has been sliced from her ankle to her knee. It gapes open, revealing her flesh and muscle. Blood gushes from the hole in her chest where her nipple has been ripped off. Blood also trickles from her mouth and from the wounds on her neck, stomach, and leg, as well as from her vagina. With her eyes open and a blank expression on her face, it is not clear whether she is alive, unconscious, or dead. Two mutilated women's corpses are hanging upside down from crosses in the background, their feet tied far apart. Blood and/or entrails fall from the vagina of one of these corpses. Various torture implements are on the ground within reach of the man, for example, long needles, scissors, rope, and knives. The woman's flowered robe lies on the ground nearby.

Comment 9. This depiction of a Japanese Jack the Ripper engaged in lethal and mutilating torture is the most gruesome picture I have ever seen. It seems doubtful that the artist could have created such a picture unless he suffered from a strong urge to torture, mutilate, and kill women. More important, however, is the issue of how such pornography affects viewers (see Russell, 1993, 1994).

Picture 10

Four photographs of women's corpses (these pictures are not simulated) are lying on a background of what appears to be wrinkled human skin that has the texture of leather (see *Hustler*, June 1990; the corpses in these pictures were described as victims of traffic accidents). Ten razor blades have been placed at the corners or edges of the photographs, as if to attach them to the skin. A severed clitoris and nipple, as well as two unidentifiable pieces of female flesh, have been fastened to the skin with fish hooks and safety pins.

One photograph shows the decapitated corpse of a naked woman lying on her back, her bloody neck and shoulders facing the viewer. Her arms, from which her hands have been severed, are folded over her large breasts.

An aerial view of another woman's naked corpse is displayed in the second photograph. She is lying on her back on the floor, her right leg sharply bent, frog-like, with her heel touching her crotch. Her left leg is missing, her trunk is ripped open, her innards are falling out of her lower stomach and pelvic area, and her genitals have been decimated. A long knife is lying on top of clothes at her side, suggesting that this woman was murdered. A deep wound from her right shoulder to below her armpit has almost severed her arm. Flesh has been cut off around her right knee, exposing bone and muscle. There are stab wounds on her right breast and long cuts on her left thigh. She appears to have lost her right eye, and blood is trickling from her nose.

The third photograph features another aerial view of a woman's naked corpse lying on her back on a bathroom floor next to a toilet. Her left arm is stretched above her head, while her right arm is bent over her chest. Blood is splattered all over her body and on the floor.

The fourth and largest photograph shows the nude severed trunk of a woman whose legs have been amputated at her knees. This truncated corpse is on its side, the thighs are closed, and the woman's pubic hair is plainly visible. There is a large bloody gash where the right thigh connects with the woman's torso. Aside from this, there is a peculiar absence of blood, suggesting that the corpse has been cleaned.

Comment 10. This picture also ranks as one of the most barbaric I have ever seen. That the women in the pictures were victims of accidents (presumably not femicides) is irrelevant to the fact that Larry Flynt chose to publish a macabre collage of photos of their mutilated corpses and body parts as masturbatory material for men.

Why do so many men (*Hustler* had a circulation of 808,667 paid subscribers in 1997) find the injury, mutilation, and femicide of women so acceptable that viewers failed to generate a public outcry after this pornographic picture was published? What would the reaction have been if comparably sadistic pictures of Black men had been published in a magazine geared to White people? What if pictures of mutilated and murdered gay men had been published in a heterosexual magazine, or comparable pictures of men had been published in a women's magazine? I'll wager that the reaction would have been far greater in these other contexts. Trying to explain why violence against women, even the most extreme forms of it, continues to be seen as harmless entertainment for men by some of the most educated people in the United States is the challenge that I tackled in two of my other books (Russell 1994, 1998).

CONCLUSION

Rape, battery, and femicide are typically considered criminal offenses. Yet the portrayal of these crimes against women is a popular form of entertainment in many countries. Millions of males regularly ejaculate to degrading pictures of women. This, in turn, intensifies their sexual response to women being abused. It is this sexual component, including the sexual gratification involved, that sets pornography apart from nonpornographic depictions that are degrading and/or violent toward women and that makes pornography particularly dangerous.

That it is considered acceptable to view this kind of material and to masturbate to it implies more than a tolerance of, and desensitization to, women's pain and degradation. It constitutes a massive hate crime against women as a gender. Would males be so cavalier about pornography, labeling it as mere free speech, if instead of the rape of women by men, pornography celebrated women cutting off men's penises and testicles? Societies that call themselves civilized cannot at the same time continue to tolerate pornography's invitation to men to rape, abuse, mutilate, and commit femicide against women.

NOTES

1. I have inserted [sic] into Clinton's quote several times to point out where he used gender-neutral terminology instead of noting that his statements apply largely to boys, not girls.
2. The source of the following descriptions and analyses of pornographic pictures can be found in Russell, 1998, pp. 98–109. The pictures described here have been reprinted in Russell, 1994.

REFERENCES

Check, James, & Ted Guloien. (1989). Reported proclivity for coercive sex following repeated exposure to sexually violent pornography, non-violent dehumanizing pornography, and erotica. In Dolf Zillmann & Jennings Bryant (Eds.), *Pornography: Recent research, interpretations, and policy considerations* (pp. 159–184). Hillside, NJ: Erlbaum.
Federal News Service. (1999, June 1). Remarks by President Bill Clinton, First Lady Hillary Rodham Clinton, Attorney General Janet Reno, & Robert Pitofsky. White House briefing on youth violence. [On-line]. *Federal News Service*. Available DIALOG File: 660.
Russell, Diana E. H. (1993). The experts cop out. In Diana E. H. Russell (Ed.), *Making violence sexy: Feminist views on pornography* (pp. 151–166). New York: Teachers College Press.
Russell, Diana E. H. (1994). *Against pornography: The evidence of harm*. Berkeley, CA: Russell Publications.
Russell, Diana E. H. (1998). *Dangerous relationships: Pornography, misogyny and rape*. Thousand Oaks, CA: Sage Publications.

Femicide in Africa

CHAPTER 6

The Shroud Over Algeria: Femicide, Islamism, and the Hijab

Rod Skilbeck

The first is a party (FIS) [The Islamic Salvation Front]. The second is a piece of fabric, the Hijjab [sic]. Both are used to weave the same material: a shroud

—Martine Gozlan, 1992, p. 57

None of us wants to wear the veil . . . but fear is stronger than our convictions or our will to be free. Fear is all around us. Our parents, our brothers, are unanimous: "Wear the veil and stay alive. This will pass."

—Fatima, a 22-year-old junior factory manager from Tlemcen (Slyomovics, 1995, p. 10)

"Katia was adamant, even if she had to die she would never wear the veil. . . . The gunman went up to them. He made a sign for the veiled girl to move away. Then he shot Katia."

—Nassima Bengana (BBC, 1994)

For most of the 1990s, Algeria was the scene of widespread and frequent terrorism as a secular government and its Islamist opponents battled for control of Algerian identity. The conflict has been fought along the lines of membership in political groupings and careers in various elite groups, as well as on the basis of racial and linguistic differences (which often equate to membership in a political group). However, in the mid-1990s overt antifemale terrorism emerged as a weapon of both sides—women were threatened and killed on the basis of what they represented as females.

Identity in Algeria has been established upon an uneasy and untenable combination of Islamic traditions, Arabic culture, traditional power hierarchies, and postcolonial modern realities. Women are defined by antagonistic patriarchal centers of power: the city, the village, and, more recently, the disaffected militant Islamist. Sexual violence against women is widespread in Algeria, as it is across the Middle East and North Africa. Where women are seen to step beyond the confines set before them by their fathers, village elders, or civilian rulers, they are punished. The civil conflict that engulfed Algeria through the 1990s saw domestic and marital femicide replaced by mass femicide—the misogynistic killing of women by groups of armed men solely on the basis of how women chose to dress.

Among these victims were three schoolgirls. Katia Bengana, 17 years old, was shot while walking to high school on February 28, 1994. A month later, 18-year-old Razika Meloudjemi and 19-year-old Naima Kar Ali were killed by a machine-gun-wielding motorcyclist at Boudouaou. These two instances of femicide encapsulate much of what is taking place in Algeria during its current unnamed crisis.

The modern Algerian state is heavily influenced by ancient, clan-based politics and the force of the military. These antimodern, undemocratic pressures undermine the notion that Algeria is a modern nation-state and bring into question the status of women as citizens. The recent rise of Islamist militancy, the arming of the extremely patriarchal Berber communities, and the seizure of power by the armed forces have revealed a deeply rooted desire among Algerian men to reestablish traditional modes of power while battling for control of the nation's power structures. As in the War of Independence against France in the 1950s and 1960s, terrorism against the civilian population has been used in order to eliminate the chance of dialogue—which would interrupt the violence.

Until 1989, Algeria was a one-party state ruled by the FLN. The FLN always was and remains a nationalist party with strong Islamic tenets—the party was formed on the back of Sheikh Abdel Hamid Ben Badis' *ulema* in the 1930s. Following pressure from Islamists in the early 1980s (and despite heated opposition from women's groups), the Family Code of 1984 was enacted, removing most rights given to women under the Charter of Algiers established after independence. Women were made minors until marriage and made to require their husband's permission in order to work. These and other laws stripping women of legal protection made domestic assault and femicide far easier for men to commit. Even 6 months before the nation's first elections, hundreds of thousands of supporters of the Islamist FIS party marched in favor of the government's legal stances on women's rights. This march in late 1989 was in response to a march by several hundred women opposed to the Family Code. The march the FIS organized the following day numbered in the tens of thousands and included thousands of women (Burgat, 1994, p. 276).

Following political reforms and a landslide victory for the FIS in late 1991, the army overturned the democratic experiment and installed its own rulers, now organized as the RND. The armed wing of the FIS and a more shadowy network known as the Armed Islamic Group (GIA) commenced guerilla activities against the paramilitary and eventually, in escalating steps, against the government, media, culture, and very identity of Algeria. Their attempts to seize power or create chaos in Algeria were met with savage repression by the military and their own guerilla groups.

For most of 1992 and 1993, communiques from the GIA warned women not to go about in public unveiled or commit other acts deemed inappropriate (such as living alone, being a divorcee, working, etc.). Public displays of these behaviors would be met with femicidal force. Meanwhile, secular guerilla units also emerged, such as the Organization of Young Free Algerians (OJAL), which promised to kill 20 veiled women (or bearded men) for any unveiled woman who was murdered (Barrouhi, 1995). Women were immediately reduced to targets for both sides—regardless of which patriarchal proscription, they adhered to they ran the real risk of being murdered because they were women.

Government controls on news from Algeria during the conflict obscure many details of the terror women were subjected to. The murder of Katia Bengana was sensationalized by the government in order to portray her Islamist killers as animals. More confusion surrounded the reporting of the murders of Razika Meloudjemi and Naima Kar Ali. Algeria's media reported that all three women were unveiled when killed. Eyewitnesses claim that Razika and Naima were actually veiled. This version of events was reported by French radio and Antenne 2 TV. The government story (that all three victims were unveiled) was run by RFI and subsequently Reuters and the *New York Times*. The FIS was quick to blame the military for Razika's and Naima's deaths and reassured its "believing sisters . . . that all appeals to kill women come from . . . heathen and bloodthirsty people [i.e., the military] to achieve their ignoble aims" (Haddam, 1994).

Women had become a commodity to be used by two antagonistic forces. The bickering over whether Razika and Naima wore veils or not as they were gunned down at a school bus stop illustrates how their political usage quickly eclipsed all humanitarian concern for their deaths. The dilemma became nongendered: How would the military deal with the Islamists, who was telling the truth, would women start wearing the veil? No mention was made of the fact that men on both sides had threatened to murder women and had carried out these threats.

Femicide could not be avoided by accommodating the demands of one terrorist group. It was inconsequential whether guilt lay with the Green Death Company, OJAL, the Death Phalanx, or the military—the reality remained that someone would want you dead if you were female and walked out the door. The immediate result was that women either fled Algeria or remained indoors—rarely straying from male protection when in public.

That this reaction of fear fits perfectly within traditional perspectives of women's proper sphere of influence is a boon for Islamists. In turn, this inflames feminist reaction. In the 1960s Algeria was one of the leading Arab states in terms of female rights and advancement. Female empowerment (apparent from time to time in Algerian history in figures such as Berber resistance leader Kahina in the seventh century or Zaynab Lalla, who ran the powerful Rahmaniyya Sufi order in the 1890s) came to the fore within the FLN during liberation, when more than 10,000 women fought for independence, including such heroes as Djamila Boupacha, Zohra Driff, and Hassiba Ben Bouali. In a reverse situation to that of the 1990s, there was also a battle of the veil, during the War of Independence, when pro-FLN women removed the hijab as a sign of protest. Hassiba Ben Bouali dressed as a European and ran guns into the casbah from 1956 until her death the next year. Following independence, the women's movement produced the powerful Union Nationale des Femmes Algerienne (UNFA), which succeeded in having 90,000 women in the work force by 1966. Despite the union's cooption into the FLN, by the 1980s 365,000 women were working in Algeria and, more important, 1.5 million girls were attending school (1979 figures) (Ruedy, 1992).

Women's education has had several results: Women are marrying at a later age, they are seen in public (the earliest Islamist protests were against women on university campuses, some of which involved acid being thrown in unveiled women's faces), and they are fulfilling the preconditions for employment within the technocratic elite. This challenges not only traditionally conceived roles for women but also the employment prospects of male graduates. The perceived challenge to male employment and study was the root of the most notorious femicidal attack in the Western world: the slaughter of 14 female students by Marc Lépine in Canada. It would appear that in Algeria, a great many young men with university training have joined the Islamist terrorist groups that regularly abduct, rape, and murder women.

Despite obvious inroads (for example, the magistrate who read the court order that dissolved the FIS in March 1992 was female) (Moghadam, 1993), Algerian women have not secured a strong position in society or the state. The advances that had been made came to a total stop with the capitulation of President Chadli BenJadid to Islamist pressure in the 1980s. The fall from power of the FLN in 1992 left the UNFA with little influence either.

Since the formation of the FIS in 1989, 40 women's groups have been founded in Algeria (among them, the Algerian Union of Democratic Women and the International Support Group for Algerian Intellectuals) to protest the curtailing of women's liberties and rights. Their members regularly receive death threats and have been targeted for assassination along with others opposed to the FIS and GIA. Ninety-four-year-old Keltoum Boudjar was killed because her son was a policeman. While the GIA and FIS had occasionally killed family members of police officers prior to February 1995, it has been the GIA's stated policy since this time to target the families of policmen purportedly in response for ill-treatment of their female supporters. Female supporters and family members of various political groupings in Algeria have been the victims of rapes and murders.

The GIA in March 1994 "began a campaign of abducting and raping young girls and women . . . even the wife of a non-fundamentalist imam was raped by members of an armed group" (Bennoune, 1994, p. 29). Young women abducted by the guerrillas are taken into the mountains, held prisoner, and raped over a lengthy period before being murdered. The medieval Islamic practice of *mouta'a*—or convenience marriage—was usually used by troops who would take enemy women hostage. A small Islamist group, The Movement for an Islamic State, split from the GIA after their leader Said Makhloufi found the GIA had passed a *fatwa* permitting *mouta'a*.

Another group splintered from the GIA after discovering plans to murder the daughter of the leader of the FIS and place the blame on the Algerian army or government. Other prominent women have been targeted also. Leading feminist and author Nabila Diahnine was shot shortly before a planned trip to Paris for International Women's Day (March 8) in 1995. Junior minister Leila Aslaoui, the secretary of state for family and national solidarity, quit her post upon the commencement of dialogue between the government and the FIS days after her bodyguard was killed. Monique Afri was targeted because of her blonde hair (i.e., foreign in appearance). Yasmina Drici (a half-French proofreader for the anti-Islamist paper *Le Soir d'Algerie*) was murdered in July 1994 while accompanied by a Polish woman. Both were foreign in appearance and unveiled, but the Pole was unharmed. Drici's work with a paper hostile to Islamists was the main motivation in the killing. As is clearly evident, clothing is not the sole reason women are selected as sacrifices to political change. Exactly who is responsible for the murders of unveiled women is difficult to say. The Algerian analyst Qusai Saleh Darwish (1994) of the Saudi paper *Al-Sharq al-Aswat* proposes the following three possibilities regarding the killings:

1. Islamists committed the acts.
2. Government agents were involved to make the militants unapproachable.
3. An extreme army faction committed the murders so as to undermine then-president Zeroual and ensure that ultra-hardline "eradicationists" generals would come to power.

As military and Islamist forces became more heavily armed and established areas of control, as foreigners left Algeria and their embassies employed more guards or shut up shop, it was women on their own who became the soft targets, attracting poor youths earning bounties for each murder or professionals looking for public spectacle. In Blida one guerilla group, "The Redeemers," used the battle cry of "All girls who go out at night will die." From the start of the civil unrest in Algeria to the end of 1994, 200 women were murdered by political terrorists (this term includes the army and their allies). The same number of women were slaughtered in just the first 7 months of 1995. During this bloody period, there was a rush by many women to take on the hijab. While this reflected the emphasis placed by the government-influenced media on Islamist outrages to the exclusion of the threat posed by OJAL, in light of the militants' programs, it was not without cause. In the last few years many women have resumed wearing Western clothing as the security situation appears to improve.

Any member of the community seen to take sides, or failing to take the right side, is targeted. This has extended to the arts—where female singers, including Chaba Fadela and Malika Domrane, have fled to France after receiving death threats. An unnamed actress from the Theatre National d'Algerie who also fled reported:

> I was afraid in the street and when I went into a supermarket. I was afraid of being murdered on stage. I was afraid at night when the phone rang and a voice told me it would soon be my turn. (Bedarida, 1995)

As Marnia Lazreg accurately observes:

> Algeria is the only nation in the Middle East where women are killed as women because they are women. Women have lost their lives for not wearing the veil, as well as wearing it. They appear now as either the symbols of Islamic authenticity or of modernity. (quoted in Ghuneim, 1995)

From another perspective, the terrorizing of women can be seen as an attempt to gain control of a very important section of Algeria. Women are seen as the custodians of Algeria's "profound" traditional values. If women take to either the Maghrebi head scarf (*haik*) or veil (*hijab* and/or *jilbab*)—even out of fear—then it reaffirms tradition's strengths. Everything that the veil stands for—modesty, obedience, sexual probity, conformity—is expressed publicly and overtly when worn. Feminist demands for autonomy and public integration are seen as part of a colonial plot to weaken the culture. A house without a woman is akin to a village in ruins. The forced veiling delivers a superficial appearance of unity—of modernity in retreat. Women are encouraged to be seen as modernized and independent or veiled and obedient. Men on both sides of the conflict find it necessary to control (or remove from sight) those varieties.

Revolution is the aim of the Islamists: a temporary inversion of societal values and attitudes to bring about a transfer of the control of the state from the educated men in their 50s running the country now to men in their 30s educated in Koranic schools. The decision by young Islamists to lay siege to the Algerian state limits possible reactions. The creation of terror by murder and threats spurs those with most to lose to fight fire with fire. The brutal war between secular military forces and Islamist guerrillas creates a narrow "space of death" in which real self-criticism, reform, and dialogue are eliminated as possible resolutions. The clan-based politics of the government, the military, the Islamists, and the Berber ethnonationalists have resulted in subnational collectives becoming the presumptions of the state, tying citizenship to tribal heads: the father. Politics and war in Algeria are the extensions of patriarchy. Traditions are imposed by the violence of guerrillas, Islamic edicts in personal laws are supported by all but one democratic party. In August 1995, the Council of Ministers unreservedly endorsed a bill on the elimination of all forms of discrimination against women—a bill that had been ignored since it was written 17 years previously and has been all but ignored since this stunt. Women's rights in Algeria have been won by few among millions and are treated as privileges by the ruling authorities.

When the GIA declared itself an alternative government (a caliphate-in-exile) in August 1994, it revealed its priorities quite clearly. Its declaration had three parts:

1. Declaration of the alternative government
2. A demand that all tax collectors cease work immediately
3. A warning that women should desist from mixed swimming or going to the beach. (GIA, 1994)

In relation to the last two proscriptions, violence was to be the penalty. Here we have in a nutshell the commodities being fought for in the Algerian crisis: political power, money, and regulation of sexual morals and relations, all backed by legitimated violence.

That Algerian women are victims and targets in this battle for power is not surprising. The politically disenfranchised are the first to be sacrificed by those in power and those hoping to obtain it. Dialogue—unwanted by many of the groups involved—can be avoided by sensational counteraccusations of murdering innocents. The symbolism of women as either upholders of tradition (modest, obedient, veiled, and at home) or as the vanguard of social change (modernizing, liberated, working, and clothes horses) makes them an obvious indicator of who is in control.

Violent conflict within a state poses many challenges to personal liberty and choice. But what came to pass on the streets of Algiers in the 1990s was an impossible decision—to veil or not to veil. The maxim of assassinated poet Tahar Djaout, "If you speak out you die/If you do not speak out you die/So speak out and die," could just as easily be applied to being female in Algeria. Women are viewed by all political players as the symbol of their nation. While these players fight to protect other symbols of the nation, all have been complicit in mass femicide, in a battle to destroy and remove a difficult symbol of the nation: a nation with a schizophrenic identity.

Acknowledgment. This article is an abbreviated version of one that appeared in the *Journal of Arabic, Islamic and Middle Eastern Studies,* 2(2), pp. 43–54, 1995. It also contains material from Rod Skilbeck, *The Poles of Permissiveness: Power, Pop and God in Algeria,* Masters Thesis, Macquarie University, 1996.

REFERENCES

Barrouhi, Abdelaziz. (1995, February 26). Vigilantes in Algeria: Militant hunt as toll rises, *Reuters World Service.*
BBC2 World Service (1994, November 19). Algeria's hidden war. Assignment 1915 GMT [radio news program].
Bedarida, Catherine. (1995, April 23). Algerian women take lonely road to exile. *Guardian Weekly,* p. 16.
Bennoune, Karima. (1994). Algerian women confront fundamentalism, *Monthly Review,* 46(4), 26–39.
Burgat, Francois. (1994). *Islamic movements of North Africa.* Austin, TX: Center for Middle Eastern Studies.
Darwish, Qusai Saleh. (1994, August 9). *Asharq al-Aswat.*
Ghuneim, Mona. (1995, June 28). Algerian women. *Voice of America* [radio program].
GIA [Armed Islamic Group] (1994, August 29). Communique. *Federal News Service.*
Gozlan, M. (1992, January 2). *L'Evenement du Jeudi,* 374, p. 57.
Haddam, Anwar. (1994, April 1). FIS [The Islamic Salvation Front] Communique, *Islamic Republic News Agency.*
Moghadam, Valentine. (1993). *Modernizing women: Gender and social change in the Middle East.* Boulder, CO: Lynne Rienner.
Reuters. (1994, April 1). Islamists blame Algerian regime for deaths. *Reuter Library Report.*
Ruedy, John. (1992). *Modern Algeria: The origins and development of a nation.* Bloomington, IN: Indiana University Press.
Slyomovics, Susan. (1995, January–February). Hassiba Benbouali: If you could see our Algeria. *Middle East Report,* 25(1), 8–13.

CHAPTER 7

Intimate Femicide and Abused Women Who Kill: A Feminist Legal Perspective

Shereen Winifred Mills

This chapter focuses on two phenomena, *intimate partner femicide*, that is, *the killing of women by their intimate male partners*, and abused women who kill their partners. Very little research and literature exist in South Africa on either phenomenon, particularly not the judicial treatment of such cases.

The term *femicide* was developed by feminists to highlight the fact that some killings are gender-motivated, founded on particular beliefs about women, such as that women are possessions of men.

Underpinning both phenomena to be investigated is the social problem of abuse of women in the domestic sphere. Perhaps it is trite to say that these phenomena illustrate the failure of our legal system to adequately protect women from domestic violence. However, this chapter traces not only the culpability of the criminal enforcement system in failing to protect women, but how the criminal justice system is further implicated in the unjust treatment of women in these situations. This occurs on two levels—through the gender bias and sexist attitudes that inform judges' decisions and through the content of the law itself. South African courts appear reluctant to allow evidence about abuse in relationships, even though this is often essential in effectively prosecuting femicide, in explaining the singular experiences of abused women generally, and particularly the desperation of those who kill their abusive spouses. More fundamentally, the defenses in law available to women who kill their spouses are systemically discriminatory.

Thanks to extensive campaigning by women's organizations, domestic violence and its most extreme form—intimate partner femicide—have in recent years increasingly engaged public attention in South Africa. However, the plight of abused women who kill has gone largely unnoticed. Such women are treated by the criminal justice system as ordinary criminals, or worse. If rape victims are "raped" twice, in that they suffer secondary victimization in the courts, then abused women who kill are abused thrice—first by the abuser; second by society, which blames the victim for bringing the abuse upon herself; and finally by the legal system, which blames her for not leaving the abusive partner (Littleton, 1996). This flies in the face of our new constitutional order, with its emphasis on equality.

In this chapter, I first look at existing statistics on the incidence of domestic violence, intimate femicide, and abused women who kill, in order to give an overview of the problem in South Africa.

Second, I undertake an analysis of two case studies: one of intimate femicide and the other of an abused woman who killed her abusive spouse. I also examine the impact of unrecognized judicial bias and the gendered nature of the defenses available to persons who kill their intimate partners. I do so in the context of international jurisprudence, particularly feminist legal arguments about how the disparate treatment of women and men who kill their intimate partners by the judicial system impacts negatively on abused women who kill.

Third, I look at responses to intimate femicide and abused women who kill from a constitutional perspective, specifically the right to equality and the right to freedom and security of the person, enshrined in the South African Bill of Rights (Constitution of the Republic of South Africa Act, No. 108 of 1996).

Finally, I outline the steps taken by nongovernmental organizations, such as the Justice for Women Alliance, in order to highlight disparities in judicial treatment of men and women who have killed their intimate partners, and offer suggestions for improvements to the law and the operation of the judicial system.

VIOLENCE AGAINST WOMEN IN SOUTH AFRICA

Violence against women in South Africa must be looked at in the context of violence in South Africa in general. South Africa is reputed to be one of the most violent countries in the world. Such violence is gendered, with men more likely than women to be perpetrators.

Research on domestic violence in South Africa conservatively estimates that between 18% and 25% of women are involved in abusive relationships. According to Human Rights Watch (cited in Bollen et al., 1991), these figures underestimate the extent of the problem. Other research puts the estimate as high as 60% (Joubert, 1997). The incidence of domestic violence appears to increase sharply in rural areas. In a case study done in the rural Southern Cape (one of the nine provinces of South Africa), it was estimated that an average of 80% of rural women are victims of domestic violence (Artz, 1999). This coincides with the lower socioeconomic status of women in the rural areas, who are predominantly Black and poor. Furthermore, four women a week are forced to flee their homes because their lives are in danger, about 70% of all violence takes place in the home, and a mere 4% of women who have sought police protection in these situations will do so again (Olckers, 1994).

Lisa Vetten's (1996) research on intimate femicide identified 130 cases for the period 1993 to 1994 in the Gauteng area (one of nine provinces in South Africa) alone. Vetten obtained these cases, which she considered incomplete, from court inquests for 1994 and news reports from 1993 to 1995. Analysis of these cases revealed that women are more likely to be murdered by male family members and friends than by strangers, with husbands and boyfriends posing the greatest threat to women's lives, and that in Gauteng, at least one woman is killed every 6 days by her intimate male partner.

Vetten's study also found that up to half of the men who committed femicide subsequently committed suicide. They often killed others as well, particularly family members, including children. The femicides frequently appeared to be precipitated by the woman's decision to end the relationship (almost 20% appear to have been directly related) or by her alleged infidelity. The woman's decision to terminate the relationship often had little effect on alleviating her male partner's sexual jealousy and violent response. Separated or divorced women were sometimes killed by the estranged partner when they began new relationships, as also were the new male partners on occasion. Finally, a history of violence in the relationship existed in many of the cases. Women were murdered even when they had court orders or interdicts against their partners to prevent the violence.

A closer look at the data revealed that men who committed intimate partner femicide came from a variety of backgrounds, ranging from wealthy businessmen and academics to taxi drivers and the unemployed. Policemen constituted nearly 20% of the sample. The majority of deaths were caused by gunshot wounds. Stabbing, beating, bludgeoning, strangulation, and torching accounted for the rest. (A review of recent intimate femicide cases shows that men with means often hire paid killers to murder their wives.)

The average age of the women murdered was 30 (the youngest victim was 14 and the oldest, 41). At age 30, women are most likely to be married, caring for dependent children, economically active, and developing their work skills. These deaths are thus not only a tragic waste of individual women's lives, but also an irreplaceable loss to children, families, the community, and the economy. In addition, 12% of the women in the group surveyed were 20 years old or younger, suggesting that young women become involved in abusive relationships while still adolescents.

According to Vetten's study, the heaviest sentence handed down to a man who committed intimate partner femicide during the period surveyed (1993–1994) was 14 years. This man had killed the woman and her two children—of whom he was not the father. This must be seen in light of the fact that until 1995, when capital punishment was abolished by the Constitutional Court in *S v Makwanyane & another* [1995(3) SA 391(CC)], the death penalty was considered a fit sentence for murder. Since then, a sentence of 25 years is prescribed by the Criminal Procedure Act of 1977 (there is limited judicial discretion depending on mitigating factors).

Abused women who kill receive sentences ranging from correctional supervision to the death penalty. According to Vetten's 1994 study (1996), women often receive long sentences. In addition, she states that it seems

> African women are receiving the heaviest sentences of all. A review of the way in which trials are conducted suggests that the South African legal system is not equipped with the jurisprudence to understand the dynamics of abuse; nor are judges and magistrates comfortable with hearing expert testimony around domestic violence. (Vetten, 1997, p. 2)

The double burden of discrimination borne by Black women (Crenshaw, 1989; Harris, 1990) is one that bears closer scrutiny in the South African context, where Black women comprise the largest historically disadvantaged group and continue to suffer the effects of such disadvantage, particularly socioeconomic disadvantage. The prejudice against African women reflects patterns of inequality in relation to access to justice.

It appears from a follow-up study currently in progress that many women who kill their male partners do so after enduring years of abuse at the hands of their partners (Vetten & Ngwane, 2000). Such intimate partner killing is highly gendered—women kill their intimate partners far less frequently than do men. It is also rare for a woman to kill others in addition to the male partner. It seems clear that men and women kill in different circumstances and for apparently different reasons (Stubbs, 1996). On a preliminary analysis of the data, not a single case of a woman beating her male partner to death in a jealous rage could be identified. However, the converse occurs fairly frequently.

Men in the latter scenario either plead not guilty on the basis of non-pathological criminal incapacity or insane automatism, or plead guilty but allege factors such as sexual infidelity and thus provocation to mitigate their sentence. While these findings are still tentative, they point to an area of the law that may be susceptible to the manipulation of stereotypes about men and women, manipulation that has the potential to bias the law and judicial thinking in favor of men. More fundamentally, the differences in the context of, and reasons for, femicide are not reflected in legal doctrine in South Africa. Such differences have been neither acknowledged nor explored. For this reason, there is no case in South Africa where the defense of self-defense has succeeded for an abused woman who has killed her abusive spouse (Wolhuter, 1998).

Case Study 1: Intimate Femicide

The case of *S v Ramontoedi* (Case No. 188/96 [Witwatersrand Local Division], 1996) is achingly poignant. Ratsapana Sandy Ramontoedi, a prison warder, shot and killed his 26-year-old wife Yvonne during a maintenance inquiry about child support at the Johannesburg maintenance court. Ratsapana shot her in an office of the maintenance court when the prosecutor left the room, leaving her alone with him. Her 3-year-old son was waiting in the corridor outside the office with her sister. Her request for maintenance for the couple's minor child appears to have prompted the shooting. Her husband denied paternity and accused her of having an affair. In the months preceding her death, he had threatened her life on a number of occasions, assaulted her, and shot at her at least once. She reported her husband's abuse and death threats to her local police station. Yvonne feared for her life and had requested a police escort on the day of her appearance in court. Her husband followed her and the police escorts to court, shouting abuse and threats. When Yvonne arrived at court, she reported his threats to the prosecutor. Despite all these attempts to protect herself, Ratsapana's gun was not removed from him at court.

At the trial, Ratsapana was found guilty of murder. He pled not guilty on the basis that his wife's wounds were self-inflicted, ensuing from a struggle for the gun. However, there was no sign of struggle in the room, and ballistic and forensic evidence showed that the deceased was shot three times, at close range.

No evidence was led by the prosecution of Ratsapana's prior abusive behavior. On the basis of provocation, the judge found that a sentence of correctional supervision was appropriate, sentencing Ratsapana to a mere 3 years to be served as community service over weekends in installments of 20 hours each. This finding of provocation was unsupported by evidence. At no point during the trial was provocation raised, either as a defense or in mitigation of sentence.

It is clear from the tenor of the judgment that the judge was overly sympathetic to Ratsapana throughout the trial. On the facts of the matter, the accused was a dangerous man who arrived at court, armed and aggressive, and carried out his threat to kill his wife at the first opportunity that presented itself. Although the court found that he had the requisite intention to murder in the most serious form of "dolus directus" (Sentence of October 1, 1997, p. 2), it failed to find premeditation, insisting that "this was a spur of the moment shooting and there could not have been any planning to it" (Sentence of October 1, 1997, p. 3). The judge dismissed the testimony of Yvonne's mother and two sisters of previous death threats by Ratsapana, accusing the women of a conspiracy (Judgment of June 23, 1996, p. 7). He noted in passing that Yvonne had thought it necessary to obtain a police escort on the day of the hearing.

The judge proceeded to deal with the issue of provocation, correctly stating that Ratsapana "genuinely held" the suspicion that his wife was having an affair with Radebe, an elderly church pastor (Judgment of June 23, 1996, p. 10). He summed up Ratsapana's version of what happened: that Ratsapana had been summoned to court "for support for a child that was not his—the deceased was *in fact* [emphasis added] having an affair with another man, which affair has broken up his marriage" (Judgment of June 23, 1996, p. 11). It was already clear at this stage that the judge regarded Ratsapana's version as definitive, notwithstanding that no evidence had been led, aside from Ratsapana's testimony, that his wife was having an affair. In his sentencing, Ratsapana's version of what happened became transformed into hard fact. The judge maintained that there was a

> great deal of provocation, not as a figment of accused's imagination or suspicions but well-grounded in fact. The probabilities are that the deceased was indeed having an affair with Radebe over some time and had deliberately deceived the accused for some considerable time prior to the shooting, and that the "serious provocation" continued for a long time before the shooting itself occurred. (Sentence of October 1, 1997, pp. 2–3)

It is evident that the judge put Yvonne on trial and that he did not think it necessary to give her a fair trial. In his mind, she was labeled "adulterer," and while he did not go so far as to say she deserved to die, the tragedy of her death and the loss to her family did not seem to concern him. Indeed, he did not address this aspect in his judgment, except to refer to the unacceptably high incidence of interfamily killings in South Africa. In light of the judge's justifications of Ratsapana's murderous behavior, his reluctance to punish Ratsapana evidenced by the token sentence handed down, it is hardly surprising.

The judge ended his defense by saying, "because of the accused's reluctance to tell the truth of exactly how the shooting of the deceased took place, the court is in the dark as to what that provocation actually was and the degree of it" (Sentence of October 1, 1997, p. 3). This statement directly contradicts the judge's previous reasoning. To vindicate Ratsapana, he now sought to locate the provocative act at the moment of the killing, since the test for provocation—which is subjective—requires loss of self-control as a result of the provocative conduct and implies a sense of immediacy. The judge was not deterred by the fact that there were independent witnesses who stated that the shooting took place almost immediately after the prosecutor left the room (Judgment of June 23, 1996, p. 9). There was in fact no time for Yvonne to provoke him, only time enough for her to be shot three times, once directly in the head—the shot that caused her death. Nevertheless, he managed to find provocation, although the more likely inference to draw was that there was no provocation at the scene of the crime and that Ratsapana's reluctance to tell the truth was precisely for that reason: He planned to kill Yvonne, and did so.

Finally, at the end of his judgment, the judge castigated the police for leaving the deceased unprotected at the court, knowing that the accused was in an aggressive mood (Judgment of June 23, 1996, p. 29). He absolved Ratsapana of all responsibility for his behavior, blaming the police instead. But for their "extraordinary" dereliction of duty, he maintained, they could have prevented Yvonne's death. According to the judge's reasoning, the police should have foreseen an act despite the judge's decision that it was both "unplanned" and "provoked." He completely failed to take Yvonne's fears of imminent death seriously.

Discussion

This case is remarkable for a number of reasons, not least because of the police's failure to take Yvonne's fears seriously by providing her with the protection she requested. It sends abusive men the unequivocal message that the legal system excuses men who commit intimate partner femicide out of jealousy. The prosecutor's failure to lead evidence of past abuse in the relationship, as well as evidence of the social context of wife abuse in South Africa, allowed the judge to treat the femicide far too lightly. It permitted him to view it as an aberration, unlikely to happen again because Ratsapana was not likely to meet another woman as duplicitous as Yvonne. On the contrary, research shows that men who abuse their wives are likely to go on to abuse women in their subsequent relationships (Coker, 1992). In addition, by focusing on Yvonne's behavior, he shifted the responsibility for Ratsapana's violence to *her*. Such victim blaming by the judiciary is not exclusive to South Africa. Keller (1996) cites two U.S. task forces that concluded that judges in that country often have the perception, in cases such as this one, that the woman provoked the man into killing *her*.

Possibly the most shocking aspect of the judgment is the explicit gender bias in the tenor of the judgment. It is clear that the judge identified with Ratsapana in a way that clouded his judgment—his reasoning being that any reasonable man would be justified in acting the same way, given the provocation of adultery. Underlying his reasoning are patriarchal attitudes of women as possessions and his stereotypes of women as deceitful and conniving. In addition, he held the unexamined opinion that it is appropriate for a man to respond violently to such an "attack" on his manhood.

With regard to the issue of adultery as provocation, the gender bias goes much deeper. Wife abusers who kill frequently invoke reasons such as infidelity or desertion for inciting their violent reaction because there is a tradition surrounding adultery that either excuses wife murder or provides "the archetypal illustration of adequate provocation" (Coker, 1992). The effect is to shift the focus from the abuser to the victim's behavior. This obscures the true cause of wife abuse and femicide, which involve power and control. Abusive men who kill their wives are often extremely dependent, possessive, controlling, and jealous (Ratsapana clearly fits this profile). The violence they inflict is purposive—a means of retaining control over their wives. Much of the purported provocation is imagined, based on patterns set much earlier in the relationship (Raeder, 1996).

The concept of provocation is based on the assumption that a reasonable man can be provoked into committing femicide by his wife's insubordinate behavior, adultery being the most extreme act of insubordination (Coker, 1992). Provocation in South African law operates either as a complete defense or in mitigation of sentence. The distinction drawn by the court in *S v Ramontoedi* between men who murder their wives with premeditation and men who are provoked by their wives' adultery—and are thus less culpable— is dubious. It stems from the misconception that violence in response to perceived provocation—that is, adultery—is uncontrollable. The fact is that the causal chain leading from male anger to male violence is a social construct (Raeder, 1996). The two are not rationally connected. Women rarely, if ever, get away with saying they were provoked to violence by their husband's adultery. The use of violence reflects the power imbalance between the parties and the abuser's assessment that a violent reaction is socially appropriate (Coker, 1992). "Hot-blooded" intimate partner femicides are as invidious as "cold-blooded" stranger killings and must be regarded as such. If women are able to abstain from violent behavior in situations of their husbands' infidelity, then men can reasonably be expected to do the same. The scenario of the "out-of-control" man and the "provocative" woman in the context of abusive relationships has its roots in the myth of women having the seductive power to make men lose control sexually. And, as in the case of rape, this myth is based on the belief that men are emotional victims who are not responsible for their sexual conduct, whereas women are held morally responsible for their own conduct *and* that of males (Coker, 1992). Such beliefs allow the law to ignore the interplay of power and control, domination and subordination, in the abusive relationship (Mahoney, 1996).

Case Study 2: Abused Woman Who Killed

In contrast to the outcome of *S v Ramontoedi*, in the case *S v Boucher* (Case no. 179/96 [WLD], 1997), an abused woman called Elizabeth Boucher who killed her husband, by shooting him, was sentenced to 18 years in prison. Very little weight was placed on Elizabeth's testimony that her husband had abused her and her girl children during her marriage, including sexually assaulting one of her young daughters. No evidence was led in her defense on the frequency and effect of such abuse on her. Elizabeth's allegation that she lived in a state of fear of her husband was preempted by the state's allegation that he, in fact, feared her.

The crisis point in the relationship was reached when Elizabeth decided to leave her husband. Her evidence made it clear that she feared for her life in the week preceding the fatal shooting and that she believed that her life was in danger when she shot her husband. Elizabeth maintained that the shooting was preceded by assault, attempted rape, and threats that if her husband could not have her, no one else would. The court dismissed her plea of self-defense, and she was found guilty of "cold-blooded" murder.

Discussion

The conduct of the trial was prejudiced against Elizabeth in two ways. First, it is clear from the evidence and the judgment that the judicial officers and assessors had very little understanding of the effects of prolonged abuse on Elizabeth. Thus expert evidence about this should have been introduced. Second, the test for self-defense adopted by the court was whether a "reasonable man in the position of the accused" would have acted similarly. Not surprisingly, considering South Africa's criminal jurisprudence of defense, there was no interrogation of the gendered nature of the test. The standards applied to Elizabeth in the case were gender-neutral; she was tried as a man would have been tried. However, it is clear that the application of a formal notion of equality was not sufficient to ensure that Elizabeth Boucher received fair and equal treatment. The evidence should have been presented in the context of the lived experiences of abused women, and questions should have been raised about the systemic gender bias or discrimination entrenched in the law itself.

1. Expert Evidence. There is extensive legal writing and legal precedent in the United States, Canada, Australia, and the United Kingdom on the need for expert evidence in cases of abused women who kill [see the landmark Canadian decision of *R v Lavallee* 1990, Volume 1, Supreme Court Reporter, p. 852]. Since abuse of women in intimate relationships is so prevalent in South Africa, it might be assumed that women's experiences of abuse are common knowledge. However, the development of legal principles, particularly in the area of violence, has largely ignored women's lives. Thus expert evidence is necessary to educate judges and magistrates (Stubbs, 1996). The purpose of such expert evidence would be to educate the judiciary about experiences and characteristics that battered women have in common

> in order to refute widely held myths and misconceptions concerning battered women that would interfere with [their] ability to evaluate the woman's action fairly. Expert testimony can present a different picture by demonstrating that the battered woman was a victim. (Schneider, 1996, p. 312)

The latter aspect is of particular importance in South Africa, where it is clear from the case under scrutiny, as well as other cases, that the status of these women as victims at the time of the killing is accorded little, if any, weight at their trials (Nathoo, 1999). (Nathoo's analysis of the successive imposition of identities as victim, then perpetrator, then again victim on the women is based on interviews with women in Johannesburg Prison.)

In Elizabeth Boucher's case, the court conceded that the relationship between the parties was "stormy" and that it could not rule out the possibility of aggression in the course of the relationship (Judgment of February 17, 1997, p. 468A). However, the court failed to make any causal connection between Elizabeth's psychological state at the time of the killing and the history of aggression inflicted on her during her marriage to Deon. The evidence made it clear that there was a history of abuse in the marriage, but the effect of such abuse on Elizabeth's state of mind was given no weight in the assessment of her guilt.

According to the evidence, Elizabeth reported a number of cases of assault and malicious damage to property to the police. She testified to at least five such reports over the 18-month period of her marriage (Judgment of February 17, 1997, p. 159). Certainly she was well known to the police at the local station. A policeman testified that he remembered Elizabeth calling for assistance when she was with Deon. Elizabeth briefly described a few incidents of the abuse. For example, after an incident in 1995, she said that she required x-rays. This reveals the seriousness of Deon's assault. She appeared more profoundly affected by a later incident in the same year, when Deon deliberately fractured the leg of her 7-year-old daughter, Nikita, and sexually abused her 15-year-old daughter, Jo-Anne. Deon was arrested for and later acquitted of these acts (Judgment of February 17, 1997, p. 160).

Regarding the 2 weeks leading up to the fatal shooting, Elizabeth described increasingly bizarre behavior by Deon: He threatened to shoot her, then decided to hang her instead (the police corroborated this with evidence of a rope hanging in a passage of their home). He told her that he had enjoyed breaking Nikita's leg and that "Jo-Anne was fresh meat," according to Deon, and that "he was not yet done with her." She responded: "In other words, I am a bad mother because I did not stand by my children." It is clear that the realization that Deon had enjoyed breaking Nikita's leg had a profound effect on her psychologically. She stood on the chair he had placed under the rope and said, "Okay, do it [kill me]" (Judgment of February 17, 1997, p. 177).

On the Saturday preceding the shooting, Deon told Elizabeth that he had been tempted to shoot her while she was sleeping and that he had begun digging a grave in the garden to bury her in. It is not clear from the evidence whether in fact there was a grave (servants who slept on the property denied having seen it), but Elizabeth insisted on its existence throughout her evidence, despite the damage that it did to her credibility as a witness. Despite her honesty and conviction about this, the court regarded it as further proof that she was lying. She testified that Deon was "worse than ever" during this period, threatening to kill his parents and his son. He described his son as a "piece of afterbirth" (Judgment of February 17, 1997, p. 159).

Elizabeth's evidence showed that she was haunted by a sense of Deon's cunningness. She constantly referred to his preternatural ability to "get" her: "Deon is very, very clever," she said (Judgment of February 17, 1997, p. 468B), "nothing can keep Deon away, he does just what he wants to" (Judgment of February 17, 1997, p. 180). In the week leading up to the fatal shooting, it is clear that she feared for her life. She asked her domestic worker and her sister to sleep in the house with her after an attempted assault by Deon the Saturday preceding the shooting. She woke them up on her return from work every night to ask if everything was fine and constantly insisted that they not let Deon into the house (Judgment of February 17, 1997, p. 14). She also testified that she called around to ask people to stay in the house with her for her safety and asked Deon's family to get help for him (Judgment of February 17, 1997, p. 181). On the Monday preceding the shooting, she called an attorney and asked if he would draw up a will for her, her instructions being that all her possessions should go to her daughters if anything should happen to her (Judgment of February 17, 1997, p. 187). The following day she called the police and asked if they could serve an interdict on Deon and also if they could provide her with protection. She was told that they did not have sufficient staff (Judgment of February 17, 1997, p. 188).

This is perhaps the most difficult aspect for courts to believe—how an abused woman knows, after enduring years of abuse, that the next act will be fatal to her. Expert evidence is needed to explain to the court the power dynamics in the relationship, the cumulative nature of the experience of abuse, and the abused woman's intimate knowledge of the abuser that enables her to "read" his mood and predict an attack (Sheehy, Stubbs, & Tolmie, 1992).

The courts also have difficulty understanding why abused women do not leave their abusers. Reasons why many women stay in abusive relationships have been well documented, including factors such as fear of retaliation, lack of economic resources, lack of social support, and feelings of isolation caused by the abuse (Dutton, 1993). Women who *do* leave often return to the abuser because of his threats and their lack of social support. The court in Elizabeth's case was no exception. The judge remarked that "the accused had already seen an attorney about divorce, and the parties were separated, so she [Elizabeth] was aware of ways to solve the problem [of abuse] without resorting to violence" (Judgment of February 17, 1997 p. 468B). Elizabeth did try to leave, and it was her decision to leave that prompted her husband's final violent attack on her. Research shows that most women are killed by their partners once they have left the relationship (e.g., Dutton, 1993). This preoccupation with why abused women stay ignores their lived experience and the personal and societal context of power in which they are enmeshed. The concepts of victimization and agency that underlie assumptions about leaving or staying need to be challenged (Mahoney, 1994).

2. Self-Defense. It is clear from the discussion above that there are a number of difficulties faced by an abused woman who attempts to show that her act of killing her abusive husband was a reasonable and necessary response to his behavior. Such conduct threatens "deeply held stereotypes of appropriately submissive female conduct and of patriarchal authority" (Schneider, 1996, p. 312). It is essential for these stereotypes to be exposed to the judiciary for what they are.

Expert evidence would have been invaluable in helping the court to recognize and understand Elizabeth's state of mind at the time of the fatal shooting and to prove that her conduct was reasonable and constituted self-defense. The court held that

> the question whether an accused acted lawfully in self-defense in the circumstances is determined objectively, the test being that of the fictional reasonable person in the position of the accused. The accused fails this test even on her own version. (Judgment of February 17, 1997, p. 394)

Elizabeth, like other abused women who kill, did not kill in the manner presumed by traditional self-defense doctrine. She let a man, whom she claimed to fear, into her house, and she fired three shots at him when he attempted to assault her. The traditional doctrine was developed in the context of a dispute between equals—the traditional bar-room brawl between men. The doctrine, based on the male norm, fails to accommodate the experience of women who kill their partners in response to ongoing violence. In rigidly applying the objective "reasonable man" test to Elizabeth's actions, the court failed to examine the gender bias of the test and to take into account the complex social reality of abused women who kill their abusers (Schneider, 1996).

As a starting point, women who kill to escape the threat of death or serious injury, as Elizabeth did, should have the same defense available to them as men who kill for the same reasons. The difference between men and women in this respect is that men are relatively safe in the private sphere and are more likely to have physical superiority over their attackers. This difference accounts for the often nontraditional ways in which women kill; therefore, it should not be used prejudicially against women in the court (McColgan, 1993).

The Constitutional Framework for Equality

Violence against women is treated in constitutional jurisprudence as discrimination against women or as an infringement of the right to equality on the grounds of sex and gender. Section 9 of the South African Constitution provides that neither the state nor private persons may "unfairly discriminate directly or indirectly against anyone on one or more grounds, including race, gender, sex" [Section 9(3) & (4)]. In addition, the right of everyone to be "free from all forms of violence from either public and private sources" is recognized in section 12. Individuals who are victims of violence are thus supposed to be afforded constitutional protection not only from agents of the state but also in the private sphere, where women and children are most vulnerable (The Law of South Africa, 1997, para 235, fn 12).

Equality is a core value of the South African Constitution. The constitutional court has held that

> in the light of our own particular history, and our vision for the future, a Constitution was written with equality at its centre. Equality is our constitution's focus and its organizing principle. [The *President of the RSA v Hugo 1997* (4) South Africa Constitutional Court at para 74]

With regard to equality as a right, South Africa's constitutional court judgments indicate that it is committed to a substantive understanding of equality that aims to redress inequality (Albertyn & Goldblatt, 1998). This commitment involves a contextual analysis that is based on eliminating the effects of discrimination. In a case of discrimination against women, the court would be required to examine the social context of inequality and disadvantage (both present and historical) and how it is related to systemic forms of domination within society [*The National Coalition for Gay and Lesbian Equality and Other v Minister of Justice and Others* 1999 (1) South African Law Reports (6) at para 60–64; *City Council of Pretoria v Walker 1998* (3) Butterworths Constitutional Law Reports 257 Constitutional Court at para 62].

The concept of equality, as espoused by critical feminist theorists, aims to

> locate its understanding of the law and legal concepts in the lived experience of women and men. Equality, therefore, has to address the actual conditions of human life. (Albertyn & Goldblatt, 1998, p. 252)

The right to equality, interpreted substantively, places a positive duty on the state not only to prevent domestic violence but also to engage with, and eliminate, gender bias on the part of the judiciary, as well as to examine systemic discrimination in the law (Wolhuter, 1998, p. 2). This means looking at the extent to which the law is based on the values not only of the dominant sex but also of the dominant race and class. As stated previously, poor Black women constitute the single largest historically disadvantaged group in South Africa. It is thus essential to challenge existing norms and to infuse the law with the diversity of such women's experiences (Albertyn, 1994; Wolhuter, 1998).

The South African constitutional court has recognized the dynamics of power and control that inform wife abuse, holding that,

> To the extent that it is systemic, pervasive and overwhelmingly gender-specific, domestic violence both reflects and reinforces patriarchal domination, and does so in a particularly brutal form. (*S v Baloyi* 1998 South African Constitutional Reports, p. 9)

These problems are thus being addressed, but such decisions are not translating into basic judicial decision making.

Precedent (and, indeed, inspiration) for the task ahead can be found in the Canadian case of *R v Lavallee* (1990, 1 SCR 852), which provides an analysis of the gendered nature of the law of self-defense within the context of the constitutional right to equality. The court looked at the accused's act of self-defense within the specific context of the history of violence in the relationship and within the broader social context. It also looked at the need for expert evidence to educate the judiciary about the experiences of abused women. The most significant aspect of the judgment was that, in looking at the requirement of "imminent danger," the court took account of the experience of abused women and held that consideration should be taken of the cumulative effect of abuse on the accused.

CONCLUSION

The advent of a new democratic constitutional order in South Africa, with its emphasis on the right to equality and the formation of a Commission on Gender Equality (an independent body established in 1997 to promote gender equality), has had many positive implications for the rights of women. It has opened the way for civil society to advocate for reform in society's treatment of women. Women's rights groups have become more organized around the issues of rape, abuse of girl children, domestic violence, and intimate partner femicide, and these issues have become the focus of much media attention. This has led in recent years to the state's addressing some of these issues as a matter of public concern (The Law of South Africa, 1997, para. 235). There have been increased efforts to secure services and legal reform for survivors of gender-based violence, as well as efforts to provide gender-sensitization training to key service providers such as police and magistrates.

Notwithstanding these improvements, it is clear from the cases analyzed that the South African system of law enforcement, and ultimately the judicial system, has continued to fail women in effectively protecting them from violence. This failure, it has been argued, is a major contributing factor to the incidence of both intimate partner femicide and abused women who kill their partners. Both phenomena are often a tragic consequence of ineffective policing and prosecution of domestic violence cases, and both reflect society's attitude toward violence in the home.

Gender bias in favor of men and sexist notions about what constitutes "proper" behavior for women and their place in society continue to influence the manner in which such cases are dealt with in courts. In addition, the legal principles that underlie defenses available to the accused in murder trials are premised on male notions of what constitutes "reasonable" behavior. Such defenses, when used for abused women who kill, do not work effectively or at all because they are based on the dominant norm of the White male and because they fail completely to address the singular experience of abused women who kill. This subtle form of systemic discrimination will prove difficult to overcome.

Work on the phenomena of intimate partner femicide and abused women who kill in the context of the right to equality is still in its very early stages in South Africa. What is clear, however, is that if we adhere to a constitutional definition of substantive equality, a strong case can be made for major improvements to the law and state actions.

Acknowledgments. The author wishes to thank Lisa Vetten for her invaluable pioneering contribution and Beth Goldblatt for her incisive comments.

REFERENCES

Albertyn, Cathi. (1994). The discriminatory and gendered nature of the law and institutions of criminal justice. In Saras Jagawanth, Pamela-Jane Schwikkard, & Brenda Grant (Eds.), *Women and the law* (pp. 15–21). Pretoria, South Africa: HSRC Publishers.

Albertyn, Cathi, & Beth Goldblatt. (1997). Gender. In Willem A. Joubert (Ed.), *The law of South Africa* (LAWSA), *10*, Part 2 (pp. 139–189). Durban, South Africa: Butterworths.

Albertyn, Cathi, & Beth Goldblatt. (1998). Facing the challenge of transformation: Difficulties in the development of an indigenous jurisprudence of equality. *South African Journal on Human Rights, 14,* 248–276.

Artz, Lisa. (1999). *Violence against women in rural Southern Cape: Exploring access to justice within a feminist jurisprudence framework.* Unpublished master's thesis, University of Cape Town.

Bollen, Sandra, Lillian Artz, Lisa Vetten, & Antoinette Louw. (1991, September). Violence against women in metropolitan South Africa: A study of impact and service delivery. Institute for Security Studies Monograph Series, No. 41 (pp. 1–102). Pretoria: South Africa.

Coker, Donna K. (1992). Heat of passion and wife killing: Men who batter/men who kill. *Southern California Law Review and Women's Studies, 2,* 71–130.

Constitution of the Republic of South Africa Act (No. 108 of 1996).

Crenshaw, Kimberle. (1989). Demarginalizing the intersection of race and sex. In Katharine T. Bartlett & Rosanne Kennedy (Eds.), *Feminist legal theory: Reading in law and gender* (pp. 57–71). Boulder, CO: Westview Press.

Dutton, Mary Ann. (1993). Understanding women's responses to domestic violence: A redefinition of battered women syndrome. *Hofstra Law Review, 21,* 1191–1240.

Harris, Angela P. (1990). Race and essentialism in feminist legal theory. *Stanford Law Review, 42,* 581–616.

Keller, Wendy. (1996). Disparate treatment of spouse murder defendants. *Southern California Law Review and Women's Studies, 6,* 255–284.

Littleton, Christine A. (1996). Women's experience and the problem of transition: Perspectives on male battering of women. In D. Kelly Weisberg (Ed.), *Applications of feminist legal theory to women's lives: Sex, violence, work and reproduction* (pp. 327–328). Philadelphia: Temple University Press.

Mahoney, Martha. (1994). Victimization or oppression? Women's lives, violence, and agency. In Martha A. Fineman & Roxanne Mykitiuk (Eds.), *The public nature of private violence: The discovery of domestic abuse* (pp. 59–92). New York: Routledge.

Mahoney, Martha. (1996). Legal images of battered women: Redefining the issue of separation. In D. Kelly Weisberg (Ed.), *Applications of feminist legal theory to women's lives: Sex, violence, work and reproduction* (pp. 341–342). Philadelphia: Temple University Press.

McColgan, Aileen. (1993, Winter). In defense of battered women who kill. *Oxford Journal of Legal Studies, 13*(4), 508–529.

Nathoo, Harnishakumari. (1999). Abused women who kill. *National Feminist Magazine, 12,* 48–50.

Olckers, Ilze. (1994). Battery: Towards a legal strategy. In Saras Jagawanth, Pamela-Jane Schwikkard, & Brenda Grant (Eds.), *Women and the law* (pp. 90–101). Pretoria, South Africa: HSRC Publishers.

Raeder, Myrna S. (1996, May). The admissibility of prior acts of domestic violence: Simpson and beyond. *Southern California Law Review, 69,* 1463–1517.

Schneider, Elizabeth. (1996). Women's self-defence work and the problems of expert testimony in battering. In D. Kelly Weisberg (Ed.), *Applications of feminist legal theory to women's lives: Sex, violence, work and reproduction* (pp. 311–321). Philadelphia: Temple University Press.

Sheehy, Elizabeth, Julie Stubbs, & Julia Tolmie. (1992). Defending battered women on trial: The battered woman syndrome and its limitations. *Criminal Law Journal, 16,* 369–394.

Stubbs, Julie. (1996). Self-defense and defense of others. In Regina Graycar & Jenny Morgan, *Work and violence themes: Including gender issues in the core law curriculum* (pp. 1–15). Canberra, Australia: Department of Employment, Education and Training.

Vetten, Lisa. (1996, Winter). Man shoots wife. *Crime and Conflict,* pp. 6–27.

Vetten, Lisa. (1997). *The legal system and spousal killings.* Paper presented to the Portfolio Committee on Justice and the Ad Hoc Committee on the Improvement of the Quality of Life and Status of Women, Cape Town, South Africa.

Vetten, Lisa, & Colette Ngwane. (2000). *Research results on femicide and abused women who kill.* Unpublished manuscript.

Wolhuter, Lorraine. (1998). Altering our range of vision: A feminist reconstruction of South African domestic violence law. *South African Criminal Law Journal, 11,* 1–22.

Quilt commemorating femicide victims in Southern Africa published on the cover of Watts, Osam, & Win's booklet *The Private Is Public* in 1995. (Original photograph by Margaret Walker. Photograph of original by Margaret Benes.)

CHAPTER 8

Femicide in Southern Africa

Charlotte Watts, Susanna Osam, and Everjoice Win

> It makes sad reading when cattle rustlers are given stiffer punishment than those who murder women.
>
> —Rude & Kazunga (1995)

Members of Women in Law and Development in Africa (WiLDAF) in five Southern African countries—Botswana, South Africa, Swaziland, Zambia, and Zimbabwe—undertook a study in each country on femicide as part of preparing for the United Nations World Conference on Women held in Beijing in 1995 (see Galloway, 1995; Mkhonta & Aphane, 1995; Pillay, Vetten, & Moeketsi, 1995; Rude & Kazunga, 1995; and Sejoe-Galetshoge, 1995). We named the study "the FEMICIDE project"—*femicide* being *the killing or murder of women because they are female.*

The specific objectives of this study were:

1. To collect and collate the names, ages, and other pertinent details of women and girls who have been victims of femicide, including how, why, when, and where each was killed and what the killer's sentence was in cases that went to court.
2. To document these cases in a register to serve as evidence of femicide.
3. To produce a quilt (like the AIDS quilt) displaying the names of these women to be taken to Beijing and also to be used in awareness-raising campaigns at national levels. Both the register and the quilt personalized femicide and ensured that the victims would not be reduced to faceless, nameless statistics.

4. To demonstrate the magnitude, manifestations, and other factors related to femicide.
5. To contribute to the discourse on femicide by analyzing it from an African perspective.
6. To look at how the state has played an active or passive role in the perpetuation of femicide through its actions and inaction.
7. To use this information for advocacy and lobbying both at national and international levels, and to inform the Special Rapporteur on Violence Against Women at the United Nations.

WiLDAF envisioned women in Southern Africa showing African leaders and other human rights groups that femicide and other violence against women is a feature of African societies and that there is a need for states and society to take immediate action to stop this gross violation of women's human rights.

WiLDAF chose to focus on femicide for a number of reasons. First, femicide lies at the end of a continuum of violence against women. Second, femicide also shows the misogyny that often underlies violence against women. Third, the ways in which women were brutalized shows the extent to which some men consciously regard women as lesser beings deserving of torture. Fourth, focusing on femicide provided WiLDAF with an indication of the degree of seriousness with which society and, much more importantly, the state regards violations of women's rights and violence against women, especially its most ultimate expression in femicide. Finally, we wanted to recommend what kinds of interventions need to be made to combat femicide.

METHODOLOGY

Although violence against women is known to exist in the countries studied by WiLDAF, there is no officially assembled data on the extent of this problem in any of these countries. Data on assault or homicide, when available from court or police statistics, are often not disaggregated by sex or the victim–perpetrator relationship. Similarly, death records and health service statistics often record only the immediate cause of death or injury rather than the long-term events that culminated in murder. This dearth of information reflects the lack of government commitment to dealing with violence against women in general and femicide in particular. Furthermore, the absence of detailed information makes the problem invisible, enabling governments to deny its seriousness. Consequently, they fail to explore their role in preventing femicide.

This lack of data required that WiLDAF gather information on femicide from a range of formal and informal sources. WiLDAF members in each country in Southern Africa compiled statistics on femicide from whatever sources of information were available to them. More specifically, the data sources were as follows: court records (Zimbabwe, Botswana, South Africa); police records (Zambia, South Africa); magazine and newspaper reports (Zambia, South Africa, Swaziland, Botswana); and oral sources (Zambia). For each case identified, researchers tried to compile details about the woman or girl murdered, the circumstances surrounding her death, and the adequacy of the judicial and societal response.

The study compiled information on femicides occurring between 1983 and 1993. Of the 754 femicides analyzed, 35% (263) were from Zambia, 33% (249) were from Zimbabwe, 12% (90) were from Swaziland, 10% (78) were from Botswana, and 10% (74) were in South Africa. Time and resource constraints largely determined the time scales over which femicide records were compiled and the number of cases analyzed in each country.

TYPES OF FEMICIDE CASES IDENTIFIED

The studies identified the following types of femicide:

1. *Intimate femicide.* Women killed by boyfriends or husbands in so-called domestic disputes.
2. *Femicide by other family members.* Femicide by male family members and in-laws who, by custom in Southern African societies, often feel that they have a right to control females.
3. *Sexual femicide.* Rape is sometimes followed by murder—either to cover up the crime or to get rid of witnesses. Some rapists also derive pleasure from killing their victims.
4. *Witch femicides.* Another example of femicide is the killing of women accused of being witches, sometimes by burning, as happens in South Africa, or by stoning, as occurs in Zimbabwe. These femicides occur predominantly in rural areas.
5. *Ritualistic femicides.* Some femicides appear to be ritualistic in nature, linked to a belief in the power of female sexual organs. In these cases, women are killed in order to cut out these organs. WiLDAF documented such cases in Zambia, Zimbabwe, and South Africa.
6. *Suicides by women experiencing violence.* In a few cases, women's suicides qualified as femicides when there was strong evidence that they had killed themselves to escape intolerable levels of violence by their husbands or other male members of their families.

7. *Women killed by thieves.* Thieves often see women as vulnerable targets, both within their homes and on the streets. Therefore the Zambian study chose to include deaths of women who had been murdered by thieves in their femicide registers (Rude & Kazunga, 1995).

THE CIRCUMSTANCES SURROUNDING FEMICIDE

The Immediate Cause of Death

The investigators were particularly shocked and disturbed by the brutal nature of many of the femicides. A number of cases included extreme cruelty and mutilation of women's bodies: Some had been beheaded, some had a breast cut off, some had their faces slashed repeatedly with a knife, and some had nails driven into their eye sockets (Rude & Kazunga, 1995). Common weapons of assault included machetes, iron bars, knobkerries, and hoes. Women were mutilated with a range of sharp objects, including knives and spears.

Most of the femicides were premeditated. The range of weapons and methods used in the femicides highlight how the offenders intended to torture and brutalize the women, and in many cases, to ensure that the victim did not survive.

Age Range of Femicide Victims

WiLDAF's studies showed that there is no age at which a woman is safe from femicide. Femicide victims ranged from a few months old to over 80 years. However, women were found to be most at risk of femicide between the ages of 21 and 40. At this age in Southern African societies, most women are married and have children and other relatives to support. The murder of a woman is a tragic waste of her life and also has a devastating impact on her children and extended family. Women are generally sexually active between the ages of 21 and 40; these are the years when male control over women's sexuality and freedom is at its peak. In most cases, the primary reason given by men for murders that occurred during these years was the woman's alleged sexual infidelity.

Elderly women, who might be expected to have gained status and power in society, are also vulnerable to femicide. One reason for their vulnerability may be their becoming more dependent on others for economic support. Another may be their acquisition of assets that younger family members would like to have. The study found that these older femicide victims had commonly been accused of being witches prior to being murdered. For example, of the 42 cases of femicide among women over 50 in Zimbabwe, most were aunts, mothers, and grandmothers whom male relatives had accused of being witches (Galloway, 1995). The fear of witchcraft places elderly women in a vulnerable situation, with men being able to use the excuse of suspected witchcraft as a justification for any violent act they commit against them—including femicide.

These examples illustrate how some sexist men see women changing with age from being temptresses or prostitutes to being witches or sorceresses. At both ends of this spectrum, women are perceived as dangerous and as a threat to men, thus justifying their destruction.

Relationship of Perpetrator to Victim

In each country, the majority of femicides were perpetrated by men who were, or had previously been, the victims' husbands or boyfriends, accounting for between 40% and 60% of the cases analyzed in each country. In many instances, these femicides were preceded by a history of partner violence. As Galloway (1995) notes, "When women are the victims of homicide, it is usually the final and most extreme form of violence at the hands of a male partner." In some cases, women were killed for rejecting their male partners. Although Rude and Kazunga (1995) note that traditionally a boyfriend is not expected to exercise ownership over his girlfriend in African culture, boyfriends also commit partner femicides. This shows that men kill women even when they don't have the excuse, which they frequently use, of such an act being part of "our culture." It also demonstrates that the main factor underlying violence against women, including femicide, is men's desire for power and control over them.

In contrast to the situation in Western societies, members of the extended family often hold important positions of power within the family in Southern Africa. For example, the male relatives of a woman's husband often have the right to "discipline" her in her husband's absence. The Zimbabwean study indicates how this power imbalance can lead to femicide. Specifically, about a quarter of the femicides identified in Zimbabwe were committed by a male relative of the dead woman.

Women in different age groups were subject to different kinds of femicide. For example, young women appeared to be most vulnerable to femicide by a male intimate partner, while very young girls were most vulnerable to femicide by their fathers and other male members of the immediate and extended family. In Zimbabwe, these young girls were killed because their male relatives wanted to punish them for such offenses as alleged theft, coming home late from school, or not bringing home the right amount of change for money they had been given to make a purchase.

Elderly women were found to be vulnerable to femicide by younger male relatives. In the absence of a husband, sons in Swaziland have always been expected to protect and provide for their mothers. However, Swaziland researchers Faith Mikhonta and Doo Aphane (1995) noted that sons killing their mothers was a disturbing new trend in that country. Likewise in Zambia, most women over 50 were killed by their children or relatives.

In Zimbabwe, attacks by strangers constituted a relatively small percentage of femicides (6%). The higher percentages found in Botswana and South Africa may reflect higher levels of all violent crimes in those countries, or they may be artifacts of the small number of cases analyzed or biases arising from the sources of information used. Regarding femicides committed by male strangers, WiLDAF researchers suspect that they were often preceded by rape. Vetten (1995) notes that this possibility is almost never explored by forensic doctors.

Alleged Motives and Circumstances of Femicides

Although all the words and deeds that supposedly provoke femicide are usually well within women's right to say and do, blame for femicides is often heaped on the victims by using their behavior to justify their murder. Court and newspaper records indicate that simple, and sometimes absurd, excuses are made by men accused of femicide.

An analysis of the excuses given by men in different countries for committing femicide reveals a number of important trends. During women's reproductive years they are most commonly accused of sexual infidelity. For example, in over a third of the cases in Zimbabwe, suspected adultery was the main reason given for femicide. In those cases where there were sufficient records detailing the alleged reasons for femicide in Botswana, 34% of the assailants alleged that the woman they killed had been unfaithful. In most cases this accusation was unsubstantiated.

These examples reveal a double standard in expectations for men and women. While a woman typically tolerates adultery by her male partner, infidelity by a wife is viewed by men as one of the worst possible humiliations (Galloway, 1995). Galloway (1995) notes, "It is culturally acceptable for a man to beat his wife when he suspects adultery." Hence, the community frequently sanctions a man's violence against his wife if he reports that he suspects she was unfaithful to him. This gives men the power to beat or murder their wives and then to use the accusation of suspected adultery to justify their actions, rendering married women particularly vulnerable to femicide.

The researchers from Swaziland report that men believe that they also have a right to assault their wives when certain services (such as sexual intercourse) have not been rendered by them.

Alcohol was commonly used to explain a man's diminished responsibility for his actions in cases of femicide. For example, in Swaziland, family arguments or misunderstandings preceded most of the femicides, particularly when one or both of the partners were drunk. In court the presence of alcohol was seen as lessening the responsibility of the perpetrator for the crime. Being drunk is regarded as an extenuating circumstance that lessens the gravity of, and sentence for, femicides.

Although it was not included in the femicide study, the researchers received information on more than 60 femicides from the Zimbabwean police in Harare Province. Of these, 44 of the women and girls had committed suicide. In the majority of these cases the reason given for the suicides was so-called domestic disputes. Some of the women killed themselves by setting themselves afire after dousing themselves with paraffin or by taking an overdose of antimalaria tablets. In none of the cases was anybody held accountable for these deaths. By taking no action, the state implicitly condoned the deaths of these women. For example, a young woman committed suicide after having been subjected to an extreme violation. She was drugged by a businessman who cut off her private parts for a business charm (an object that is believed to bring good luck in business). The businessman was never charged for lack of evidence. Cases in which women have committed suicide as a result of violence against them must be taken into account by the state.

In summary, many factors, including tradition, culture, and the use of alcohol by men, make women vulnerable to femicide. Because violence against women is condoned in certain circumstances, when this violence leads to femicide the common perception of the murderer is that he went too far in the heat of the moment or that he was drunk at the time. Thus, the general sanctioning of minor forms of violence ultimately allows society and the state to excuse extreme and brutal forms of femicide.

Patterns of Conviction and Sentencing

Once it had been established in court that the accused committed the crime, the trial often centered around whether there was some extenuating circumstance that could provide a partial excuse for the femicide. The excuses presented were often flimsy and unsubstantiated. The studies reveal, however, that these excuses gained sympathy for the perpetrator that carried weight in court, particularly when he was the intimate partner of the femicide victim. Analyses of the convictions of men in each of the five countries indicate that even if the initial charge was murder, most were reduced to the lesser charge of culpable homicide or even common assault. These verdicts were justified on the grounds of alleged victim provocation or extenuating circumstances.

In the majority of cases, the common defenses raised were those of provocation, intoxication, or insanity. For example, Galloway (1995) notes that in most cases in Zimbabwe, "the defenses of provocation and intoxication are raised simultaneously, usually the man being so drunk that any action by his wife will provoke him." In Swaziland, initial charges of murder were almost always reduced to lesser charges. For example, in a case in which a grandson said that he killed his grandmother because he suspected her of bewitching him, the judge found that his belief in witchcraft was an extenuating circumstance.

The insanity plea is normally entered in cases in which the femicide was committed in a very violent and horrific manner. This suggests that the judiciary (and society) cannot believe that a sane person could kill someone in such a way. In such cases, it is important to ask: Why is it that when men get so insane, they kill women—not men? When an insanity plea has been made, the focus shifts from punishing the offender to finding him less culpable for what he did. By reducing the charges to something other than murder, the judiciaries in all the states displayed the attitude that the deaths of these women were not to be treated seriously.

In each country, the sentencing patterns revealed that men who commit femicide are typically sentenced to short jail terms. In Zambia, a year or two for a charge of manslaughter was the typical penalty. The sentencing patterns for Botswana and Zambia show that the majority of offenders received sentences of 6 years or less. In Swaziland, the sentences handed down ranged from acquittals and suspended sentences to periods of imprisonment of usually less than 10 years. In Botswana, femicide was most frequently punished by a sentence of less than 6 years (Sejoe-Galetshoge, 1995). In reference to Zambia, Rude and Kazunga (1995) note that "it makes sad reading when cattle rustlers are given stiffer punishment than those who murder women."

In general, the charges and sentences meted out in cases of femicide were found to be particularly lenient when the perpetrator was the husband or a male relative of the deceased women.

The inadequate and in some cases negative response of the state to violence against women can also be understood from an analysis of some of the statements made by the judiciary when passing sentence in femicide cases. Table 8.1 lists comments made by the judiciary in Zambia in cases of intimate partner femicide and the sentences that were handed down (Rude & Kazunga, 1995). The judiciary often used the supposed presence of extenuating circumstances and provocation to pass particularly lenient sentences.

In one highly publicized case in Zimbabwe in which a man brutally beat and killed his wife with a stick because she insulted him, the trial magistrate held that the deceased "was asking for trouble in behaving like she did" and

Table 8.1. Comments on Cases of [Partner] Femicide Made by the Judiciary in Zambia (Watts et al., 1995, p. 41)

"He could not reasonably be expected to be in control of his mental facilities. The husband did what any reasonable man would have done in the circumstance."

—Case of Kasuba, 1993, whose husband got a 2-year sentence for shooting her

"The deceased was to blame."

—Case of Kazhila, 1989, whose husband got 1 year for killing her

"The provocation offered by your wife was such that any self-respecting person would lose control. The facts reveal that you did not use a lethal weapon, you only used your fists. I feel this case calls for maximum leniency."

—Case of Mulampa, 1986, whose husband got a 3-year suspended sentence

One husband got 18 months for manslaughter but was told not to be violent when he remarries, "because you may not be so lucky next time!"

—Case of Nata, 1985

"The accused was a responsible citizen with six children and parents to look after and so gets an 18-month sentence, suspended for 2 years, on the condition that he is not found guilty of any offense involving violence."

—Case of Nshingano, 1986

---

concluded that she was therefore looking for her own death (*S. v. Chapusa*). The murderer was found guilty of culpable homicide and sentenced to pay a fine of $250. However, this verdict was later overturned by the high court. This outcome highlights how sentencing patterns and the condemnation meted out to men found guilty of femicide are strongly influenced by the attitudes of the judge presiding over the case.

Many people in Southern African societies still believe that men have a right to beat their wives. Law enforcement officers and the judiciary are subject to the same forces of socialization and culture and therefore tend to hold similar views about violence against women. The findings clearly illustrate how the patriarchal view that men own women greatly influences the administration of justice in cases of femicide, with judges often sympathizing and condoning the femicide committed.

The lack of strong penalties against men who commit femicide is of great concern. By excusing violent femicides in the way some of the judges did, and by failing to treat femicides as murder, the state is failing in its responsibilities. The right to life is protected by international law and is the most fundamental of all human rights. Yet femicide victims are not protected, despite their lives often ending in gruesome torture, pain, and suffering. These acts violate the right to freedom from torture and from cruel, inhuman, or degrading treatment or punishment. These are rights guaranteed in the African Charter on Human and Peoples' Rights and by some United Nations bodies. Hence, the state has the duty to ensure that all citizens are protected.

The kind of violence that men perpetrate on femicide victims highlights the inequality between men and women. The state reinforces this inequality. Looking at why men committed the femicides, it is clear that women are often killed for trivial reasons. In Southern Africa this is justified on cultural, traditional, or religious grounds, and the state has condoned these excuses for femicides. By failing to uphold human rights norms and principles that it freely and willingly assumed, the state is implicitly and explicitly failing in its obligations to victims of femicide.

Acknowledgments. The femicide project was the brain-child of Darlene Rude, who worked with the Young Women's Christian Association of Zambia. It was she who got the YWCA to start on this project in Zambia. Thank you, Darlene, for inspiring a whole subregion to take up this study. To Mary Kazunga and all the staff at the "Y," our sincere gratitude for having the courage to take the lid off what many would not dare expose.

Sincere gratitude and thanks go to the following women who conducted the studies in different Southern African countries: Doo Aphane, Amelia Bazima, Whitney Bell, Monica Clear, Skha' Dube, Sheila Galloway, M. Kazunga, Faith Mkhonta, Caroline Moeketsi, Sanu' Moya, Salina Mumbengegwi, Nomsa Ncube, Emilia Noormohamed, Anu Pillay, D. Rude, Doreen Sejoe-Galetshoge, Nanisa Sigauke, Lisa Vetten, everybody at Women's Action Group, and Eunice Njovana and all at the Musasa Project.

We would also like to thank all the funders who supported the project in the five countries. Special thanks to all the police, ministries of justice, and other state functionaries who gave us access to information and moral support.

Let us continue to claim the public spaces that have been denied to us for so long and let us make the world listen to our analysis of our lives from our own perspective(s).

NOTE

This chapter consists of edited excerpts from Charlotte Watts, Susanna Osam, and Everjoice Win, *The Private Is Public: A Study of Violence Against Women in Southern Africa*, Havare, Zimbabwe: Women in Law and Development in Africa, 1995.

REFERENCES

Galloway, Sheila. (1995). *Femicide project*. Unpublished WiLDAF Country Report on Zimbabwe.

Mkhonta, Faith, & Doo Aphane. (1995). *The femicide report*. Unpublished SWAGA & WLSA Country Report for Swaziland.

Pillay, Anu, Lisa Vetten, & Caroline Moeketsi. (1995). *Femicide project*. Unpublished POWA Country Report on South Africa.

Rude, Darlene, & Mary Kazunga. (1995). *Report on the femicide research*. Unpublished WiLDAF Country Report on Zambia.

Sejoe-Galetshoge, Doreen M. (1995). *Violence against women*. Unpublished WiLDAF Country Report on Botswana.

Vetten, Lisa. (1995). *"Man shoots wife": A pilot study detailing intimate femicide in Guateng, South Africa*. A project of People Opposing Women Abuse (POWA) in South Africa and the NGO Secretariat for Beijing. [No information on publisher available.]

Watts, Charlotte, Susanna Osam, & Everjoyce Win (1995). *The private is public: A study of violence against women in Southern Africa*. Havare, Zimbabwe: Barnaby Printers.

CHAPTER 9

AIDS as Mass Femicide: Focus on South Africa

Diana E. H. Russell

Male sexual privilege is what drives the [AIDS] epidemic.
—Mark Schoofs, 1999, p. 68

In this country [South Africa], rape is not just a devastating act of violence. It can be a death sentence.
—Kelly St. John, 2000, p. A1

The lethal impact of AIDS on many women and girls must be recognized as a form of mass femicide that is devastating women throughout the world. These femicides are occurring as a result of the overlap of four gender-related problems: AIDS, male sexism and male domination, genital mutilation, and rape.

The combination of male sexism and male domination has played a significant role in causing the rapid spread of AIDS in the Caribbean. According to Jeannie Relly (2000), the ministry of health in Trinidad and Tobago reported that seven out of eight people infected with HIV/AIDS between the ages of 10 and 19 are female. The Jamaican health minister attributed the spread of AIDS to "the irresponsible sexual behavior of our men" (p. A15). Peggy McEvoy, AIDS policy team leader for a Caribbean program, explained that "married women face high risks because their partners are unfaithful and will not use condoms" (cited in Relly, 2000, p. A15). If the women insisted that their husbands use condoms, "Their husbands would kick them out," McEvoy explained. She further added, "Many women are also unaware that their husbands are having extramarital affairs" (cited in Relly, 2000, p. A15).

The causes of women's vulnerability to AIDS in the Caribbean are common in most parts of the world. I consider the global spread of AIDS to be chiefly due to sexist male behavior within a patriarchal context. Although some unknown percentage of women who die of AIDS are not necessarily victims of femicide (those who become infected by dirty needles, for example), many more are.

THE GLOBAL DISTRIBUTION OF HIV/AIDS

A recent global estimate of the number of people in the world living with AIDS is 34.3 million, and approximately 24.75 million of these infected individuals are living in Africa, compared to:

- 900,000 in North America
- 1.3 million in Latin America
- 520,000 in Western Europe
- 420,000 in Eastern Europe and Central Asia
- 530,000 in East Asia and the Pacific
- 5.6 million in South and Southeast Asia
- 15,000 in Australia and New Zealand
  (United Nations AIDS Program, see map in Perlman, 2000a, p. A6)

According to another source, two-thirds of the people in the world who are infected with HIV/AIDS live in Africa (Shaw, 1999). The highest rates of infection in the world are currently found in seven Southern African nations, including South Africa, where "at least one-fifth of the population is infected" (UNAIDS Program, cited in Perlman, 2000a, p. A6; Russell, 2000a, specifies 20% of adults as infected). Hence, the primary focus of this analysis will be on the particularly devastating impact of AIDS in Southern Africa.

In sub-Saharan Africa, new figures show that "55% of all infected adults are women" (Schoofs, 1999, p. 68). And according to data compiled by the UNAIDS Program: "For every 10 African men with the disease there are 12 infected women" (Reuters, 1999, p. 4).

The causal relationship among male sexism and male domination, genital mutilation, rape, and the AIDS epidemic in Africa are now addressed in this order.

MALE SEXISM, MALE DOMINATION, AND AIDS

Heterosexual males' sexist and misogynist beliefs and behavior toward females in patriarchal societies are a major cause of the spread of AIDS and, hence, of increasing rates of femicide.[1] The earlier passage on the spread of

AIDS in the Caribbean gave examples of common manifestations of male sexism and male domination that can have lethal consequences for females when their male partners have HIV/AIDS:

1. Males who refuse to wear condoms with their female partners despite engaging in sexual relations with others (male and/or female).
2. Males who engage in sex with others (male and/or female) but fail to divulge their nonmonogamous behavior to their female sex partners. This deprives these women of the opportunity to protect themselves from contracting HIV, to protect any children they may have from the same fate, and to save their own lives by refusing to engage in sexual relations with their partners.

Other examples include:

3. Husbands who feel themselves entitled by patriarchal law or custom to expect, demand, and/or force their wives to engage in sex with them, and who act on this conjugal right.
4. Men who are ignorant of their HIV-positive condition and who do not wear condoms or refuse to wear them.
5. Men who have sex with prostituted women. These women are at very high risk of having HIV/AIDS, especially if they fail to wear condoms. Many women—including prostituted women—do not know the importance of wearing condoms for protection and/or they accommodate their customers, who may dislike or refuse to wear them. Some men are also ignorant of the importance of condoms, whereas others consider sex with condoms less satisfying and put their own enjoyment above women's preference and/or safety.

The women and girls who contract HIV/AIDS from their male partners because of their sexist attitudes and behavior, and/or because of their superior power and dominant status, are—when they die—victims of femicide.

Village Voice journalist Mark Schoofs (1999), who won the Pulitzer Prize in 1999 for his series of articles on AIDS in Africa, devoted one article to "Death and the Second Sex." This article on femicide provides devastating evidence of male domination in Southern Africa and how this relates to AIDS. For example, Schoofs notes that "African women subordinate their sexual safety to men's pleasure" (p. 67). "Throughout Southern Africa, where the AIDS epidemic is worse than anywhere in the world," many African women practice "dry sex" to please their husbands (p. 67). Some women dry out their vaginas with soil mixed with baboon urine; others use "detergents, salt, cotton, or shredded newspaper" (p. 67). Schoofs describes the way in which Sipewe Mhakeni dried out her vagina:

> Mhakeni used herbs from the Mugugudhu tree. After grinding the stem and leaf, she would mix just a pinch of the sand-colored powder with water, wrap it in a bit of nylon stocking, and insert it into her vagina for 10 to 15 minutes. The herbs swell the soft tissues of the vagina, make it hot, and dry it out. That made sex "very painful," says Mhakeni. But, she adds, "Our African husbands enjoy sex with a dry vagina." (p. 67)

Other women also reported that having dry sex was painful. Furthermore, "research shows that dry sex causes vaginal lacerations and suppresses the vagina's natural bacteria, both of which increase the likelihood of HIV infection. And some AIDS workers believe the extra friction makes condoms tear more easily" (p. 67).

Schoofs reported that Southern African girls "are socialized to yield sexual decision-making to men" (p. 67). Prisca Mhlolo, who was in charge of counseling at an organization for HIV-positive Zimbabweans, noted that women are not even allowed to say, "Can we have sex?"—so it's even more difficult for them to bring up the subject of condoms. For example, Mhlolo's husband, who had infected her with AIDS, objected to her suggesting that he wear a condom when he developed open herpes sores on his penis, accusing her of having found a boyfriend.

Because women in Southern Africa "are unable to negotiate sex," they have to "risk infection to please the man," Schoofs observed. He quotes Mhlolo as commenting that this situation "is part of our culture . . . and our culture is part of why HIV is spreading" (p. 68). Schoofs maintains that African men "retain the mindset of polygamy," which was practiced in their traditional cultures. Now, instead of men practicing polygamy in those African nations where it is illegal, they "have many partners through commercial sex or 'sugar daddy' relationships that lack the social cohesion of traditional marriages" (p. 68).

Dr. Michel Carael, lead researcher of a U.N. study released in September 1999, found that HIV "spread more quickly in places where girls became sexually active at an earlier age" (cited by Shaw, 1999, p. A15). According to a UNAIDS report, "Older men, who often coerce girls into sex or buy their favours with sugar-daddy gifts, are the main source of HIV for the teenage girls" (Reuters, 1999, p. 4). For their part, some "young girls think the older men can provide for them," according to Anne Buve of the Institute of Tropical Medicine in Antwerp, Belgium (cited in Shaw, 1999, p. A15). Their relationships with older men, whether forced, coerced, or bought, increase their vulnerability to contracting HIV. As Peter Piot, executive director of the Joint U.N. Program on HIV/AIDS, points out, "Gender inequality—including women's economic dependence on men—is a driving force of the AIDS epidemic" (Associated Press, 2000a, p. A6).

GENITAL MUTILATION AND AIDS

Despite a number of different factors that contribute to the perpetuation of genital mutilation in many regions of the world, I concur with Efua Dorkenoo's (1999) view that "the roots of the practice lie in the patriarchal family and in [the patriarchal] society at large" (p. 95). As long as gender inequity persists in societies that practice female genital mutilation and the more extreme the gender inequity is, the more difficult it will be to combat this sometimes lethal operation.

Although "there have been no comprehensive global surveys of the prevalence of female genital mutilation" (Dorkenoo, 1999, p. 91), experts Fran Hosken and Nahid Toubia estimate "that there are at present more than 120 million girls and women who have undergone some form of female genital mutilation" (cited in Dorkenoo, 1999, p. 87). According to several sources cited by Dorkenoo (1999), most of these mutilated girls and women live in 28 African countries. However, this operation is also performed:

> in the Southern parts of the Arabian peninsular and along the Persian Gulf and, increasingly, among some immigrant populations in Europe, Australia, Canada, and the United States. . . . It has also been reported to be practiced by . . . the Daudi Bohra Muslims, who live in India—and among Muslim populations in Malaysia and Indonesia. (Dorkenoo, 1999, p. 87)

The World Health Organization's (WHO) Technical Working Group defines female genital mutilation as "the removal of part or all of the external female genitalia and/or injury to the female genital organs for cultural or other nontherapeutic reasons" (cited in Dorkenoo, 1999, p. 88). This WHO group differentiates four types of female genital mutilation, ranging from the mildest type I form, which involves the removal of the clitoral hood, to complete clitoridectomy. In type II operations part of the labia minora is removed along with the clitoris. Type III, known as infibulation,

> involves the complete removal of the clitoris and labia minora, together with the inner surface of the labia majora. The raw edges of the labia majora are then stitched together with thorns or silk or catgut sutures, so that when the skin of the remaining labia majora heals, a bridge of scar tissue forms over the vagina. A small opening is preserved . . . to allow the passage of urine and menstrual blood. (cited in Dorkenoo, 1999, p. 88)

Type IV is a new category devised to cover other surgical practices, for example, "cauterizing by burning of the clitoris and surrounding tissue" and the introduction of substances into the vagina to tighten or narrow it (Dorkenoo, 1999, p. 88).

Dorkenoo (1999) estimates that 80% of all the female genital mutilations performed qualify as type II, whereas about 15% constitute type III. This most extreme form of female genital mutilation is widely practiced in Somalia, Sudan, Ethiopia, Eritrea, northern Kenya, and small regions in Mali and northern Nigeria (Dorkenoo, 1999).

Despite the intense interest of many AIDS researchers in discovering why this disease is such a mammoth scourge, particularly in Africa, the likely connection between AIDS and genital mutilation has received very little attention. Yet because HIV is transmitted by HIV-infected sperm or blood entering the bloodstream of someone who was formerly free of the virus, the tendency of mutilated genitals to bleed puts genitally mutilated women at high risk of catching this disease.

The more severe the form and the more widespread the practice of female genital mutilation, the more this atrocity contributes to the massive numbers of women and girls infected by HIV. Many subsequently die— the victims of femicide. Unknown numbers of female genital mutilation victims also die from non-AIDS-related infections, particularly those related to childbirth.

The age at which female children are subjected to genital mutilation varies widely in different societies. In some groups, this operation is performed on babies only a few days old; in others, on girls about 7 years old; in yet others, on adolescents. The crude implements frequently used to perform these unnecessary, dangerous, and sometimes fatal operations are often used on a number of girls on the same occasion, with only a superficial water rinse of the knife or razor blade. Hence, if one child has AIDS, all the other girls are likely to get it, too.

Women who have been infibulated have often been sewn up so tightly that intercourse can easily cause their mutilated genitals to bleed. This means that they are far more at risk of being infected by AIDS. In addition, genital bleeding is common among infibulated women who have intercourse because of the friction involved, their vulnerability to vaginal tearing, and their lack of lubrication due to a deficiency of sexual desire. Bleeding also occurs because newlywed men frequently cut open their brides' tightly sewn vaginas on the wedding night to accommodate their penises and/or use their penises to force their way in. Women are also sewn up when their husbands leave home for an extended time and cut open again when they return. In addition, pregnant women have to be cut open to give birth, after which they are tightly sewn up again. If a husband resumes intercourse before his wife's wounds have healed, bleeding is especially likely to occur.

Hence, the horrific compulsory patriarchal custom of the most severe types of genital mutilation imposed on millions of girls in Africa causes females of all ages to be at much greater risk of dying because of the lethality of AIDS. The likelihood that the less severe forms of genital mutilation also result in more bleeding than occurs in nonmutilated genitals is an empirical question that is in urgent need of research.

Genital mutilation also causes numerous other fatal health complications aside from AIDS. Unknown numbers of young girls die from infections as a result of the often unhygienic methods used to perform this excruciatingly painful operation. Unknown numbers of infibulated women die during childbirth or because of fatal infections caused by being repeatedly cut open and sewn shut. Therefore, genital mutilation is also a form of mass femicide in its own right.

Because genital mutilation is designed to suit men's sexual needs and to maintain their inordinate control over women, AIDS deaths resulting from this practice qualify as femicide. Genital mutilation and other patriarchal customs such as vaginal drying (described above) contribute to this tragic male-perpetrated reality. How important these factors are as contributors awaits urgently needed research.

RAPE AND AIDS

Sub-Saharan Africa, where 10% of the world's population reside, "has almost 70% of the world's HIV/AIDS sufferers," according to Reuters (1999, p. 4).

There are no reliable statistics on the prevalence of rape in Africa. However, South Africa has been identified as having one of the highest rates of rape in the countries in which rape rates have been estimated. For example, Radhika Coomaraswamy, the United Nations Special Rapporteur on violence against women, noted that since the South African police estimate that only approximately 2.8% of the rapes that occur there are reported to them, then "South Africa would . . . probably have the highest level of rape among countries which have taken the initiative to collect statistics on violence against women" (1997, p. 3).

More recent sources are far less equivocal. "South Africa has . . . the world's highest per capita rate of rape," states Kelly St. John (2000, p. A1). As high as rape rates are in the United States, St. John maintains that "a woman [in South Africa] is five times more likely to be raped than in the United States" (p. A5); Daniel Wakin (1999) gives the comparable figure of three times more likely. In addition, approximately one in eight South African adults was infected with HIV in 1999 (Wakin, 1999), and "HIV/AIDS is spreading faster in South Africa than anywhere else in the world" (St. John, 2000, p. A5).

The prevalence of the AIDS virus "makes sexual assault increasingly lethal" in South Africa (Wakin, 1999, p. A10). In the fall of 1999, "five insurance companies began selling 'rape insurance'" in South Africa (St. John,

2000, p. A5). One firm sells a policy "whose benefits include a triple cocktail of antiretroviral drugs for 28 days and free HIV testing for a year after a rape" (St. John, 2000, p. A5).

For reasons unknown, violence against women, including rape, has escalated since ex-president Nelson Mandela and the African National Congress came to power in April 1994. For this and other reasons, there has been considerable international publicity about the high rape rate in South Africa. In a country with a high rape rate as well as a high rate of AIDS, there will be a very high rate of rape-related AIDS. Hence, the very high rates of rape in South Africa have undoubtedly contributed to the severity of the AIDS epidemic there, as well as to the epidemic of rape-related femicides (Cape Town is now sometimes referred to as "rape town" [Anne Mayne, personal communication, October 24, 2000]).

Another factor that contributes to both the rape rate and the rate of AIDS in South Africa is the belief of some males in the myth that an HIV-infected man "can cure himself of HIV if he has sex with a virgin" (St. John, 2000, p. A5), which only young children can be presumed to be. Some AIDS-free men also choose to rape girls rather than women because they assume that young girls will be free of AIDS. Hence, growing numbers of female children are becoming victims of this form of femicide when they contract the fatal disease.

African men in some other African countries also believe the myth about the curative effect of sex with virgins, which only young children can be counted on to be. Michel Carael of the U.N. AIDS office in Geneva was the lead researcher in a random-sample study of 1,000 men and 1,000 women in each of four towns situated in Zambia, Kenya, Cameroon, and Benin. The researchers found that "the prevalence of the virus in very young girls is a major dynamic in this epidemic" (cited in Shaw, 1999, p. A15). They also reported that

> the younger a girl was having her first sexual experience, the more likely she would be to contract the disease [HIV]—partly because of the belief among many sexually active men that young girls are "safe," and even that sex with a virgin can cure AIDS. (cited in Shaw, 1999, p. A15)

STRATEGIES TO PREVENT AIDS

The more prevalent AIDS is, the more at risk rape and genital mutilation victims are to catching this fatal disease from AIDS-infected rapists and sex partners. Therefore when rape rates rise, so does the prevalence of AIDS for females—and hence femicide. Given the epidemic proportions of rape, AIDS, and genital mutilation, this means these problems cause geometrically rising numbers of femicidal casualties in the world today.

South African president Thabo Mbeki has been heavily criticized by many leaders and AIDS specialists in Western nations, including in his own country, for his insistence that AIDS is not caused by HIV (e.g., see Cauvin, 2000; Jeter, 2000). He maintains that "poverty is a greater enemy than the virus" (Russell, 2000b, p. A1; also see Russell 2000d, p. 8). "The notion that immune deficiency is only acquired from a single virus cannot be sustained," Mbeki told *Time* magazine (Associated Press, 2000b). More extreme yet, a progressive South African newspaper reported that "Mbeki told an ANC [the governing political party] parliamentary caucus that the United States and pharmaceutical companies have conspired to establish a false link between HIV and AIDS to promote the sales of anti-retroviral drugs" (cited by Jeter, 2000, p. D4).

Mbeki has also been heavily criticized in South Africa and internationally for his rejection of expensive anti-viral medication as the means of dealing with the escalating AIDS problem in his country. Nor did his position waver when he was offered the anti-AIDS drugs at a substantially lower price. However, his denial of the causal relationship between HIV and AIDS was not the only reason for his stance. Joseph Kahn (2000) reports that

> even at 90 percent discounts, a typical cocktail of AIDS-suppressing drugs might cost $2,000 a year for a single patient in Africa, more than four times the average per capita income in many of the worst-afflicted countries.

Besides stating that a medical strategy is not affordable in South Africa even at this allegedly bargain-basement price, Mbeki also argues that AIDS in Africa appears to be significantly different from its manifestations in Europe and the United States, where it has been concentrated among gay men. He even wonders "if there are different biological circumstances affecting Africa" (Russell, 2000a, p. A16).

I feel strongly that Mbeki should provide free anti-AIDS medication for pregnant and child-bearing women in South Africa, as well as victims (male and female) of rape, incestuous and extrafamilial child sexual abuse, and other forms of sexual assault. However, I think he is correct to reject the costly pharmaceutical approach practiced in the United States that focuses on prolonging the lives of everyone who is already infected with the AIDS virus and whose illness is covered by medical insurance or Medicare, rather than focusing on the prevention of the disease.

However, on July 7, 2000, Boehringer Ingelheim, "an international pharmaceutical company that markets a powerful antiviral AIDS drug" that has proven effective in preventing the "transmission of the AIDS virus from pregnant women to their infants," announced "that for the next five years, it will donate free supplies of the drug to every nation in the developing world that asks for it" (Perlman, 2000b, p. A1). Despite the fact that this offer totally undermines Mbeki's economic reasons for rejecting a pharmaceutical approach to AIDS for pregnant mothers in South Africa, he turned it down (Russell, 2000c).

Mbeki's shocking refusal to accept Boehringer Ingelheim's gift when it was first offered to him was irrational and indefensible. Almost six months later on February 1, 2001, Mbeki finally reversed his decision and accepted Boehringer Ingelheim's five-year donation of drugs for pregnant women who are infected with HIV (Jeter, 2001, pp. A9–A10). Based on pediatricians' estimate of 70,000 babies a year who are born with HIV in South Africa, or who "contract it shortly after birth," Mbeki's delay in accepting Boerhringer Ingelheim's offer on June 7, 2000, has resulted in 35,000 babies contracting HIV (Jeter, February 2, 2001, p. A9).

However, there is also an almost entirely neglected feminist rationale for rejecting an exclusively pharmaceutical approach to the HIV/AIDS problem in South Africa and many other African and non-African countries. Ignorance of the connection between common sexist and misogynist sexual practices and the etiology of HIV/AIDS seriously undermines the efficacy of prevention strategies that emphasize medication above all else. Common male attitudes regarding manhood, male sexuality, and male entitlement to dominate their female sex partners are not influenced by medication. As Geeta Rao Gupta, president of the Washington, D.C.-based International Center for Research on Women, said

> gender roles that disempower women and give men a false sense of power are killing our youth and women and men in their most productive years. (Russell, 2000d, p. A8).

Hence, the first order of business requires educating people about the role of sexism and male domination in the spread of HIV/AIDS. Policies have to be developed to work on eradicating these manifestations of patriarchy. It is not enough to conduct educational campaigns that focus only on the need to avoid risky sexual behavior, such as the need to use condoms—particularly when engaging in anal sex—the need to find out about the sexual histories of potential sex partners, the danger of having sex with many different partners, and how to recognize the symptoms of HIV/AIDS.

It is also of utmost importance that those responsible for knowingly infecting another person with HIV/AIDS when engaging in voluntary sex should be prosecuted for murder or femicide. Prosecutions would add the necessary teeth to ensure that educational campaigns are taken more seriously. Although some men with HIV/AIDS have been prosecuted in the United States for deliberately infecting their sex partners (e.g., see Sherman, 1991), these cases represent only a tiny fraction of the enormous number of guilty men whom I refer to as *AIDS perpetrators*. One is hard pressed to find any evidence that fear of prosecution restrains AIDS carriers from risking transmission of the disease to their sex partners.

Pornographer Larry Flynt has been accused by William Rider—Flynt's chief of security for more than seven years and "one of his closest confidants"—of having another man inject his wife Althea with the AIDS virus (Rider, 1997, p. 48). (Rider also reports that "Flynt threatened to give AIDS to a number of employees" [p. 52].) Althea, who was also convinced of Larry's role in this crime, subsequently died of a combination of this disease and a drug overdose. If this charge was followed up by the police, it appears to be a well-kept secret. Nor has it resulted in a public scandal. It seems unlikely that such a charge would have been equally ignored had Althea been accused in an equally credible account of injecting Flynt with the lethal virus.

Letting these men off the hook is an outrageously sexist reaction to a serious femicidal crime. It reveals a shockingly casual attitude about the millions of women and girls who have died because of men's sexist and duplicitous behavior.[2] Patriarchy so devalues women's lives that the behavior of HIV/AIDS-positive male femicide perpetrators is not taken seriously.

It is vital that the femicidal nature of the AIDS epidemic be recognized. Hopefully, this chapter will contribute to the achievement of this important goal.

Acknowledgment. I would like to thank Tammy Gordon for her very helpful editing of this chapter.

NOTES

1. There is also a biological factor that contributes to males more readily infecting women with AIDS than vice versa. Schoofs (1999) points out that "because a man ejaculates into a woman men are more likely to transmit the virus, whereas women are more likely to contract HIV without passing it on" (p. 68). However, my analysis focuses on nonbiological factors.

2. Although I think that women as well as men who are guilty of this offense should be prosecuted, this should not include women whose actions are controlled by another (e.g., if their husband or father insists that they have sex with another man despite their HIV-positive status).

REFERENCES

Associated Press. (2000a, June 7). U.N. meeting on women's rights deplores sex traffic, rise in AIDS. *San Francisco Chronicle*, p. A15.
Associated Press. (2000b, September 11). South Africa's president insists that HIV alone cannot cause AIDS. *San Francisco Chronicle,* p. A8.

Cauvin, Henri. (2000, October 17). South African leader to curb comments over AIDS' origin. *San Franciso Chronicle*, p. A15.

Dorkenoo, Efua. (1999). Combating female genital mutilation: An agenda for the next decade. *Women's Studies Quarterly*, 27(1–2), 87–97.

Jeter, Jon. (2000, October 13). Mbeki's HIV stance wins few friends. *San Francisco Chronicle*, p. D4.

Jeter, Jon. (2001, February 1). South African reverses stand on AIDS drugs. *San Francisco Chronicle*, pp. A9–A10.

Kahn, Joseph. (2000, July 19). U. S. to lend Africa $1 billion for AIDS drugs. *San Francisco Chronicle*.

Perlman, David. (2000a, June 28). AIDS making Africa a land of living dead. *San Francisco Chronicle*, pp. A1, A6.

Perlman, David. (2000b, July 8). AIDS drugmakers to give medicine to poor nations. *San Francisco Chronicle*, pp. A1, A7.

Relly, Jeannie. (2000, February 26). Societal norms, poverty blamed for rapid spread of AIDS in the Caribbean. *San Francisco Chronicle*, p. A15.

Reuters. (1999, November 24). Gloom as AIDS toll rises. *Cape Times* (South Africa), p. 4.

Rider, William. (February 1997). The real Larry. *Penthouse*, 28(6), pp. 46, 48, 50, 52, 101.

Russell, Sabin. (2000a, July 7). AIDS experts to meet in eye of epidemic. *San Francisco Chronicle*, pp. A1, A16.

Russell, Sabin. (2000b, July 10). Mbeki's stand angers delegates. *San Francisco Chronicle*, p. A1.

Russell, Sabin. (2000c, July 14). Moms passing HIV to kids is urgent topic. *San Francisco Chronicle*, A15.

Russell, Sabin. (2000d, July 15). Meeting accomplished its purpose—and provided some hope. *San Francisco Chronicle*, p. A8.

Schoofs, Mark. (1999, December 1–7). AIDS: The agony of Africa: Part 5: Death and the second sex. *Village Voice*, pp. 67–72.

Shaw, Angus. (1999, September 15). Teen sex linked to AIDS in Africa. *San Francisco Chronicle*, p. A15.

Sherman, Rorie. (1991, October 14). Criminal prosecutions on AIDS growing. *National Law Journal*, 14(6), pp. 3, 38.

St. John, Kelly. (2000, May 22). When rape is a death sentence. *San Francisco Chronicle*. pp. A1, A5.

Wakin, Daniel J. (1999, October 12). Women fearing rape, HIV turn to new insurance. *San Francisco Chronicle*, p. A10.

Femicide in
Other Nations

CHAPTER 10

Intimate Femicide in Israel: Temporal, Social, and Motivational Patterns

Simha F. Landau and Susan Hattis Rolef

Over the past two decades, female partner battering has become an issue of general public concern. Researchers and practitioners alike agree that like most forms of violence in the family, female partner battering is a widespread phenomenon and, as such, should be considered a serious social problem. Be that as it may, only a small fraction of such cases are known to the police and/or other social agencies due to reluctance on the part of victims to report to the authorities. In Israel, for instance, it has been officially estimated that about 10% of all married women are, or have been, victims of female partner battering (Landau, 1991). A more recent survey reports that 16% of adult Jewish females are physically abused at home (Sadan, 1993).

This chapter focuses on the most extreme form of female partner abuse, namely, intimate femicide (the killing of women by their male partner or ex-partners). As in the case of homicide in general, the statistics on the incidence of intimate femicide are far more accurate than those for nonfatal violence against women in intimate relationships. Intimate femicide should be seen as "the tip of the iceberg" of the much deeper and, more often than not, hidden problem of violence against women. It is, therefore, somewhat surprising that this topic has received so little attention in the literature on violence against women. Clearly, intimate femicide should be studied as a topic in its own right and not simply as part of homicide research in general. The results of such research, in turn, will surely bear important implications for practitioners and policy makers.

In Israel, violence against women has featured quite prominently on the public agenda over the past decade or so. Reported cases of female partner battering, especially the killing of women by their partners, are subject to extensive coverage by the media. Increased awareness of the problem and the initiative of a number of women members of the Knesset (the Israeli Parliament) led in 1995 to the establishment of a special Parliamentary Committee of Inquiry for the Investigation of the Killing of Women by their Intimate Partners (Dayan & Livnat, 1996). However, due to the fact that the general elections in Israel were brought forward (from November 1996 to May 1996), this committee had to terminate its work sooner than planned, and a somewhat incomplete report was submitted in June 1996.

The present study analyzes the data collected by this committee in greater depth. The data cover all cases of intimate femicide committed in Israel during the years 1990–1995: 76 cases in all.[1] The main data sources were police records, court files, and daily newspapers, as well as material collected from voluntary organizations involved in the prevention of violence against women and the provision of assistance for the victims of such violence. The relatively small number of cases in this study put limitations on the application of statistical analyses. However, the fact that we are dealing here with an entire "population" (rather than a sample) diminishes the need for statistical significance tests. It should be noted that the incidence of the converse case—women killing their male partners—is extremely rare in Israel. During the 6-year period covered by our data, there were only four such cases. Of these four cases, two were clear cases of killing an abusive male partner. This low rate is in sharp contrast to findings in other countries, especially the United States, where the killing of men by their female partners represents a substantial proportion of intimate homicides. For example, a study conducted in Jacksonville, Florida (Rasche, 1993), reported that 38% of homicides involving spouses were committed by females, and a study in Chicago (Block & Christakos, 1995) found males and females equally represented in such homicides. However, most women who kill their husbands do so in self-defense.

This chapter focuses on the following three aspects of intimate femicide: the temporal distribution of these cases during the period 1990–1995, the differential representation of various population groups in intimate femicide, and the motives/reasons given for intimate femicide.

THE TEMPORAL DISTRIBUTION
OF INTIMATE FEMICIDE: 1990–1995

Let us first look at the incidence of intimate femicide in Israel. Table 10.1 presents the annual rates of intimate femicide for the years 1990–1995.[2] This table shows that the highest rate for intimate femicide occurred in 1991. There

Table 10.1. Numbers and Rates of
Intimate Femicides in Israel: 1990–1995*

Year	Intimate Femicides	
	n	Rate per 1,000,000 pop.
1990	15	3.22
1991	19	3.84
1992	6	1.17
1993	12	2.28
1994	13	2.41
1995	11	1.98
Total	76	2.48

Source: Adaptation of Table 1 in Landau & Rolef, p.77.
Adapted with permission of the authors

was a sharp decrease in 1992, and subsequently the rate moderated between these two extremes. More specifically:

- The rate of intimate femicides in 1991 (3.84 per 1,000,000 population) increased by 19.3% in comparison to the rate in 1990 (3.22).
- The rate of intimate femicides in 1992 (1.17) was more than three times lower than that of 1991 (3.84).
- The rate of intimate femicides in 1995 (1.98) was 17.8% lower than that in 1994 (2.41).

Although caution should be exercised in attempting to explain short-term statistical trends of rare events such as intimate femicide in Israel, some of the findings of our study do seem to lend themselves to explanation within a wider social context and in terms of relevant developments on the macrolevel.

Our findings suggest that the marked increase in intimate femicides in 1991 can be attributed to the heightened stress on the national macrolevel surrounding the Persian Gulf War, which broke out at the beginning of that year. This war was unique in that, unlike many other previous wars, the whole country became a "front," with the civilian population being forced to endure prolonged periods encapsulated in sealed rooms. Among the most frequently reported symptoms during the Persian Gulf War were anger and rage (Landau, 1998b), reflecting the frustration and helplessness felt by large sections of the population due to the passive role imposed upon Israel by its allies. The accumulated stresses of this war were expressed in violent behavior after it ended: An alarming increase in female partner battering was reported in the months following the war (Landau, 1998b). Greenberg and Stanger (1991) report that between February and August 1991, more than 12 Israeli women were killed by their husbands, adding:

> Many Israelis blame the increase [in intimate femicide] on the psychological stress triggered by the war. Men trained to lead tank columns and infantry units were forced to sit at home with their families while coalition forces took on the job of defeating Iraq. With many businesses closed, people could not work or shop. Shut up in tiny sealed rooms under threat of Scud missile attacks, family tensions escalated. . . . There was an emasculation of the Israeli male. . . . They felt fear and helplessness. Their anger built up. (p. 15)

Landau (1994) reports a similar increase in all homicides triggered by domestic conflict in 1991. Reports from hotlines during and immediately after the war provide support for the interpretation of the 1991 intimate femicide figures mentioned above: There was a marked increase in calls from women venting their frustrations over smoldering male aggression toward them that appeared to be heightened by the war ("Tensions, Threats," 1991).

The sharp decrease in intimate femicide in 1992 may have been a consequence of an important development in coping with female partner battering on the societal level: the enactment of the Law for the Prevention of Family Violence by the Knesset in 1991. According to this law, based on her word alone, a woman can obtain an immediate court order barring a violent husband from the home for a 7-day period. At the end of the 7-day period, the restraining order can be extended for a period of up to 3 more months, subject to appearance before the court by both parties, if the evidence of abuse is judged sufficient. The order can be prolonged for a second 3-month term following an additional court confrontation. This relatively simple legal procedure provided battered women with a fast-acting instrument to ward off imminent physical danger from an abusive male partner. The law was widely discussed and publicized in the media. Voluntary women's organizations distributed (free of charge) booklets about the law (including detailed instructions for action) through social welfare agencies, day-care centers, hospital emergency rooms, and other relevant channels. More important, the law facilitated radical changes in the practice of social agencies dealing with victims of female partner battering (the police, social welfare agencies, hospitals, etc.).

It is worth noting that the impact of this law went beyond the immediately relevant formal agencies. For instance, in addition to an increase in the number of complaints filed by battered women, there has also been an increase in the number of men required to undergo group treatment programs for violent husbands (Fishkoff, 1992). Thus, the combined effects of this law—the empowerment of battered women, together with the more general consciousness-raising of the public (including battering husbands) regarding the problem of male violence in the family—may have contributed to the sharp decrease in intimate femicides in 1992. This is also the impression of practitioners dealing with battered women ("Fewer Wives," 1993).

As might be expected, the strongest effect of this new legislation was observed in 1992, immediately after its enactment. In the 3 years that followed (1993–1995), the rates of intimate femicide increased, but only moderately, reaching a level far below not only the 1991 rate but also that of 1990 (the year before the Persian Gulf War). The long-term impact of the new law on the frequency and the severity of violence against women clearly requires separate evaluation research.

DIFFERENTIAL PRESENTATION OF POPULATION GROUPS

In addition to the disparate distribution of spousal homicides based on gender, cultural and structural factors contribute to the fact that violence is more prevalent in some sectors of the population than in others. Intimate femicide is no exception in this respect. Table 10.2 shows the proportions of the population groups in Israel and their respective representation among intimate femicide offenders.[3]

The main social/ethnic division in Israel is between the Jewish majority and the non-Jewish (mostly Muslim-Arab) minority. As can be seen in Table 10.2, the Jewish population is slightly underrepresented among intimate femicide offenders, whereas the non-Jewish population is overrepresented by about one-third. This finding is in line with previous research showing higher

Table 10.2. Proportions of Various Social Groups in the Population and Among Intimate Femicide Offenders, 1990–1995 (in Percent)

Social group	Average proportion in the population	Proportion among intimate femicide offenders	Over/under representation among intimate femicide offenders
1. Jews	81.4	75.0	−7.9
2. Non-Jews	18.6	25.0	+34.3
3. Immigrants from the former Soviet Union	12.5	19.7	+57.6
4. Immigrants from Ethiopia	0.9	9.1	+922.2

rates of violent crime among the non-Jews in Israel in comparison to their Jewish counterparts (Landau, 1975; Zonshein, 1976). In fact, in the studies mentioned above, the overrepresentation of non-Jews among all homicide offenders is considerably higher than their overrepresentation in the cases of intimate femicide found in the present study. This "lower than expected" rate of non-Jews among intimate femicide offenders in our study may well be due to the fact that, in the case of a wife's infidelity, Middle Eastern Muslim culture calls for the killing of the "guilty" woman for having "brought shame upon the family name" by a member of her own parental nuclear family, usually her father or a brother, not her husband. Hence, the "lower than expected" rate of intimate femicide in this group (Kressel, 1981; Landau, 1998a).

The most salient findings in Table 10.2 relate to the high overrepresentation of two specific groups of immigrants in intimate femicide: those from the former Soviet Union and those from Ethiopia. As can be seen, immigrants from the former Soviet Union are overrepresented by almost 60%, and the proportion of immigrants from Ethiopia involved in intimate femicides is 10 times higher than their proportion in the total population in Israel. Some background information regarding these two distinct population groups is clearly called for in attempting to explain their high rates of intimate femicide.

During the period 1990–1995, there was a huge influx of almost 600,000 immigrants from the former Soviet Union. In 1994, this population group comprised 14% of the total Israeli population (as compared to 7.2% in 1983). On the whole, the fact that many of these newcomers were skilled, middle class, and well educated helped them in their adjustment to the new environment. However, uprooting from the country of origin and readjusting to the new country and culture inevitably constitute a stressful process. In a study on the psychological well-being of immigrants from the former Soviet Union (Lerner, Mirsky, & Barasch, 1992), it was found that this social group scored significantly higher on a "demoralization scale" than a representative sample of veteran Israelis. The same study reports that the proportion of immigrants who reported psychological distress increased sharply between pre-emigration and arrival in Israel.

Official figures confirm these findings: During the years 1990–1991, the yearly psychiatric admission rates of immigrants (the vast majority of them from the former Soviet Union) were 40% higher than those of the general Israeli population (Popper & Horowitz, 1992). Our findings are in line with the studies mentioned above: They suggest that stress related to the adjustment of immigrants from the former Soviet Union inevitably took its toll, contributed to increased tension within families and between partners, and, in turn, led to the overrepresentation of this group among intimate femicide offenders in Israel.

The adjustment problems of the ex-Soviet Jews, no matter how stressful, appear almost trivial in comparison with those of the Ethiopian immigrants. This group, reunited with the mainstream of Jewry after total isolation for more than 2,000 years, arrived in Israel in two main waves: in 1984–1985 (Operation Moses) and in 1991 (Operation Solomon). All in all, close to 50,000 Ethiopian immigrants came to Israel, and by 1994 the size of this community had reached 57,000. Many of them came alone, without families. The Operation Moses immigration involved a long and arduous journey, much of it by foot, via Sudan, plagued by hunger, illness, and persecution. As many as 30% of those who set out on the long trek perished before reaching their "Promised Land."

The adjustment of Ethiopian Jews to life in Israel was highly problematic, even traumatic, for both the immigrants and, to a large extent, for the absorbing society: Israeli society as a whole felt compassion for this "Lost Tribe" due to the suffering they had endured on their journey to Israel. However, the official demand of the rabbinate (Israel's officially authorized supreme authority regarding religious affairs), who doubted their Jewishness, that they undergo conversion ceremonies was perceived by the Ethiopians as a severe affront in view of their faithful adherence to Judaism over the millennia despite constant persecution. Their sense of alienation was further exacerbated by negative reactions by some Israelis to their dark complexion.

The adjustment of the Ethiopian immigrants, most of whom came from small rural communities, to the realities of the modern, essentially Western-oriented Israeli society had extensive repercussions on their extremely patriarchal family structure. In many cases, the power of the male patriarch in the family was undermined. The high rate of unemployment among these immigrants contributed to demoralization, family disputes, and mostly male acts of violence. Arieli and Ayche (1993) reported that 10% of the adult Ethiopian community in their study had visited local mental health clinics. Another study (Arieli, Gilat, & Ayche, 1996) reports that the rate of suicide among Ethiopian immigrants was much higher than among the general population: In 1986 it was six times higher and in 1991 and 1992, three times higher.

Our findings suggest that the extremely high overrepresentation of Ethiopian immigrants among intimate femicide offenders is yet another indicator of the men's extremely violent acting-out toward their wives in reaction to the stress they experienced while adjusting to modern Israeli society.

MOTIVES/REASONS FOR INTIMATE FEMICIDE

Any attempt to classify motives is quite problematic. Indeed, the literature on motives in homicide is fraught with inconsistencies in the terminology used. A host of terms with different meanings are used by researchers, among them *intent, reason, motive, cause, justification, excuse,* and *explanation* (Landau, Drapkin, & Shlomo, 1974; Rasche, 1993). In the present analysis we focused on the immediate interactional reason for the fatal attack. In most cases, more than one motive or reason was given by the male offender and/or by persons who knew the couple (e.g., relatives, neighbors, social welfare agency personnel) for the killing of his female partner. Other people were also important informants in cases in which the male offender committed suicide without leaving information about his motivation. The reasons reported are grouped into the following three categories:

- *Possessiveness.* This includes the subcategories of jealousy, protecting family honor, victim threats to abandon the partner, and suspicion of the victim's infidelity. This category was mentioned in 75% of the cases.
- *Arguments/conflict.* This includes the subcategories of arguments and quarrels over a variety of issues, including money. This category was mentioned in 45.9% of the femicide cases.
- *Other.* This includes the subcategories of male offenders having mental problems, drinking problems, and/or drug problems in the offender, as well as other motives. These reasons were mentioned in 55.6% of the intimate femicides.

Table 10.3 shows the various combinations of motives/reasons given in the present study. As can be seen in this table, "possessiveness" is the dominant motive, but it is given as a single motive in only one-quarter of the cases, appearing mostly in combination with other motives (in descending order); "other" (20.5%), "other" plus "arguments/conflict" (16.4%), or "arguments/conflict" (13.7%). "Arguments/conflict" and "other" as single or combined motives without "possessiveness" appear in only a small number of intimate femicides.

Table 10.3. Motives/Reasons for Intimate Femicide

	n	*Percent*
1. Possessiveness	18	24.7
2. Possessiveness and arguments/conflict	10	13.7
3. Possessiveness and other	15	20.5
4. Possessiveness, arguments/conflict, and other	12	16.4
5. Arguments/conflict, and other	8	11.0
6. Arguments/conflict	4	5.4
7. Other	6	8.3
Total	73	100.0

Table 10.4. Distribution of Motives/Reasons for Intimate Femicide by Population Group of Male Offenders (in Percent)

Motive/ reason	Population Group				
	Jews	Non- Jews [6]	Immigration from former Soviet Union	Immigration from Ethiopia	Total
1. Possessiveness	71.4	83.3	73.3	85.7	75.0
2. Arguments/conflict	50.0	33.3	60.0	28.6	45.9
3. Other	60.7	38.9	60.0	57.1	55.
n	56	18	15	7	74

Table 10.4 presents the distribution of the motives/reasons by population group. The main findings of Table 10.4 can be summarized as follows:

- Among non-Jewish male offenders and those of Ethiopian origin, "possessiveness" is particularly high and "arguments/conflict" is relatively low. The similarity between these two population groups with regard to "possessiveness" has to do with their more extreme patriarchal character and the inferior status of women in these groups.
- "Other" motives (which are mainly indicative of personal pathologies of the male offender) are relatively low among non-Jewish male offenders. Among offenders of Ethiopian origin, however, the prevalence of this category is very similar to that among all Jewish male offenders and male offenders from the former Soviet Union.

Thus, with regard to motive, male offenders of Ethiopian origin are the only population group to be strongly represented on motives of an extreme patriarchal cultural nature ("possessiveness," similar to non-Jewish offenders), as well as motives of an individual-pathological nature ("other," similar to the Jewish male offenders). This may be seen as just another indicator of men's reaction to the traumatic adjustment of this social group following their immigration to Israel.

Table 10.5 presents the relationship between motive and the victim–offender relationship. As can be seen, the most salient finding in Table 10.5 is that "arguments/conflict" among divorced or separated couples and ex-nonmarried partners is twice as frequent as among married couples or non-married partners living together. This difference is hardly surprising because the status of divorce or separation implies a background of conflict between the partners. Of special interest is the finding that among ex-

Table 10.5. Motives/Reasons for Intimate Femicide by Victim–Offender Relationships (in Percent)

	Victim–offender relationship		
Motive/ reason	Married or partners	Divorced, separated, or ex-partners	Total
1. Possessiveness	77.6	69.6	75.0
2. Arguments/conflict	34.7	69.6	45.8
3. Other	55.1	56.5	55.6
n	49	23	72

partners, "possessiveness" still appears as a motive in about 70% of the cases: In spite of the official or unofficial separation, the male partner does not relinquish his "ownership" of the woman. This finding seems to be indicative of the deeply culturally embedded patriarchal norm of males' domination over females in society.

DISCUSSION

The findings of this study strongly suggest a relationship between intimate femicide in Israel and specific major events or processes experienced by Israeli society during the period investigated. Our findings are in line with the stress–support theoretical model proposed by Landau and Beit-Hallahmi (1983), which postulates that violence in society will be positively related to stress factors and negatively related to support systems. This model has received considerable empirical support in a series of studies. A positive relationship was found between homicide (on the aggregate level) and various stress factors in Israeli society on the macro social level, such as economic stress (inflation, unemployment) and security-related stress (casualties in wars and security-related incidents) (Landau & Pfeffermann, 1988; Landau & Raveh, 1987). In another study, rates of homicide in Israel were found to be positively related to subjective measures of stress in the population (dissatisfaction with the economic, political, or security situation) and negatively related to subjective support measures (solidarity between various social groups in society), as predicted by the model (Landau, 1988, 1997; for more details, see also Landau, 1994; Landau & Beit-Hallahmi, 1983).

In terms of the stress–support model discussed above, the Persian Gulf War and the trials and tribulations of immigration can be seen as constituting stress factors and, as such, were found to be related to an increase in intimate femicide, as predicted by the model. The Law for Preventing Family Violence can be seen as constituting a support system for battered women and, as such, was found to be related to a decrease in intimate femicide, as predicted by the model.

The sharp decrease in intimate femicide in the period immediately following the enactment of the Law for Prevention of Family Violence is indicative of the potentially positive effect of changes in legislation and in social policy on violence in the family (including intimate femicide). However, as our figures show, the drastic reduction in intimate femicide following this legislation was quite short lived. A careful follow-up study is necessary to evaluate its long-term impact.

Intimate femicide in Israel is a relatively rare crime, and therefore it is quite difficult to recommend specific measures for its prevention. However, because this phenomenon should be seen as representing "the tip of the iceberg" of the much wider problem of male violence in the family, measures that deal with this wider problem are also likely to have a mitigating effect on the frequency of intimate femicide. Most important, a concerted effort is needed for the delegitimation of violence against women in society. Specific attention should be paid to those social groups that are subject to stress (new immigrants, marginal social groups, etc.) as well as to those sectors of society in which the more extreme patriarchal structure exposes women to more extreme abuse. Our findings show that in view of the unique features of intimate femicide, this type of crime should be studied separately, not as part of the more general crime of homicide. Finally, it should be emphasized that the study of intimate femicide in Israel is only in its infancy. More research has to be conducted in this field. We have yet to analyze our data by relating it to situational factors, previous criminal records of male offenders, prior violence in the relationship, help-seeking behavior by the victim or offender, and treatment by the criminal justice system of these cases. In-depth examinations of sociocultural differences among various sectors of the population as well as sociohistorical changes are also pending.

The conclusions reached should be treated with some caution due to the relatively short time period covered by this study. The time span of the research on this topic needs to be expanded in order to increase our knowledge and understanding of this social problem.

Acknowledgment. The authors would like to thank Tali Efrati for her assistance in the data analysis.

NOTES

This is an edited version of Simha F. Landau and Susan Hattis Rolef's article, "Intimate Femicide in Israel: Temporal, Social, and Motivational Patterns," *European Journal on Criminal Policy and Research*, 6, pp. 75–90, 1998. An earlier version of this paper was presented at the 9th International Symposium on Victimology, Amsterdam, August 1997.

1. Originally there were 79 cases, but 3 of them were omitted from the analysis because they were committed in 1989.

2. The size of the population during these years was obtained from the Central Bureau of Statistics (1991–1997).

3. Data on the proportions of various population groups in the total population and on immigration to Israel were obtained from the Central Bureau of Statistics (1996).

REFERENCES

Arieli, Ariel, & Seffefe Ayche. (1993). Psychopathological aspects of the Ethiopian immigration to Israel. *Israeli Journal of Medical Science*, 29, 411–418.

Arieli, Ariel, Itzhak Gilat, & Seffefe Ayche. (1996). Suicide among Ethiopian Jews: A survey conducted by means of a psychological autopsy. *Journal of Nervous and Mental Disease*, 184, 317–319.

Block, Carolyn Rebecca, & Antigone Christakos. (1995). Intimate partner homicides in Chicago over 29 years. *Crime and Delinquency*, 41, 492–526.

Dayan, Yael, & Limor Livnat. (1996). *Report and conclusions of the parliamentary committee of inquiry for the investigation of the killing of women by their intimate partners.* Jerusalem: Knesset.

Fewer wives slain by spouses in 1992. (1993, January 5). *The Jerusalem Post.* [electronic edition]

Fishkoff, Sue. (1992, July 10). The fight begins at home. *The Jerusalem Post.*

Greenberg, Sheldon H., & Theodore Stanger. (1991, August 19). Israel's men on the verge. *Newsweek*, 118, pp. 15, 24.

Kressel, Gideon. (1981). Sororicide/filiacide: Homicide for family honor. *Current Anthropology*, 22, 142–158.

Landau, Simha F. (1975). Pathologies among homicide offenders: Some cultural profiles. *British Journal of Criminology*, 15, 157–166.

Landau, Simha F. (1983). Is Israeli society more violent than other societies? In Alouph Hareven (Ed.), *On the difficulty of being an Israeli* (pp. 171–200). Jerusalem: Van Leer Foundation.

Landau, Simha F. (1988). Violent crime and its relation to subjective social stress indicators: The case of Israel. *Aggressive Behavior*, 14, 337–362.

Landau, Simha F. (1991). Police response to spousal violence in Israel: Some preliminary findings. In Gunther Kaiser, Helmut Kury, & Hans Jorgen (Eds.), *Victims and criminal justice: Legal protection, restitution and support* (pp. 719–735). Freiburg: Max-Planck Institute.

Landau, Simha F. (1994). Violent crimes in a society at war: Israel and the Intifada. In Jesus M. Ramirez (Ed.), *Violence: Some alternatives* (pp. 63–84). Madrid: Centreur.

Landau, Simha F. (1997). Crime patterns and their relation to subjective social stress and support indicators: The role of gender. *Journal of Quantitative Criminology, 13*, 29–56.

Landau, Simha F. (1998a). Crimes of violence in Israel: Theoretical and empirical perspectives. In Robert Freedman (Ed.), *Crime and criminal justice in Israel: Assessing the knowledge base towards the 21st century* (pp. 97–120). Albany, NY: State University of New York Press.

Landau, Simha F. (1998b). Security-related stress: Its effect on the quality of life in Israel. In Daniel Bartal, Dan Jacobson & Aaron S. Klieman (Eds.), *Concerned with security: Learning from Israel's experience* (pp. 289–310). Greenwich, CT: JAI Press.

Landau, Simha F., & Benjamin Beit-Hallahmi. (1983). Aggression in Israel: A psychohistorical perspective. In Arnold P. Goldstein & Marshall H. Segall (Eds.), *Aggression in global perspectives* (pp. 261–286). New York: Pergamon Press.

Landau, Simha F., & Susan Hattis Rolef. (1998). Intimate femicide in Israel: Temporal, social, and motivational patterns. *European Journal on Criminal Policy and Research, 6*, 75–90.

Landau, Simha F., Israel Drapkin, & Arad Shlomo. (1974). Homicide victims and offenders: An Israeli study. *Journal of Criminal Law and Criminology, 65*, 390–396.

Landau, Simha F., & Danny Pfeffermann. (1988). A time series analysis of violent crime and its relation to prolonged states of warfare: The Israeli case. *Criminology, 26*, 489–504.

Landau, Simha F., & Adi Raveh. (1987). Stress factors, social support and violence in Israeli society: A quantitative analysis. *Aggressive Behavior, 13*, 67–85.

Lerner, Yaacov, Julia Mirsky, & Miriam Barasch. (1992). *New beginnings in an old land: The mental health challenge in Israel* (JDC, Research Report F-21). Jerusalem: Falk Institute.

Popper, Miriam, & Ruth Horowitz. (1992). *Psychiatric hospitalization of immigrants: 1990–1991* (Statistical Report No. 7). Jerusalem: Ministry of Health, Mental Health Services.

Rasche, Christine E. (1993). "Given" reasons for violence in intimate relationships. In Anna Victoria Wilson (Ed.), *Homicide: The victim/offender connection* (pp. 75–100). Cincinnati, OH: Anderson.

Sadan, Sasha. (1993, April 29). Survey shows 16% of adult Jewish women suffer beatings. *The Jerusalem Post*. [electronic edition]

Tensions, threats against women heightened by war. (1991, February 22). *The Jerusalem Post*. [electronic edition]

Zonshein, Eliezer. (1976). *A profile of homicide in Israel*. Unpublished master's thesis, Tel-Aviv University, Tel-Aviv, Israel.

CHAPTER 11

Femicide: An International Speakout

Diana E. H. Russell

This chapter presents an edited version of women participants' contributions to a workshop titled "A Speakout on Femicide" that I organized for the International Conference on Violence, Abuse, and Women's Citizenship in Brighton, England, in November 1996. This workshop was one of the very few that was only open to women. I made this a condition of attendance because I share the belief of many feminists that woman-only settings are necessary for women's sharing of sensitive material. Nevertheless, it took a little persuasion to get the male bodyguard of the First Lady of Botswana to abandon his job for the duration of the workshop!

About 40 women from many different countries attended the femicide speakout, sitting informally in the familiar feminist circle. Participants were required to speak in English, as was the case at all sessions on the conference program. Initially, I felt a lot of trepidation about whether such a culturally diverse group of women, who were mostly strangers to one another, would be willing to share their experiences. The fact that the victims of femicide cannot speak for themselves made this speakout different from speakouts for survivors of rape, battering, incestuous abuse, and the like. I was greatly relieved when women started sharing their thoughts about, feelings about, and experiences with femicide.

I began the speakout by defining femicide, then going on to say: "Although the victims of femicide cannot speak for themselves, those who have survived attempted femicide can. So, too, can those who have been affected or traumatized by victims of femicide whom they knew and cared about, such as an intimate partner, another family member, a friend, or a work colleague. Stranger femicide can also have a traumatic impact on women, making us fearful and more willing to restrict our lives in the hope of preventing this ultimate form of victimization. Hearing the experiences of those of you who've been affected by femicide will help to raise awareness of this important but terribly neglected form of violence against women. This, in turn, should motivate both individual and organized actions to try to combat femicide."

Following are a selection of the statements made by women at the workshop.

Unidentified woman, Bangladesh. I represent the Center for Children and Women Studies. My research found that most women are killed by close associates like husbands and brothers. Most of the quarrels that result in these murders are family quarrels about dowry, like the woman's husband's family demanding more dowry money after marriage. You see a lot of reports of suicides in newspapers and other media. But most of these suicides aren't really suicides. They are camouflaged cases of husbands killing their wives. For example, after killing their wives, men sometimes hang them in a tree and then go to the police station and say that their wives killed themselves. In certain areas of Bangladesh there are more reports of suicide by women than deaths or murders of women. When these murders happen in the village areas, the police stations are very far away. When the police eventually investigate the case, the husbands often bribe them to record suicide as the cause of their wives' deaths. Nevertheless, everyone in the village knows what the husbands have done.

As soon as a girl gets married, she has to go and live with her in-laws for the rest of her life. Because the in-laws aren't going to admit that their son killed her, it is very difficult—even for women's groups—to take up these cases. And there are no postmortems in the villages, so the police classify these murders as suicides. It's only if a women's group discovers some relevant new information that the woman's dead body is allowed to be taken out of the grave for examination. But other evidence is often lost by then, making it very hard to prove these cases. And there aren't many grassroots women's organizations working in these remote villages, so it's very difficult.

Although we don't subscribe to dowry practices in Islam, the influence of Hindu practices has made dowry the custom even for those who believe in Islam. This custom has become particularly prevalent among poor families. Some women's husbands throw acid in their wives' faces, causing their wives to lose their eyesight. Although the law has now been changed to punish these men, these laws aren't being implemented.

Margaret, England. I represent [as a lawyer] women at Great Easter Heights Women's Aid [a battered women's shelter] who have either been on trial for killing their abuser or who were almost killed and are now seeking criminal injuries. The point I want to emphasize is that *women don't always die directly as a result of the assault.* It's not only what has been done to them with a knife or an ax that's important; it's what they're left with at the end of all the assaults.

One woman I recently represented has been tried for hitting back at the man she lived with because he stuck a knife up her vagina. This attack left her with a fistula [an abnormal passageway between the vagina and the rectum resulting from injury, disease, or a congenital disorder]. She is likely to die as a result of this attack because fistulas cannot heal and because now she has alcohol problems as a result of the appalling abuse she suffered year after year. This woman will probably get off at her murder trial, but then she will be out on the streets with no support, no counseling, and no help whatsoever. She will die on those streets. She will not be one of the heroines. She will not be a feminist icon. She will die unnoticed and unremembered.

The husband of another woman I've been working with attempted to strangle her. It was just a matter of luck that she was found lying on the floor with a flex [an electric cord] tied tightly around her throat. She has been denied criminal injuries because she didn't cooperate fully with the police, who for years have refused to arrest her husband when he was beating lumps out of her. She's now suffering from *profound* depression, anxiety, sleeplessness, intrusive thoughts, hypervigilance and all the other signs of post-traumatic stress [disorder]. Where is her life?! (*said very indignantly*). Her life has been taken from her as surely as if he had plunged a knife in her heart. *So femicide for me is not just about being dead. It's about the extinction of a woman's right to live a full, happy, and safe life.* I think this kind of destruction *has* to be part of the organized fight against femicide.

Joyce Andersen, Botswana. We in Botswana have a network with other southern African countries, like Zimbabwe, Zambia, Swaziland, and South Africa, to coordinate our work on the problem of femicide. We have talked about what femicide is and about its causes, and we have formulated strategies to assist those who suffer because of it. And we have listed all the cases of women being battered to death or driven to suicide by depression and economic problems. We have also organized a network that produces programs to assist women who are abused as well as to assist the families of femicide victims.

We have also collaborated with our governments and with the women's NGOs [nongovernmental organizations] and informed them about the problem of femicide in our countries. We want the people in our countries to be aware of what femicide is, including *all the women who belong to the living dead.*

Norma Hoteling, United States. I am a survivor of prostitution and the director of an organization called the Sage Project in San Francisco that is run by and for survivors of prostitution. My work is motivated by my friends who died on the streets because they were prostitutes. Although San Francisco is considered very sophisticated, hip, and progressive, I know that if I had died on the street there, nobody would have cared. They probably would have said, "One more dead hooker! Thank God she's gone!"

Our debates about prostitution have all been without the voices of dead women and without the voices of women who have been so hurt by prostitution that they find it hard to talk about their experiences. So we decided to create a quilt for the women who became femicide victims because they were prostitutes, as a way of giving a voice to them. Two very good friends of mine—Laura and Cheryl—are on the quilt. Now we have five more patches to add to it. I thank God that I survived my years in prostitution.

A lot of us survivors are going through a lot of grieving right now because 2 weeks ago we lost another one of our sisters to the streets. Three prostituted women have been brutally murdered in San Francisco in the last year, and a number of others have died of drug overdoses. They are all lost to this world—like so many other women and children. These are the crimes that I believe we have to focus on.

Unidentified woman, Asia. I visited a fistula clinic where young mothers who were married at the ages of 11 and 12 had been torn very, very badly during childbirth because their bodies are too tiny for a baby to come out. So they became fistulous. Consequently, they are rejected by their husbands and by society. It is so sad when you see how tiny these girls are, and when you look into their eyes and realize that there is nowhere for them to go besides the clinic. To me, *they are the living dead. This is a femicide that you can see.*

Ruth Resnick, Israel. We started a shelter in Israel in 1978 when a woman was murdered by her husband of 3 months. The following year, on July 18, 1979, a woman named Camila Knocish was murdered on our shelter grounds. This is when the fact that women can be killed by their husbands first hit the Israeli public. They were especially shocked that this atrocity happened on the shelter grounds. When I visited the dead woman's family during the week of bereavement, they told me that she had been forced to marry this man because he had threatened to kill her family if she refused. He was insanely jealous—as are most violent men. This murder forced us to move our shelter which we named after this woman.

On the 25th of November last year [1995], there was a session in parliament in which well over 100 names of femicide victims who had been murdered in the past 5 years were displayed.

Albertine, Antigua, the Caribbean. I want to share with you the death of a very good personal friend of mine called Era Hecta. We were schoolmates together. She was very active in the women's movement in Antigua and the wife of the opposition leader there. She and her husband befriended a man they were trying to rehabilitate because he had often been in prison for stealing. One day when my friend's husband was out of the country and she was on a farm outside the capital with this man, he raped and killed her. I felt really devastated by this. It seems so incredible that someone she befriended would attack her in this way. What happened to my friend remains ever present to me. We are now trying to start the first shelter in Antigua for abused women which we will name after her.

I also want to make the same point that my sister here just made. I am a psychiatrist and I often work with abused women in Antigua. *The depression I see from constant years of abuse is a kind of death.* We are not just talking about the physical taking of life but the emotional taking of life, and I dare to say—the spiritual taking of life. These women cannot really enjoy life because their self-esteem is so low. They have no quality of life whatsoever. *We ought to look at femicide in this broad context.*

Susan, England. I find it hard to speak. I suffered at home for over 20 years watching my father try to kill my mother. It was unbelievably frightening to me, and I feel it's taken a terrible toll on me which is still going on. I'm talking about depression, relationship problems, you *name* it, my life feels like a mess. My mother stuck with my father for 27 years before she finally left him.

Living in that situation was horrific. I used to see the carving knife on the landing, and my father would chase my mother upstairs with it. I would hide her in my bedroom and put the chest of drawers against the door, and I'd tell her to get into my bed. Then I'd go out of my bedroom to take the knife off him. That happened dozens and dozens of times in my life. It's beyond words to describe this situation. My father never actually killed my mother, but the constant threat was almost as bad because I never knew what he'd do. I felt I could never go out—that I had to stay at home with my mother because who knew what would happen if I went out and left her alone. I realize now that it made me hypervigilant. I had to always be watching because he might come home early, or he might do something, or she might say something, and all these sort of things could trigger him to go off. *To put this on a child destroys you.* I am still trying to find out more about the effects that all this has had on me, and the effects that this type of situation has on children in general. What I went through is still very painful to me.

Selena, Zimbabwe. I am here with others who have worked on the Femicide Project in southern Africa. I would like to share with you some of the suicides that aren't recognized as femicides—just as a previous sister said. After the women receive payment for having toiled in the cotton fields, the men just squander the money away. This drives the women to extremes. Most of them take their own lives by drinking the insecticide that is sprayed on the cotton. *These are femicides, because they are driven to kill themselves by the men who deprive them of their economic means of survival. But their deaths are reported as suicides—not as femicides.* And they are the ones who are blamed for killing themselves.

Another kind of femicide sometimes happens when women are accused of witchcraft by their close relatives. For example, there is a case in our femicide register in Zimbabwe where an elderly woman was accused by her son of bewitching his children. So she drowned herself in a pool. When women die like that, they are blamed for it. So women are dying silently without the cause of their deaths being recognized. *The economic factors causing femicides as well as accusations of witchcraft need to be looked at more carefully.*

Vivian, Sudan. My origins are Syrian, but I was born in the Sudan. I live in a very small town there. It is the custom in the Sudan for girls aged 13 and 14, sometimes before they even get their periods, to get married. Some of these young married girls commit suicide or attempt suicide because of the vulgar way their husbands approach them sexually, especially on the first night.

One of these young girls was a friend of mine; we had studied together at school. We were happy when we learned that she was getting married. But a couple of weeks later, we heard that she was dead. After talking to friends and relatives from the community, we found out that her husband had used a knife to have sex with her on her first night. Using a knife to cut open the girl or woman's vagina was the custom in earlier times. Because of tradition, this man was never found guilty. He said that his young wife had not cooperated willingly with his sexual advances. This made him frustrated, so he had to be rough with her.

My friend lost her life like other young married girls do. *I agree with the other women here who've said that suicides in these circumstances are actually femicides.*

Unidentified woman, Scotland. I really don't want to say this, but I think I have to. Eleven years ago Anne—a really good friend of mine who lived in Scotland—went missing. Months later she was found naked and wrapped in a piece of carpet and stuffed in a canal about 5 minutes from the house where she lived. Police officers investigated her murder. After examining the forensic evidence, they ascertained that she had been very severely sexually violated by at least three men and that these attacks had taken place in her own house. I know that Anne wouldn't have allowed strangers into her house, and there was no evidence of forced entry. But the murderers have never been found. I probably knew these men. I probably drank with them—which is a terrible thought. And the fact that men can do this and get away with it really distresses me.

Anne's death obviously had a severe effect on her family. As a woman here said earlier, Anne won't be a feminist icon, but I'd like to ask you to remember her and to remember that she was a wonderful person.

Unidentified woman, England. When I heard the last woman speak, I realized that I'm still carrying a sense of injustice about a friend of mine who was murdered in her own home when she was 31 by a man who lived in the flat below her. Another friend and I found her naked and brutally beaten and battered. The police eventually found the man who murdered her, but he was only sentenced to 5 years in prison! And he got out in 4½ years!

When I saw my dead friend's sister on the street as I was driving the other day, she looked as if she were an old lady of about a 100 although she is only about 45. Her whole family is still suffering because justice was not done—because her murderer is out of prison today.

Unidentified woman, England. Like other women here, I want to talk about the *women who aren't necessarily dead, but whose total sense of self has been annihilated from very early childhood*. I work in a mental health system in Exeter. I'm part of a small group of women, colleagues, and friends who try to provide better services for women who hit the mental health services and who have experienced childhood sexual abuse. I recently completed a research study and interviewed a lot of women and heard their life stories about the torture they had experienced from very early childhood—sexual, physical, and emotional, you name it! They described how their sense of reality and their sense of self were consistently and systematically destroyed. Then as adults they were often led to commit acts of self-harm. Many of them attempted suicide, and some of them succeeded. As another woman here said, *often suicide is actually femicide*. And when they hit the so-called mental health care services, these services often confirm the women's lack of a sense of self by refusing to listen to their experiences and often refusing all services to them. I think more of us should be speaking out about these problems, but unfortunately these services are mostly controlled by men and a medical profession that is predominantly male, so it's very difficult to get women's voices heard.

Monica, Ireland. It has been a really difficult year for femicides in the south of Ireland, where I work in Women's Aid. Sixteen women have been murdered already this year, 10 of them in their own homes. One woman had caustic soda poured over her, causing her death. Her husband and her son have been charged with her murder. Sons have been involved in the murders of their mothers in two other cases. In one of them, the woman had obtained an order of protection.

What concerns me is that we ask women to use the legislation. This makes them believe that the state will protect them from their abusive husbands. But when they *do* take out an order, they are not given telephones, so they cannot get help when they need it. So all of us working in refuges must ask ourselves—how are *we* going to take responsibility for protecting these women *ourselves*, or will we continue to give them the illusion that the state will provide this protection?

Unidentified woman, England. It is not enough to gender the crime; we have to gender the perpetrator, too. Bea Campbell has pointed out that 87% of the perpetrators that turn up in court are men. This is never indicated in the crime figures.

Unidentified woman, Scotland. Like my sister from Edinburgh, I want you to remember five women I knew who were all murdered in Glasgow in the past few years. One of them, called Leona, I knew very well. They all worked in prostitution, and all of them had been sexually abused when they were very young. I've come to realize that prostitution isn't just about selling sex; it's about the continuation of the abuse. All the women I work on behalf of were destroyed because some man stuck his dick up them when they were only 6 or 7 years old. Sometimes this happened nightly. Five of these women were murdered, but no one has been convicted.

Remember that the Yorkshire Ripper case was only treated seriously when a nonprostitute was murdered. There is so much misogyny toward women who service men sexually. They get battered not only by their punters [pimps] but by the partners they live with. I want you to remember these women. I wish Leona was here right now. She was a really amazing young woman and I am really, really sad that she had to die in such appalling circumstances.

Unidentified woman, England. The stories we have heard here today are the ones we know about. But there are hundreds and hundreds that we don't know about. A lot of children and young women are missing or go on the streets, where they are driven into prostitution and then often disappear.

CONCLUSION

I was very moved by the willingness of so many women to share their experiences. Although I did not include the pleas by a few women during the speakout to come up with strategies to combat femicide, my closing statement focused on the action issue.

"Unfortunately, our time is now up. I want to thank you all very much for coming to this speakout, particularly those of you who shared your experiences and ideas. And I want to urge you to educate other women about femicide and to press for its inclusion in all campaigns and actions to combat violence against women and girls.

"Although individual actions can be effective, actions by organizations—even very small organizations—tend to be far more effective. Some of our countries have rape crisis centers to help rape survivors and shelters to help survivors of battering. In the United States, there are also national rape and battery organizations to formulate policies for local crisis centers or shelters as well as to formulate policies and strategies on a national level. But there are no comparable organizations for dealing with femicide. For example, there are no organizations to assist the survivors of attempted femicide (unless they identify as battered women or rape victims)—including the survivors of attempted suicides that are disguised femicides, as well as those who have been traumatized or otherwise negatively affected by both disguised and overt femicides.

"Yes, there have been campaigns around particular cases of femicide in some countries, for example, the so-called Yorkshire Ripper in England [from 1975 to 1981]. These campaigns are important, but they only last as long as it takes to solve the case, or as long as the motivation of the campaigners lasts in the face of the failure to solve it. We need ongoing organizations against femicide that recognize and work on the broad scope of this form of violence against women—such as partner femicides; intrafamilial femicides; femicides by acquaintances, friends, and unrelated authority figures; and stranger femicides. We need to be creative in thinking up effective ways to organize against this massive global problem—a problem that has been nameless for too long.

"I want to urge those of you who are really concerned about the problem of femicide to plan with others who share your concern ways of organizing against femicide in your country. If we mobilize to combat femicide in the same way that we have mobilized against other forms of violence against women, then the millions of femicide victims throughout the world need not have died in vain."

ANALYSIS

One of the most striking features about the testimonies at the speakout is how many women considered it important to expand the word *femicide* beyond physical annihilation to include *psychic murder* and male-provoked suicides. *Femicidal suicide* is the term that I proposed we use in Chapter 2 for women who are driven to kill themselves by men and/or the patriarchal system.

The phrase *the living dead* to describe some of the causalities of patriarchy by workshop members is particularly poignant. One woman participant also suggested that gender-based economic deprivation imposed by men can drive some women to kill themselves or to starve to death. This form of disguised or covert femicide became commonplace in Afghanistan when the patriarchal Taliban Muslim fundamentalists became the rulers in 1996 and forbade women from working or obtaining an education.

Although the contributions to this volume focus on femicide as physical annihilation, the articulation of more subtle forms of femicide by several speakout participants is a particularly provocative contribution to theoretical debates about how best to define *femicide*.

CHAPTER 12

Female Infanticide in China: The Human Rights Specter and Thoughts Toward (An)Other Vision

Sharon K. Hom

Crimes of gender and cultural practices that have an adverse and often deadly impact on women are present across all cultural and socioeconomic groups. These include widespread physical abuse, genital mutilation, bride burning or "dowry deaths," the use of amniocentesis to abort female fetuses, and the high female mortality rate. According to one United Nations (1986) study, the lives of 75 million women and children are affected by female genital mutilation; about 1 million female children die each year due to neglect, and there are approximately 5 million perinatal deaths per year. The statistics cannot begin to reflect the suffering, pain, and human costs of these practices. As Lori Heise noted, "The risk factor is being female" (Heise, 1989, p. B4).

Female infanticide in China is arguably not a general norm of social practice but rather an extreme and persistent form of abuse and devaluation of female life. However, as a crime of gender (that is, gender in part as "the cultural definition of behavior defined as appropriate to the sexes in a given society at a given time . . . a set of cultural roles" [Lerner, 1986, p. 238]), it suggests disturbing insights into ideological, structural, and political factors that contribute to maintaining the inferior status of Chinese women. By underscoring the life-and-death consequences of ideology and the contingent construction of social life (e.g., law, government policy, or the family), female infanticide provides a radical lens through which broader questions of social justice and gender-based oppression can be analyzed.

FEMALE INFANTICIDE:
SPHERES OF VIOLENCE AND GHOSTS AT THE WELL

"You must not tell anyone," my mother said, "what I am about to tell you. In China your father had a sister who killed herself. She jumped into the family well. We say that your father has all brothers because it is as [if] she had never been born." (Kingston, 1975, p. 3)

Overview: Female Infanticide in China

I define *female infanticide* broadly as the induced death (euthanasia) of infants by suffocation, drowning, abandonment, exposure, or other methods. In China, reported methods also include crushing the infant's skull with forceps as it emerges during birth or injecting formaldehyde into the soft spot of the head (Chang, 1988).

Infanticide "has been practiced on every continent and by people on every level of cultural complexity. . . . Rather than being the exception, it has been the rule" (Williamson, 1978, p. 61). As Laila Williamson (1978) points out, infanticide has satisfied important familial, economic, and societal needs. For example, in Imperial China, Japan, and Europe, it was used as a method of controlling population growth, avoiding starvation, and preventing social disruption. Although not viewed as cruel or violent by the societies that practiced it in the past, infanticide is now considered a crime by national governments all over the world (Williamson, 1978). Because there are very few cases of preferential male infanticide as a universal social practice, infanticide is a reflection of the deadly consequences for females of the cultural domination of patriarchal values and culture.

Female infanticide in China existed as early as 2000 B.C. "Girls were the main, if not exclusive victims of infanticide and tended to have a higher infant mortality rate in times of poverty and famine" (Croll, 1980, p. 24). Yet despite the view of infanticide as homicide throughout the different Chinese dynasties, there appears to be little evidence in recorded texts of actual liability or criminal punishments imposed upon parents who killed their infant children.

In 1985, Michael Weisskopf, an American reporter, extrapolating from demographic information compiled by a 1982 Chinese national census, suggested that there were almost 300,000 cases of female infanticide during 1982 and 345,000 in 1983. Although the *Renmin Ribao* (1983) had already reported that "the phenomenon of butchering, drowning, and leaving female infants to die is very serious" (p. 4), and numerous official references to the problem can be found in the Chinese media, the government nevertheless demanded a retraction from Weisskopf. The Chinese government claimed that the reports were exaggerated and that there were only rare cases, which were checked and corrected immediately.

Since the public reemergence of female infanticide in the post-Mao era, only a few well-publicized cases were prosecuted in the early 1980s. Despite Chinese official condemnation and outrage at the crime of female infanticide, and despite legislative pronouncement prohibiting the practice (see U.S. Department of State, 1991; Marriage Law, 1980), the reality remains that female infanticide continues (see Kristof, 1991; "Surge," 1990). The extent of the practice is difficult to document in part because about 80% of the Chinese people live in poor, rural areas where the only effective deterrent to infanticide may be the willingness of neighbors to report suspicious circumstances. The scope of female infanticide is even more difficult to quantify. Nevertheless, Reuters ("Surge," 1990) reported that the practice of drowning girl babies had revived again in China's Guangxi province, resulting in a ratio of newborn girls to boys of 100 to 121. And Nicholas Kristof (1991) suggested that newly released 1990 official Chinese census data "support previous suspicions that 5 percent of all infant girls born in China are unaccounted for" (p. A1). Although many reports, both foreign and official Chinese, differ in their analysis of the extent of, and responses to, female infanticide (e.g., Chengzun, 1985, cited in Chang, 1987; Weisskopf, 1985), Chinese government officials do not deny the reemergence of what they regard as a shameful legacy of feudal China.

Although female infanticide in China is arguably a crime within the existing legal framework of domestic civil and criminal law and is clearly officially condemned by Chinese leaders, their tendency to narrowly define female infanticide in isolation from the broader question of gender inequality and violence against women limits their analysis of the problem and the possible responses. Chinese literature, official government rhetoric, and Western analyses of female infanticide focus on the persistence of feudal thought and practices as the cause of the problem. This approach reflects a tendency to characterize female infanticide as the "unfortunate consequence" of Chinese population control and modernization policies. This conception of female infanticide and its resulting explanations need to be reexamined. How the problem is conceptualized filters our capacity to imagine solutions and alternative visions that might inform these approaches. Expanding and contextualizing female infanticide more broadly may help to break the hold of the coercive hegemonic narrative about Chinese women's lives dictated by the authoritarian power-holders and may also promote a questioning of the assumptions of legitimacy held by the existing social institutions and practices.

Reconceptualizing Female Infanticide as Social Femicide

I use the term *social femicide* to suggest that an existing social order is implicated in practices that result in female deaths and devaluation of female lives.

Maxine Hong Kingston has written powerfully and eloquently to break the silence in her family about the past, in which women who broke the social rules paid for their "transgressions" with their lives. In the story of No Name Woman, Kingston's aunt, impregnated by a man whose identity she protects with her life, is violently attacked and terrorized by the villagers. Finally, overwhelmed by desperation and the exhaustion of giving birth in a pigsty, she throws herself and her newborn female infant into the family well. In the suicide and the "infanticide," there is not only a killing of another, but a killing of the self, an acceptance of the diminished value of female life, her daughter's and her own. Tragically, these two deaths are not limited to Kingston's semi-autobiographical memories of a family past; they are also reminders of the difficulty of eradicating this gender-based violence in the domestic, national, and global spheres.

Because the impact of particular incidents of violence has ramifications beyond the individual victim, female infanticide must be reconceptualized as more than a privatized, prohibited social practice caused by the remnants of feudalism. The killing of infant girls is a form of violence against the infant herself, the mother, and all women in the society in which the practice occurs. Female infanticide is a gender-based discriminatory judgment about who will survive.

At the familial and societal level, the mother was often subjected to enormous pressure to bear a son or face abuse and humiliation. For example, Maria Chang (1988) reports that women in China are systematically abused and discriminated against for giving birth to girls. Two examples she cites include a Tianjin woman who suffocated her female infant and then committed suicide after repeated physical abuse by her husband and mother-in-law for giving birth to a girl, and the femicide by a Chinese man of his wife and two daughters because, he declared, he was too young to be condemned to a life without sons. Women are blamed for the female sex of the child, and

> unsuccessful wives have been poisoned, strangled, bludgeoned and socially ostracized. . . . [Some have been driven] to suicide, others into mental institutions. . . . The pressure on women is so great that many openly weep on learning they have given birth to a girl. (Chang, cited in Weisskopf, 1985, p. A1)

In its deadly persistence, female infanticide may operate as a terrorist practice of control over women to keep them in their prescribed reproductive role as the bearers of sons.

Reminders of the persistence of female infanticide are present in media stories, in official pronouncements, and in the content of numerous education campaigns attempting to eradicate these abuses. In the insidious and implicit ideological messages conveyed, female children, women, and men may be conditioned to accept the legitimacy or, perhaps worse, the inevitability of this practice. Both Chinese socialist ideology and the two key social institutions of power, the Chinese Communist party (CCP) and the Chinese family, reflect authoritarian and hierarchical assumptions that legitimate the supremacy of a male-engendered vision of the "natural" order of society (Hom, 1992b).

At the same time, it is important to clarify the actors involved in female infanticide and not leave my proposed reconceptualization adrift in a sea of unmediated social forces or faceless individuals, institutions, or ideologies. If viewed narrowly as the killing of female infants, the guilty responsible parties appear to be the mother herself, or the father, relatives, midwives, or medical workers who might get involved. (See Chang, 1988, for a discussion of "state sanctioned" infanticide performed by hospital doctors and medical personnel.) An appropriate "solution" to this privatized conception of the problem would be to criminalize this behavior and to focus on education, deterrence, and punishment of individuals. This "solution" in fact describes the Chinese government's approach. In addition to general criminal and civil prohibitions against female infanticide and the maltreatment of children, education and propaganda campaigns are the Chinese government's primary strategies in responding to the persistence of the female infanticide problem that continues to haunt the implementation of China's population-control policies.

Although legal prohibitions and protections are clearly significant in terms of norm building and contributing to a climate of equality for girls and women, the isolated privatized criminalization of the problem is not enough to eradicate the practice or the underlying ideological and structural causes of the problem. If viewed as a form of social femicide that occurs as a result of the existence of spheres of violence against women, female infanticide would be viewed as more than a crime committed by individuals. Within a "spheres of violence conceptualization," female infanticide, the forced abortion of female fetuses against the consent of the pregnant woman, the abortion of supernumerary children, the abuse of wives who "fail" to bear sons, suicides by despondent women, and malnutrition of female versus male children are all forms of the devaluation of female life.

All of these forms of abuse against females are in fact inevitable and foreseeable gender-based consequences of official Chinese policies adopted in the context of the existing structural, ideological, and cultural realities. Nor is this the first time Chinese policies have had foreseeable and disastrous consequences for women. After the introduction of marriage and divorce reforms in 1949 and 1950, there followed an alarming rise in the number of suicides, femicides, and other acts of violence against women who had attempted to use their newly guaranteed "rights" to file for a divorce. In a survey of 59 counties in Shanxi province in 1949 by the Women's Association, out of 464 female fatalities, 97% were related to the women's efforts to get a divorce. These fatalities included suicides by women denied divorces (40%), suicide because of abuse inflicted upon women by their families for initiating divorce proceedings (20%), death as a result of women's torture and abuse by their family (25%), and suicide in relation to family disputes about divorce (12%). This pattern was repeated in other parts of China, resulting in more than 10,000 female fatalities in central and southern China alone (Chang, 1988; Tieding, 1951).

Although the authorities were supportive of women's rights and social reforms in the family sphere, their failure to prepare or educate the masses to accept such legislative changes and policies resulted in women bearing the costs of the resistance to these changes. Government leaders cannot simply point to a formal system of law and policy to avoid responsibility for promulgating policies that have deadly gender-based consequences. They have also failed to adequately plan for the inevitable resistance and reaction of the Chinese people.

These social femicides implicate government policy makers and leaders at the institutional and ideological levels and also raise questions about their responsibility for the impact of their policy decisions. Reconceptualizing female infanticide as social femicide encourages a more appropriate social response to this widespread problem.

The Explanations

The litany of American social science and official Chinese explanations for the persistence of female infanticide and the devaluation of female lives is familiar: a thousand-year-old feudal tradition, deeply imbedded cultural norms that place prime social value on sons, the social instrumentalist role of children (children are viewed as hedges against their elderly parents' future starvation and abandonment), structural factors (e.g., the lack of an adequate social security system coupled with the predominantly patrilocal villages maintains the pressure on the male children to be the insurance for the future of their parents), and policies shaped by economic and collective survival concerns (e.g., the one-child policy). In addition to these familiar social science explanations, I have suggested elsewhere that the gap between Chinese legal norms and actual practice and the problematic role of Chinese law as an institution contribute to the difficulty in eliminating deeply entrenched patriarchal values and abusive practices (Hom, 1992b).

Although China has achieved significant social and economic progress and advances in its efforts to build a system of law, it appears that women and female infants are still the most vulnerable to sacrifice for the survival of the whole as defined by a predominantly male leadership.

CONCLUSION

Earlier, I suggested that female infanticide needs to be reconceptualized as part of a sphere of violence against women globally as well as in China. Resulting from a complex interaction of structural, ideological, and cultural factors, this violence against women is a crime of gender, that is, social femicide—the practice of killing females. However, by acknowledging the global dimensions of the violence, theorists, policy makers, and government leaders cannot engage in self-righteous condemnation of other countries' abuses while ignoring the same abuses in their own countries. The global dimensions of violence against women indicate that the human costs of patriarchal ideology and institutions are clearly not limited to any culturally specific context.

Anthropological perspectives provide a useful critical framework for an analysis of the universality of women's oppression. They point to the universal asymmetry in cultural evaluation of the sexes reflected in food distribution, economics, linguistics, and the relative importance assigned to women and men, with men as the locus of cultural power (Rosaldo, 1983). These factors are all relevant in understanding the subordinate social status of Chinese women.

How does the killing of female infants raise questions of global violence against women? First, violence against women exists globally and appears to be embedded in cross-cultural gender relations of inequality and oppression. While women represent 50% of the world's population, they perform nearly two-thirds of all the working hours, receive only one-tenth of the world's income, and own less than 1% of the world's property (World Conference, 1985). As one feminist activist and theorist has observed:

> Sex discrimination kills women daily. When combined with race, class, and other forms of oppression, it [female infanticide] constitutes a deadly denial of women's right to life and liberty on a large scale throughout the world. The most pervasive violation of females is violence against women in all its manifestation. (Bunch, 1990)

In addition to female infanticide, other forms of violence and abuse flow from the commodification[1] and exploitation of female lives, such as prostitution, rape, and the abduction and sale of women and female children[2]

(U.S. Department of State, 1990). Female infanticide is a part of these concentric spheres of violence against women. Thus, a revised analysis of female infanticide must first be situated within the broader global and Chinese reality of violence and sexual discrimination against women.

NOTES

This chapter is an edited excerpt of one section of a longer article originally published under the same title in *Columbia Human Rights Law Review*, *23*(2), pp. 249–314, 1992. The full article examines gender-based violence in China within a domestic Chinese law and international human/women's rights framework and suggests alternative feminist vision(s), values, and decision making.

1. The category "commodity" refers to material or terms or concepts, such as labor power, that are objects of exchange or commerce. Commodification refers to a process by which persons or things are transformed into exchangeable market/marketable "things." For example, the trafficking of girls and women is a commodification of female life.

2. Selling women was such a "growing problem" that the Chinese government listed it as one of "six evils" to be eradicated. (The "six evils" are prostitution, pornography, abducting women and children, taking and trafficking in drugs, gambling, and superstition.) Citing unofficial sources and Chinese sources, the U.S. State Department Country Report estimates tens of thousands of cases of wife selling and the abduction of 16,000 women and 900 children in Shandong province between 1981 and 1988 (Harbin Jiang People's Radio Network, 1991; *Renmin Ribao*, 1989).

REFERENCES

Bunch, Charlotte. (1990). Women's rights as human rights: Towards a re-vision of human rights. *Human Rights Quarterly*, *12*, 486–498.

Chang, Maria Hsia. (1988). Women. In Yuan-li Wu, Franz Michael, John F. Copper, Ta-ling Lee, Maria Hsia Chang, & A. James Gregor (Eds.), *Human rights in the People's Republic of China* (pp. 250–267). Boulder, CO: Westview Press.

Chang, Dae. (1987). Violence against women in the family: A national and international perspective. *International Journal of Comparative and Applied Criminal Justice*, *11*, 153–157.

Croll, Elisabeth J. (1980). *Feminism and socialism in China*. New York: Schocken Books.

Harbin Jiang People's Radio Network. (1991, December 27). Kidnappers sentenced to death by Harbin Court. FBIS-CHI-92–001.

Heise, Lori. (1989, April 9). The global war against women. *Washington Post*, p. B4.

Hom, Sharon K. (1992a, Summer). Female infanticide in China: The human rights spectre and thoughts towards (an)other vision. *Columbia Human Rights Law Review*, *23*(2), 249–314.

Hom, Sharon K. (1992b). Law, ideology and patriarchy in the People's Republic of China: Feminist observations of an ethnic spectator. *International Review of Comparative Public Policy, 4,* 173–191.

Kingston, Maxine Hong. (1975). *The woman warrior: Memoirs of a girlhood among ghosts.* New York: Knopf.

Kristof, Nicolas D. (1991, June 17). A mystery from China's census: Where have young girls gone? *New York Times,* pp. A1, A8.

Lerner, Gerda. (1986). *The creation of patriarchy.* Oxford: Oxford University Press.

Marriage Law of the People's Republic of China. (1980). Chapter III (Family Relations), Article 15.

Renmin ribao (People's Daily). (1983, April 7). p. 4.

Renmin ribao (People's Daily). (1989, November 15).

Rosaldo, Michelle Zimbalist. (1983). Woman, culture, and society: A theoretical overview. In Michelle Zimbalist Rosaldo & Louise Lamphere (Eds.), *Women, culture, and society* (pp. 17–42). Palo Alto, CA: Stanford University Press.

Surge in girl baby-killing. (1990, February 22). *Chicago Tribune,* p. 19.

Tieding, Ma. (1951, June 10). *Changjiang ribao (Changjiang Daily),* p. 3.

United Nations, Working Group on Slavery of the Sub-Commission on Prevention of Discrimination and Protection of Minorities. (1986). *Report of the working group on traditional practices affecting the health of women and children* (U.N. Doc/E/CN./1986/42). New York: United Nations.

United Nations. (1993). World conference on human rights: The Vienna Declaration and Programme of Action. New York: United Nations.

U.S. Department of State. (1990). *State Department reports for 1989.* Washington, D.C.: U.S. Government Printing Office.

U.S. Department of State. (1991). *Country reports on human rights practices for 1990: Report submitted to the Committee on Foreign Affairs, House of Representatives, and the Committee on Foreign Relations, U.S. Senate.* Washington, D.C.: U.S. Government Printing Office.

Weisskopf, Michael. (1985, January 8). China's birth control policy drives some to kill baby girls. *Washington Post,* p. A1.

Williamson, Laila. (1978). An anthropological analysis. In Marvin Kohl (Ed.), *Infanticide and the value of life* (pp. 61–75). Buffalo, NY: Prometheus Books.

World Conference to Review and Appraise the Achievement of the United Nations Decade for Women: Equality, Development and Peace. (1985, July). *Women: A world report 81–83.* Gaborone, Botswana: Ministry of Home Affairs, Women's Affairs Unit.

CHAPTER 13

Woman Killing: Intimate Femicide in Ontario, 1974–1994

Rosemary Gartner, Myrna Dawson,
and Maria Crawford

In March 1988, a young mother of two was killed by her estranged husband in a town in northern Ontario, Canada. The killer had been visiting his wife, who was staying in a shelter for abused women. Convinced that she was not going to return to him, he shot her twice at close range. Later that year, in a small town outside of Edmonton, Alberta, a woman was shot to death in her home by her estranged husband, who then shot and killed himself. Miraculously, the woman's 3-year-old girl, whom she was holding in her arms when she was shot, was not wounded. These women were 2 of the 202 female victims of femicide in Canada in 1988. They shared with 68 other female victims a marital relationship with their killers. These two women also shared the experience of having been clients and friends of women who worked in shelters for abused women in Ontario.

In response to these and other intimate femicides of women they had worked with, eight women who worked in shelters for abused women met in January 1989 to share their experiences and provide each other emotional support. Within a few months, the group had named itself the Women We Honour Action Committee and set itself the task of learning more about the phenomenon of women killed by their intimate partners, or intimate femicide. With support from the Ontario Women's Directorate, they conducted what was the first study of intimate femicide in Ontario. The study had three goals: to document for Ontario the incidence of intimate femicide, including legal spouses, common-law partners, and boyfriends, both current and estranged; to describe the characteristics of the people involved in and the circumstances surrounding these killings; and to present the stories of a small number of victims of intimate femicide. That study, completed in 1992, compiled and analyzed data on all intimate femicides known to authorities in Ontario from 1974 through 1990 (Crawford, Gartner, & Women We Honour Action Committee, 1992). A second study, designed to update the data through 1994, was completed in April 1997 (Crawford, Gartner, & Dawson, 1997). In what follows, we describe the major findings of these two studies.

FRAMING THE ISSUE OF INTIMATE FEMICIDE

Intimate femicide is a phenomenon distinct in important ways both from the killing of men by their intimate partners and from nonlethal violence against women; as such, it requires analysis in its own right. This view contrasts with much of the earlier literature on "spousal violence," which treated it as a relatively undifferentiated phenomenon arising out of the intense emotions, stresses, and conflicts that often characterize marital relations (e.g., Blinder, 1985; Boudoris, 1971; Chimbos, 1978; Goode, 1969). These analyses tended to locate the sources of "spousal violence" in patterns of learning early in life, in the disinhibitory effects of alcohol consumption, and in dysfunctional patterns of communication between marital partners. This early work also devoted only limited attention and analysis to gender differences in spousal violence.

In response to this neglect of gender, a number of analysts have made gender a central feature of their accounts of spousal violence. Sex-role theorists highlight gender differences in socialization that teach males to view toughness, power, and control as masculine attributes. Evolutionary theorists argue that violence is an adaptive strategy for males facing the loss of status and control over their partners. Resource theorists view violence as the ultimate resource available to men when other means of exerting control over their partners are exhausted. General systems theorists argue that for men the rewards of violence against their wives are greater than the costs, because of society's failure to adequately sanction such violence. The arguments of these more gender-sensitive analyses resonated with the experiences of members of the Women We Honour Action Committee. Power, control, and domination were themes that they encountered daily in talking with abused women and that they detected in relationships ending in intimate femicide.

In more recent work specifically focused on women victims of intimate femicide, these themes have been elaborated on and, in the case of feminist analyses, placed in a historical and institutional context (Campbell, 1992; Kelkar, 1992; Mahoney, 1994; Marcus, 1994). For example, Wilson and Daly (1992) cite "male sexual proprietariness" as the predominant motive in the killing of wives across cultures and historical epochs:

Men exhibit a tendency to think of women as sexual and reproductive "property" that they can own and exchange. . . . Proprietary entitlements in people have been conceived and institutionalized as identical to proprietary entitlements in land, chattels, and other economic resources. (p. 85)

They go on to note: "That men take a proprietary view of female sexuality and reproductive capacity is manifested in various cultural practices," including genital mutilation practices, asymmetrical adultery laws, and bride-prices. From this perspective, an extreme, if apparently incongruous, manifestation of male proprietariness is intimate femicide. If unable to control or coerce his partner through other means, a man may exert the ultimate control over her by killing her.

Thus, male proprietariness, or male sexual jealousy, has been placed at the center of many empirical and theoretical analyses of intimate femicide. For example, research on intimate femicide and spousal homicide in Canada, Australia, Great Britain, and the United States (Daly & Wilson, 1988; Dobash & Dobash, 1984; Easteal, 1993; Polk, 1994; Wallace, 1986) has identified a common core in these killings of "masculine control, where women become viewed as the possessions of men, and the violence reflects steps taken by males to assert their domination over 'their' women" (Polk, 1994, p. 56). This empirical work challenges many of the popular notions about the characteristics of such crimes, for example, the belief that they are explosive, unplanned, and unpredictable acts of passion. At the same time, it contests the validity and coherence of the concept "spousal homicide," with its connotations of sexual symmetry in violence, by revealing distinct differences between intimate partner killings by men and those by women. As Dobash, Dobash, Wilson, and Daly (1992) note:

Men often kill wives after lengthy periods of prolonged physical violence accompanied by other forms of abuse and coercion; the roles in such cases are seldom if ever reversed. Men perpetrate familicidal massacres, killing spouses and children together; women do not. Men commonly hunt down and kill wives who have left them; women hardly ever behave similarly. Men kill wives as part of planned murder-suicides; analogous acts by women are almost unheard of. Men kill in response to revelations of wifely infidelity; women almost never respond similarly. (p. 81)

DATA SOURCES

We began our data collection by searching death records kept by the Office of the Chief Coroner for Ontario. Coroner records provide a centralized source of information on all deaths in Ontario and a means of identifying and accessing records for deaths identified by the Coroner's Office as homicides. These files frequently contain copies of police reports as well as medical reports on the condition of the body, the way in which the woman was killed, and the violence she suffered—details often not available from other sources. However, coroner records, like all official sources of information on homicide, are imperfect measures of the actual number of deaths due to homicide. For example, cases of femicides and homicide in which no body has been found will not typically appear in coroner records. As a consequence, we expect our estimates of the incidence of intimate femicide to undercount the true incidence, an issue we discuss in more depth below.

We were able to cross-check and supplement data from coroner records by reviewing police homicide investigation files for many of our cases. In the second study, we were also able to review data from Crown Attorney (i.e., prosecutors) files on many of the cases in which charges were laid between 1991 and 1994. In both studies, we supplemented the data we collected from official sources with information from media accounts of some of the intimate femicides and of trials of some of the alleged offenders. Our final data-collection instrument was designed to provide codes for approximately 52 variables, as well as space to record a narrative of the case where further information was available.

THE INCIDENCE OF INTIMATE FEMICIDE
IN ONTARIO, 1974–1994

Between 1974 and 1994, 1,206 women aged 15 and older were killed in Ontario, according to official records. In 1,120 (93%) of these cases, the crimes were solved and the killers were identified. In 705 (63%) of the solved cases, the killers were the current or former legal spouses, common-law partners, or boyfriends of their victims. Thus, in Ontario over this 21-year period, male partners were responsible for the majority of all femicides and an average of 34 women were victims of intimate femicide each year. These data indicate that the focus in official publications and some academic research on "spousal homicides" of women provides an incomplete picture of the more general phenomenon of intimate femicide. For example, excluding killings of women by their estranged common-law partners or by current or former boyfriends underestimates the total number of intimate femicides by about 25%.

The actual number of intimate femicides in Ontario during these years is undoubtedly higher than this. Intimate partners were certainly responsible for some portion of the cases in which no offender was identified or in which we had too little information to determine the precise nature of the relationship between victim and offender. Adjusting for excluded cases, we estimate

that intimate femicides may have accounted for as many as 76% of all femicides in Ontario between 1974 and 1994. However, since it is impossible to
know the number and characteristics of excluded cases, the analyses that
follow focus only on those 705 cases in which the offender was officially
identified as the current or former intimate partner of the victim.

TRENDS IN INTIMATE FEMICIDE

Between 1974 and 1994, the rate of intimate femicide (i.e., the number of
victims of intimate femicide per 100,000 women in the general population)
ranged from a low of 0.55 in 1978 to a high of 1.26 in 1991 but appears to
have followed no particular trend over time (see Figure 13.1). Dividing the
21-year period in half suggests otherwise, however: The average annual rate
for the second half of the period (1.02) was slightly higher than the rate for
the first half (.92).

On its own, this difference is statistically and, it might appear, substantively insignificant. However, when compared to the statistically significant
decreases in other types of lethal violence, the slightly higher rate of intimate
femicide in the latter period takes on greater importance. The annual rate at

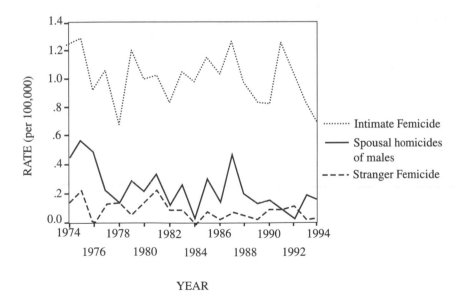

FIGURE 13.1. Trends in Rates of Lethal Violence in Ontario: 1974–1994

which women were killed by strangers or unknown assailants declined significantly from an average of 0.27 during 1974–1983 to 0.16 during 1984–1994. Moreover, the annual rate at which men were killed by their spouses also declined significantly, from an average rate of 0.31 during 1974–1983 to 0.18 during 1984–1994. In other words, *during a period when women's risks from strangers and men's risks from spouses decreased, women's risks from their male partners increased slightly.* Put another way, after 1984—a period of substantial expansion in services for abused women—men's risks of being killed by intimate partners decreased significantly whereas women's risks did not.

One possible explanation for this pattern is that while the expansion of services for abused women may have resulted in the protection of abusive men from defensive violence by their female partners, these same services may not necessarily protect women from violence by their male partners. Women are most likely to kill their intimate male partners after prolonged abuse and when they fear continued or more serious violence against themselves or their children (e.g., Browne, 1987). Where services for abused women are available, women in abusive relationships have an alternative to killing their partners. As Browne and Williams (1989) note, "By offering threatened women protection, escape and aid, [legal and extralegal] resources can engender an awareness that there are alternatives to remaining at risk" and thus prevent "killings that occur in desperation" (p. 91). Their analysis of data from the United States supports this interpretation; states with higher levels of services to abused women had lower rates of spouse killings of males, but not lower rates of spouse killings of females.

CHARACTERISTICS OF THE VICTIMS AND THEIR KILLERS

In many respects, the women killed by their intimate male partners and the men who killed them are very similar to women and men in the general population of Ontario, as can be seen from the data in Table 13.1. For example, women killed by their intimate partners were, on average, about 37 years old; 51% were employed; 80% had children; and 76% were born in Canada. These characteristics do not distinguish the victims from other women in Ontario.

In some other respects, however, victims of intimate femicide and their male killers differed from women and men in the general population. We can think of these differences as risk markers for intimate femicide because they tell us that some types of women and men face disproportionately high risks of intimate victimization or offending. Each of the markers we discuss below has also been associated with increased risks of lethal violence against women in other research.

Table 13.1. Characteristics of Victims of Intimate Femicide and Their Male Killers, Ontario: 1974–1994

Characteristics	Victims	Offenders
Total number	705	705
Average age	37	41
% born in Canada	76	70
% with children	80	77
Employment Status		
% employed	51	64
% unemployed	17	21
% homemakers	18	0
% students	5	2
% retired or on disability pension	9	13
Relationship of Victim to Offender		
% legal spouse, cohabiting	39	
% legal spouse, separated	16	
% common-law partner, cohabiting	18	
% common-law partner, separated	7	
% divorced spouse	<1	
% current girlfriend	12	
% estranged girlfriend	8	
% Aboriginal	6	6

Relationship Status

Research based on data on spouse killings from Great Britain, Australia, the United States, and Canada shows that two indicators of the status of the relationship—estrangement and common-law status—are associated with a higher risk of intimate femicide (Campbell, 1992; Dawson & Gartner, 1998; Johnson, 1996; Wallace, 1986; Wilson & Daly, 1993). We find evidence of similar patterns in our research, although data limitations restrict our analysis somewhat.

Census Canada collects information on marital separations, but only for registered marriages. According to census figures, during the years of our study, 3% of women in Ontario were separated from their legal spouses. According to our data, among the victims of intimate femicide, 16% were separated from their legal spouses. Separation, then, appears to be a risk factor for intimate femicide, since women who were separated from their partners were overrepresented among victims of intimate femicide. However, exactly how much greater the risks are for separated women cannot be determined from our data. This is because our measure of separation and the census measure of separation are not precisely comparable: The census measure captures largely long-term and relatively well-established separations, whereas our measure is more sensitive and captures short-term as well as long-term separations. Thus our measure will yield a higher estimate of separated couples. Nevertheless, we expect that even correcting for this difference, we would find separation to be associated with higher risks of intimate femicide.

Data on the prevalence of common-law unions in the general population have been collected since 1991, so we can estimate the risks to women living in common-law relationships only for the most recent years of our research. According to census data, 4% of women were living in common-law unions in 1991 in Ontario. According to our data, during 1991–1994, 21% of the victims of intimate femicide were killed by common-law partners with whom they were living. Thus, the rate of intimate femicide for women in common-law unions was approximately five times greater than the average rate of intimate femicide in Ontario in the early 1990s. Clearly, then, women in common-law unions were greatly overrepresented among victims of intimate femicide during the early 1990s, and perhaps in earlier years as well.

The higher risks associated with common-law status and estrangement have been interpreted in various ways. Compared to couples in registered marriages, common-law partners are more likely to be poor, young, unemployed, and childless—all factors associated with higher homicide rates. Compared to co-residing couples, estranged couples are more likely to have a history of woman battering (Johnson & Sacco, 1995; Rodgers, 1994). This violence may be associated both with women's decisions to leave their relationships and with their greater risks of intimate femicide. In other words, "the fact that separated couples constitute a subset of marriages with a history of discord could explain their higher homicide rates" (Wilson & Daly, 1994, p. 8).

Male sexual proprietariness could also play a role in the higher risks for common-law and estranged relationships. If, as some have speculated, "husbands may be less secure in their proprietary claims over wives in common-law unions than in registered unions" (Wilson, Johnson, & Daly, 1995, p. 343), they may be more likely to resort to serious violence to enforce those claims or to use lethal violence when those claims are challenged. Echoing a similar theme, several studies that have found elevated risks during separation have cited the male's inability to accept termination of the relationship and obsessional desires to maintain control over his sexual partner: "He would destroy his intimate 'possession' rather than let her fall into the hands of a competitor male" (Polk, 1994, p. 29).

Ethnicity

Women in certain ethnic groups have risks of intimate femicide disproportionate to their representation in the population, according to several studies. For example, in the United States, African American women face unusually high risks of intimate femicide. In Canada, such research is more difficult to do because of restrictions on the collection of crime statistics by race and ethnicity. However, Statistics Canada has collected data on Aboriginal victims of spousal homicides that indicate Aboriginal women's rates of intimate femicide are between five and ten times higher than the rates for non-Aboriginal women (Kennedy, Forde, & Silverman, 1989; Silverman & Kennedy, 1993).

We had initially hoped to explore ethnic and cultural differences in the risk of intimate femicide in our research. However, our research agreement with the Ministry of the Solicitor General prevented us from compiling statistics based upon social, cultural, regional, linguistic, racial or ethnic group from the coroners' records. Nevertheless, we were able to document the number of Aboriginal victims of intimate femicide by relying on other sources of data.

We estimate that at least 6% of the victims of intimate femicide in Ontario between 1974 and 1994 were Aboriginal women; during these years, just under 1% of all women living in Ontario classified themselves as Aboriginal. Thus, Aboriginal women in Ontario appear to be overrepresented among the victims of intimate femicide. Conversely, Aboriginal men are overrepresented as offenders, since all but four of the Aboriginal victims were killed by Aboriginal men.

A number of factors might explain the disproportionate risks of intimate femicide faced by Aboriginal women. Aboriginal Canadians, similar to African Americans, are an economically impoverished and politically disenfranchised ethnic minority. Considerable research has shown that economic, social, and political disadvantages are associated with higher homicide rates generally, as well as higher rates of serious spousal violence. In addition, Aboriginal Canadian heterosexual couples also have disproportionate rates of other risk markers for intimate partner violence, such as common-law marital status, low income, periods of male unemployment, exposure to violence during childhood, alcohol abuse, overcrowded housing conditions, and social isolation—all of which have been cited as reasons for the higher rates of family violence in Aboriginal communities (Health and Welfare Canada, 1990; Long, 1995). Some analysts situate these risk factors within a structural approach that views them as consequences of internal colonialism: "The conditions of colonialism [are] directly related to aboriginal acts of political violence as well as rates of suicide, homicide, and family violence among the aboriginal peoples" (Long, 1995, p. 42; see also Bachmann, 1993; Frank, 1993).

Employment

Men's unemployment is commonly cited as a risk factor for wife assaults and is also associated with elevated risks of intimate femicide. Women's employment status, on the other hand, does not appear to be consistently associated with their risk of violence from male partners (Johnson, 1996; Macmillan & Gartner, 1999). The association between men's unemployment and violence against their female partners traditionally has been attributed to the stresses produced by unemployment and limited economic resources. But if this were the case, one would expect to find evidence that women's unemployment is also associated with men's violence against their female partners, which is not the case. For those who see male violence against their partners as a resource for demonstrating power and control, the gender specificity of the effects of unemployment is not surprising: men who lack more traditional resources (such as economic success) may "forge a particular type of masculinity that centers on ultimate control of the domestic setting through the use of violence" (Messerschmidt, 1993, p. 149).

Our data on intimate femicide are consistent with this interpretation. For women, employment status is not associated with differential risks of intimate femicide: 51% of women in both the victim population and the general population were employed during the period of our study. For men, however, employment status is associated with differential risks. Among intimate femicide offenders, 64% were employed, whereas among males in the general population, 73% were employed. In Ontario, then, male unemployment appears to be associated with higher risks of intimate femicide offending.

Offenders' Violent Histories

Several studies have shown that men who kill their spouses frequently have histories of violent behavior, both in and outside of their marital relationships. As Johnson (1996) notes, "Although some wife killings are the result of sudden, unforeseeable attacks by depressed or mentally unstable husbands and are unrelated to a history of violence in the family, most do not seem to fit this description" (p. 183). Because of this, risk-assessment tools designed to assess battered women's risk of lethal violence typically include measures of their partners' violence against their children and outside of the home as well as threats of serious violence against their wives or others (Campbell, 1995).

We also found evidence of unusual levels of violence in the backgrounds of the male offenders in our sample. At least 31% of them had an arrest record for a violent offense, and another 30% had been arrested and charged with nonviolent criminal offenses. At least 53% of them were known to have been violent in the past toward the women they ultimately killed. This corresponds to data for Canada as a whole which indicates that in 52% of spousal homicides of women between 1991 and 1993, police were aware of previous violent incidents between the spouses (Canadian Centre for Justice Statistics, 1993). In addition, in at least 34% of the cases of intimate femicide, the husbands were known to have previously threatened their wives with violence. (In contrast, in only 6% of the cases were the victims known to have been violent toward their killers in the past; and in only 2% of the cases were the victims known to have previously threatened their husbands with violence.) At least 10% of the intimate femicides occurred while the victims' male partners were on probation or parole, or under a restraining order. This information clearly challenges the view that intimate femicides are typically momentary rages or heat-of-passion killings by otherwise nonviolent men driven to act out of character by extreme circumstances.

A Summary of Risk Markers for Intimate Femicide

Women killed by their intimate male partners and the men who kill them are drawn from all classes, all age groups, all cultural and ethnic backgrounds. However, the victims of intimate femicide and their male killers in our study did differ from other women and men in Ontario in some important respects: They were more likely than women and men in the general population to be separated from their partners, to be in common-law relationships, and to be Aboriginal. In addition, men who killed their intimate partners were also more likely to be unemployed and to have histories of criminal violence. These risk markers for intimate femicide have been noted in other research on spousal homicides and have been interpreted from within various theoretical frameworks. We suggest that they are perhaps most consistent with a framework that views intimate femicide as the manifestation of extreme (if ultimately self-defeating) controlling and proprietary attitudes and behaviors by men toward their female partners.

CHARACTERISTICS OF THE KILLINGS

Intimate femicides are typically very private acts: Three-quarters of the victims were killed in their own homes and, in almost half of these cases, in their own bedrooms. Less than 20% occurred in public places, such as streets, parks, workplaces, or public buildings. The most typical method was shooting: One-third of the victims were killed with firearms. Virtually all the other methods required direct and often prolonged physical contact between male offenders and their victims: About two-thirds of these men stabbed, bludgeoned, beat, strangled, or slashed the throats of their victims.

One of the distinguishing features of intimate femicide is the extent and nature of the violence done to the victim. Unlike killings by women of their intimate male partners, intimate femicides often involve multiple methods or far more violence than is necessary to kill the victim. For example, in over half of the stabbings, male offenders inflicted four or more stab wounds. Beatings and bludgeonings typically involved prolonged violence—leading some coroners to use the term "overkill" to describe them. In about 20% of the cases, male offenders used multiple methods against their victims, such as stabbing and strangling or beating and slashing. In about 10% of the cases, we also found evidence that the victim's body had been mutilated or dismembered.

The violence in these intimate femicides is much more likely to be sexualized than when women kill their intimate partners. Records on approximately half of the cases in our study provided sufficient information for us to determine whether sexual violence was present. In 27% of these cases we found evidence that the victims had been raped, sodomized, or sexually mutilated; in another 22% of the cases the victim's body was found partially or completely unclothed.

Consumption of alcohol by offenders and/or victims was no more common in intimate femicides than in other killings: 39% of the male offenders and 32% of the intimate femicide victims had been drinking immediately prior to the killing. In only 3% of the cases was there evidence of drug use by these men or women immediately prior to the killing.

Establishing the motives in these intimate femicides is fraught with difficulties, as suggested earlier. We made our own determination of the motive after reviewing all the information available to us. In about one-fourth of the cases we felt we had insufficient information to make a judgment about the male offender's motive. In the remaining cases, one motive clearly predominated: the male offender's rage or despair over the actual or impending estrangement from his partner. This motive characterized 45% of the intimate femicides in which we identified a motive. In contrast, women who kill their intimate partners only rarely kill out of anger over an estrangement (Browne, 1987; Daly & Wilson, 1988).

Suspected or actual infidelity of the victim was the motive in another 15% of the intimate femicides. In 10% of the cases the killing appears to have been the final act of violence in a relationship characterized by serial male abuse. In only 5% of the cases did stressful life circumstances—such as bankruptcy, job loss, or serious illness—appear to motivate the male offender; and in only 3% of the cases was there evidence that the male offender was mentally ill.

Another feature that distinguishes intimate femicide from intimate partner killings by women is the number of people who die as a result of these crimes. The 705 cases of intimate femicide resulted in the deaths of 977 persons. Most of these additional deaths were suicides by the offenders: 31% of the male offenders killed themselves after killing their female partners. But male offenders killed an additional 74 persons, most of whom were children of the victims. In addition, more than 100 children witnessed their mothers' deaths; thus, while they may have escaped physical harm, they obviously suffered inestimable psychological harm.

Our documentation of these characteristics of intimate femicide cannot sufficiently convey the complexity and context surrounding these crimes. Nevertheless, it serves important purposes. Comparing characteristics of intimate partner killings by males and females shows the distinctiveness of these two types of killings—a distinctiveness that is obscured in studies that treat intimate partner killings by men and women as instances of a single phenomenon. Compared to killings of men by intimate female partners, intimate femicides are much more likely to involve extreme and sexualized violence, to be motivated by anger over separation, to be followed by the suicide of the male offender, and to be accompanied by the killing of additional victims. These features highlight the gender-specificity of intimate partner killings and are consistent with a perspective on intimate femicide that views it as based in a larger system of gender[ed] inequality and stratification which perpetuates male control over women's sexuality, labor, and, at times, lives and deaths.

THE GENDER-SPECIFIC NATURE OF INTIMATE FEMICIDE

Among those who study homicide, it is well known that women and men are killed in different numbers, by different types of people, and in different circumstances. Women are less likely to be victims of homicide than men in virtually all societies (Gartner, 1990; Gartner, Baker, & Pampel, 1990). Canada generally and Ontario specifically are no different: Men outnumbered women as victims of homicide by a ratio of approximately 2:1 in Canada and in Ontario between 1974 and 1994.

This may appear to indicate that women have a sort of protective advantage over men—that, at least in this sphere of social life, women are not disadvantaged relative to men. However, if we consider gender differences in offending, a different picture emerges. Men accounted for 87% of all homicide offenders in Ontario during these years; in other words, males outnumbered females as offenders by a ratio of almost 7:1. When women were involved in homicides, then, they were almost three times more likely to be victims than to be offenders; when men were involved in homicides, they were more likely to be offenders than to be victims. In other words, women are overrepresented among victims and underrepresented among offenders; for men the opposite is true.

Women were also much more likely than men to be killed by someone of the opposite sex, as these figures imply. Fully 98% of all women killed in Ontario between 1974 and 1994 were killed by men. Only 17% of the adult male victims were killed by women. Thus, man killing appears to be primarily a reflection of relations *within* a gender, whereas woman killing appears to be primarily a matter of relations *between* the genders. Because women are the majority of victims in opposite-sex killings, such killings can be seen as one of the high costs to women of male dominance and desire for control in heterosexual relationships.

It is in intimate relationships between women and men that male dominance and control are most likely to erupt into physical violence. Women accounted for about 75% of all victims of spouse killings in Ontario during the last two decades. So women outnumber men among victims of spouse killings by a ratio of about 3:1. Moreover, spousal homicides accounted for over 50% of all killings of women but less than 10% of all killings of men.

If males, unlike females, are not killed primarily by their intimate partners, who are they killed by and under what circumstances? In Ontario, about 60% of male victims are killed by acquaintances and strangers; another 20% are killed by unknown assailants. Most male–male homicides are the result of arguments or disputes that escalate to killings. In many cases, both victim and offender have been drinking, and who becomes the victim and who the offender is a matter of happenstance. One classic study of homicide (Wolfgang, 1958) concluded that male–male homicides, as an instance of the more generally physically aggressive behavior of males, converge with notions of masculine identity.

When males kill their intimate female partners, their methods of and motives for killing take on a character distinctive from male–male killings— a character that denotes the gender specificity of intimate femicide. As noted above, a substantial number of intimate femicides involved multiple methods, excessive force, and continued violence even after the woman's death would have been apparent (see also Wolfgang, 1967). The violence in intimate femicides also frequently involves some form of sexual assault, a very rare occurrence in killings of men.

The motives in intimate femicide also point to its gender specificity. The predominance of men's rage over separation as a motive in intimate femicides has no obvious counterpart in killings of men—even killings of men by their intimate female partners. We agree with others who see this motive as a reflection of the sexual proprietariness of males toward their intimate female partners.

In sum, our analysis of intimate femicide and our review of other research and data on gender differences in homicide suggest that woman killing in general and intimate femicide in particular are uniquely gendered acts. By this we mean these killings reflect important dimensions of gender stratification, such as power differences in intimate relations and the construction of women as sexual objects generally and as sexual property in particular contexts. Intimate femicide—indeed, probably most femicide—is not simply violence against a person who happens to be female. It is violence that occurs and takes particular forms *because* its target is a woman, a woman who has been intimately involved with her killer.

CONCLUSION

Our overview of the extent and character of intimate femicide in Ontario between 1974 and 1994 has raised at least as many questions as it has answered. Why, for example, did women's risks of intimate femicide increase slightly when public concern over and resources available to abused women were also increasing; when other forms of lethal violence were decreasing; and when criminal justice responses to intimate femicide were becoming more punitive? Why did some women—such as those in common-law relationships and Aboriginal women—face disproportionately high risks of intimate femicide? Were there other types of women with elevated risks of intimate femicide—for example, immigrant women or disabled women— whom we couldn't identify because of the limitations of our data? Why are intimate partner killings by men and women so distinctively different? All of these questions deserve answers, but the answers will require research that goes beyond the data and analysis we have been able to present here.

There are other types of questions raised by our research that are more immediately pressing, questions about how to prevent intimate femicides. Our research has shown that intimate femicides are not the isolated and unpredictable acts of passion that they are often believed to be. Most of the killers in our study had acted violently toward their partners or other per-

sons in the past, and many had had prior contact with the police as a consequence. Many of the victims had sought help from a variety of sources. In a
substantial portion of these intimate femicides, then, there were clear signs
of danger preceding the killing, signs that were available to people who might
have been able to intervene to prevent the crime. We believe this information could be combined with what we know about the risk factors for intimate femicide—such as estrangement—to develop interventions that would
save women's lives. This is the question that has been at the core of our research and the recommendation that we tabled at the conclusion of both of
our studies. Of course, any intervention must be coupled with efforts to
address the underlying sources of intimate femicide. If, as we and others have
argued, the sources lie at least in part in attitudes and behaviors that have
been supported for centuries by patriarchal systems of power and privilege,
those attitudes and behaviors, as well as the systems supporting them, must
be confronted and contested. Some feminists argue that one means of doing
this is through refining and reformulating law as a weapon against men's
intimate violence against women. Isabel Marcus (1994), for example, argues
for identifying male violence against their female partners as terrorism and, as
such, a violation of international human rights accords. Elizabeth Schneider
(1996) suggests redeploying the concept of privacy, not to keep the state out
of intimate relationships as the concept has been used in the past, but to emphasize individuals' autonomy and independence. She argues this affirmative
aspect of privacy could frame a new feminist agenda against woman abuse.

As these and other analyses emphasize, preventing intimate femicide
will require that the public as well as those working in fields relevant to
the prevention of violence begin to see intimate femicide as a preventable
crime. From our own and others' research on intimate violence, it should
be apparent that these crimes are patterned and predictable. The danger
lies in maintaining the view that violence is inevitable, unavoidable, and
inherent in intimate relationships. Such fatalism must be challenged, so that
women's safety in and outside their homes is seen as an achievable and
preeminent goal.

NOTES

This chapter is a revised version of an article with the same title by Gartner, Dawson,
and Crawford in *Resources for Feminist Research*, 26, pp. 151–173, 1998/1999.

Major funding for the studies described in this paper was provided by the
Ontario Women's Directorate. The Ministry of Community and Social Services and
the School of Graduate Studies at the University of Toronto each provided additional funding for one of the studies. The analyses and opinions in the paper are
those of the authors and do not necessarily represent the views of any of these funders.

REFERENCES

Bachmann, Ronet. (1993). *Death and violence on the reservation: Homicide, family violence and suicide in American Indian populations*. New York: Auburn House.

Blinder, Martin. (1985). *Lovers, killers, husbands, and wives*. New York: St. Martin's Press.

Boudoris, James. (1971). Homicide and the family. *Journal of Marriage and the Family, 32*, 667–676.

Browne, Angela. (1987). *When battered women kill*. New York: Free Press.

Browne, Angela, & Kirk Williams. (1989). Exploring the effect of resource availability on the likelihood of female-perpetrated homicides. *Law and Society Review, 23*, 75–94.

Campbell, Jacquelyn C. (1992). "If I can't have you, no one can": Power and control in homicide of female partners. In Jill Radford & Diana E. H. Russell (Eds.), *Femicide: The politics of woman killing* (pp. 96–113). New York: Twayne/Gale Group.

Campbell, Jacquelyn C. (1995). Prediction of homicide of and by battered women. In *Assessing dangerousness: Violence by sexual offenders, batterers, and child abusers* (pp. 96–113). Thousand Oaks, CA: Sage Publications.

Canadian Centre for Justice Statistics. (1993). *Homicide survey*. Unpublished statistics.

Chimbos, Peter C. (1978). *Marital violence: A study of interspousal homicide*. San Francisco: R & E Associates.

Crawford, Maria, Rosemary Gartner, & Myrna Dawson, in collaboration with Women We Honour Action Committee. (1997). *Women killing: Intimate femicide in Ontario, 1991–1994*. Toronto: Women We Honour Action Committee.

Crawford, Maria, Rosemary Gartner, & Women We Honour Action Committee. (1992). *Women killing: Intimate femicide in Ontario, 1974–1990*. Toronto: Women We Honour Action Committee.

Daly, Martin, & Margo Wilson. (1988). *Homicide*. New York: Aldine de Gruyter.

Dawson, Myrna, & Rosemary Gartner. (1998, November). Differences in the characteristics of intimate femicides: The role of relationship state and relationship status. *Homicide Studies, 2*(4), 378–399.

Dobash, R. Emerson, & Russell Dobash. (1984). The nature and antecedents of violent events. *British Journal of Criminology, 24*, 269–288.

Dobash, Russell P., R. Emerson Dobash, Margot Wilson, & Martin Daly. (1992). The myth of sexual symmetry in marital violence. *Social Problems, 39*, 71–91.

Easteal, Patricia Weiser. (1993). *Killing the beloved: Homicide between adult sexual intimates*. Canberra: Australian Institute of Criminology.

Frank, Sharlene. (1993). *Family violence in Aboriginal communities: A first nations report*. British Columbia: Report to the Government of British Columbia.

Gartner, Rosemary. (1990). The victims of homicide: A temporal and cross-national comparison. *American Sociological Review, 55*, 102–106.

Gartner, Rosemary, Kathryn Baker, & Fred Pampel. (1990). Gender stratification and the gender gap in homicide. *Social Problems, 37*, 593–612.

Goode, William. (1969). Violence among intimates. In Donald J. Mulvihill & Melvin M. Tumin (Eds.), *Crimes of violence* (pp. 941–977). Washington, DC: U.S. Government Printing Office.

Health and Welfare Canada. (1990). *Reaching for solutions: Report of the special advisor to the Minister of National Health & Welfare on Child Sexual Abuse in Canada*. Ottawa: Supply & Services.

Johnson, Holly. (1996). *Dangerous domains: Violence against women in Canada*. Toronto: Nelson Canada.

Johnson, Holly, & Vincent Sacco. (1995). Researching violence against women: Statistics Canada's national survey. *Canadian Journal of Criminology, 3*, 281–304.

Kelkar, Govind. (1992). Women and structural violence in India. In Jill Radford & Diana E. H. Russell (Eds.), *Femicide: The politics of woman killing* (pp. 117–123). New York: Twayne/Gale Group.

Kennedy, Leslie W., David R. Forde, & Robert A. Silverman. (1989). Understanding homicide trends: Issues in disaggregating for national and cross-national comparisons. *Canadian Journal of Sociology, 14*, 479–486.

Long, David A. (1995). On violence and healing: Aboriginal experiences, 1960–1993. In Jeffery Ian Ross (Ed.), *Violence in Canada: Sociopolitical perspectives* (pp. 40–77). Don Mills, Ontario, Canada: Oxford University Press.

Macmillan, Ross, & Rosemary Gartner. (1999). When she brings home the bacon: Labour force participation and the risk of spousal violence against women. *Journal of Marriage and the Family, 61*, 947–959.

Mahoney, Martha. (1994). Victimization or oppression? Women's lives, violence, and agency. In Martha A. Fineman & Roxanne Mykitiuk (Eds.), *The public nature of private violence: The discovery of domestic abuse* (pp. 59–92). New York: Routledge.

Marcus, Isabel. (1994). Reframing "domestic violence": Terrorism in the home. In Martha A. Fineman & Roxanne Mykitiuk (Eds.), *The public nature of private violence: The discovery of domestic abuse* (pp. 11–35). New York: Routledge.

Messerschmidt, James W. (1993). *Masculinities and crime: Critique and conceptualization of theory*. Lanham, MD: Rowman & Littlefield.

Polk, Kenneth. (1994). *When men kill: Scenarios of masculine violence*. Cambridge, UK: Cambridge University Press.

Rodgers, Karen. (1994). *Wife assault: The findings of a national survey*. Ottawa: Canadian Centre for Justice Statistics.

Schneider, Elizabeth. (1996). Women's self-defence work and the problems of expert testimony in battering. In D. Kelly Weisberg (Ed.), *Applications of feminist legal theory to women's lives: Sex, violence, work and reproduction* (pp. 311–321). Philadelphia: Temple University Press.

Silverman, Robert, & Leslie Kennedy. (1993). *Deadly deeds: Murder in Canada*. Ontario: Nelson, Canada.

Wallace, Alison. (1986). *Homicide: The social reality*. New South Wales, Sydney, Australia: NSW Bureau of Crime Statistics and Research.

Wilson, Margo, & Martin Daly. (1992). Till death us do part. In Jill Radford & Diana E. H. Russell (Eds.), *Femicide: The politics of woman killing* (pp. 83–93). New York: Twayne/Gale Group.

Wilson, Margo, & Martin Daly. (1993). Spousal homicide risk and estrangement. *Violence and Victims, 8,* 3–16.

Wilson, Margo, & Martin Daly. (1994). Spousal homicide. *Juristat, 14*(8), Ottawa: Canadian Centre for Justice Statistics, pp. 1–15.

Wilson, Margo, Holly Johnson, & Martin Daly. (1995, July). Lethal and nonlethal violence against wives. *Canadian Journal of Criminology, 37*(3), 331–362.

Wolfgang, Marvin. (1958). *Patterns of criminal homicide.* New York: Wiley.

Wolfgang, Marvin. (1967). *Studies in homicide.* New York: Harper & Row.

CHAPTER 14

Femicide in Australia: Findings from the National Homicide Monitoring Program

Jenny Mouzos

This chapter provides an overview of the major findings of a larger study of adult femicide in Australia. *Femicide* is defined here as the killing of women regardless of the gender of the offender or the motive for the crime. This definition includes women who were killed because of opportunistic crime, such as armed robbery and mass shootings. In addition, a small minority of women are also killed by other women.

Our study analyzed data from the National Homicide Monitoring Program, which is based on all cases of homicide identified by the Australian State and Territory police services. This data set contains a total of 2,821 homicide incidents that occurred between July 1, 1989, and June 30, 1998. These incidents were perpetrated by 3,314 identified offenders, resulting in the deaths of 3,045 victims, of whom 1,125 (37%) were female and 1,913 (63%) were male. (In 7 cases, gender was unknown.)

The differentiation of homicidal violence between the sexes is evident when the gender of homicide offenders is examined. Over half of the homicides that occurred during the 9-year period from 1989 to 1998 involved the killing of males by other males (see Table 14.1). On the other hand, when females killed, they were more likely to kill males than other females. Overall, during the 9-year period, where gender was known, males accounted for 88.6% of all homicide offenders and females for only 11.4%.

Table 14.1. Distribution of Homicide Victims According to Gender of
Offenders (*n* = 2,704)*, July 1, 1989–June 30, 1998

Victim	Male Offender		Female Offender		Total Offenders	
	No. Victims	%	No. Victims	%	No. Victims	%
Male	1,464	54.2	237	8.8	1,701	62.9
Female	931	34.4	72	2.6	1,003	37.1
Total	2,395	88.6	309	11.4	2,704	100.0

* Excludes 125 unidentified offenders and 222 cases where either victim's or offender's gender was unknown/not stated.
Source: National Homicide Monitoring Program, Australian Institute of Criminology.

TRENDS IN FEMICIDE

During the period under review, females in Australia were killed at an aver-age annual rate of 1.4 per 100,000 population and males at an average annual rate of 2.4 per 100,000 population. There has been a slight declining trend in the number of femicides per year. The annual number of femicides from 1989–1990 to 1997–1998 ranged from 147 in 1990–1991 to 111 in 1996–1997. On average, there were 125 femicide victims each year.

Because of different levels of exposure to violence during the life cycle, homicide victimization varies significantly according to age (James & Carcach, 1998). Figure 14.1 shows the rate of femicide per 100,000 popula-tion for specific ages from 0 to over 80 years.

Figure 14.1 also shows that females are at a relatively high risk of femi-cide before their first birthday (the rate is 2.7 per 100,000 population) and from their late teens (a rate of 2.3 per 100,000 population) to their early 30s (with an average rate of 2.1 for females aged 18 to 31 years). The highest risk of femicide (a rate of 2.8 per 100,000 population) is between the ages of 21 and 23.

THE RELATIONSHIP CONTEXT OF FEMICIDE

The nature of the relationship between victim and offender determines the context and dynamics of femicide. It is therefore essential to examine the contexts in which femicide occurs based on the relational distance between the female and the male offender.

Source: National Homicide Monitoring Program, Australian Institute of Criminology

FIGURE 14.1. Female Homicide Victimization Rate per 100,000 Age-Specific Population July 1, 1998–June 30, 1998

Our study focused on adult femicide occurring within four types of victim–offender relationships: intimates; family; friends/acquaintances; and strangers. We excluded 137 victims aged 0–14 years as well as 113 victims whose offenders were unknown or not recorded in offense reports or in which the victim–offender relationship was different from the four categories identified above. Of the 1,125 remaining femicide victims identified over the 9-year period, 875 became the focus of our analysis.

Male offenders killed approximately 94% of the adult female victims. The vast majority of these femicides occurred in relationships with intimate partners (57.6%). Only 14.6% of adult female victims were killed by strangers, 16% by friends or acquaintances, and 11.8% by family members. However, when women kill women, the relationship is more likely to be familial or one of friends or acquaintances.

There also appear to be distinct differences in the victim–offender relationship between femicides and male homicides. For example, whereas 57.6% of women were killed by an intimate partner, men were more likely to be killed by a friend or acquaintance (45%) or a stranger (32%). In approximately 95% of these nonintimate homicides, the offender was male. In contrast, only 11% of men were killed by an intimate partner, the majority (84%) of whom were female.

These findings indicate that adult femicides in Australia are overwhelmingly male-dominated acts in which, more often than not, there is some familiarity between the victim and offender.

SPATIAL CONTEXT AND MOTIVES FOR FEMICIDES

In intimate partner relationships, approximately 90% of femicide victims were killed as a result of "altercations of a domestic nature." This term refers to domestic arguments, desertion or termination of an intimate relationship, and jealousy and/or rivalry. These were the motives for approximately 40% of the femicides. When the victims of femicide in intimate relationships were killed as a result of domestic altercations, most (77%) were killed in a private residence—either their own home or the offender's home. Less than a quarter (22.6%) of the femicide victims were killed at some other location, such as in a street or open area, in a commercial location, on public transport, or in a transport facility such as a bus shelter, tram stop, train station, or taxi stand. (All but three of these cases involved a male offender.)

In contrast, when men killed women who were strangers to them, nearly three-quarters of these femicide victims were killed at some location other than a private residence, and more than half (57%) of them were killed in the course of other crimes, including robberies, sexual assaults, abductions, and break-ins.

WEAPONS USED IN FEMICIDE

The type of weapon used to kill victims varied according to the victim–offender relationship. In intimate relationships, male offenders were more likely than female offenders to use a knife or other sharp instrument. These weapons were also likely to be used by both male and female offenders against family or friends. On the other hand, when male strangers committed femicide, they were more likely to use bodily force (assault with hands and/or feet).

FACTORS ASSOCIATED WITH THE OCCURRENCE OF FEMICIDE

There are a number of factors that are associated with an elevated risk of femicide, including location, motive, and victim–offender relationship. The likelihood of femicide varies with the degree to which these factors are related to the sociodemographic characteristics of the femicide victims and their offenders.

Age

Table 14.2 shows the mean age of femicide victims and offenders based on their relationship. The most striking finding in this table is that the offender's

Table 14.2. Mean Age of Femicide Victims and Offenders According to
Relational Context, July 1, 1989–June 20, 1998

Relational Context	Mean Age of Victims	Mean Age of Offenders
Intimates	36 years	39 years
Family	50 years	32 years
Friends/acquaintances	36 years	31 years
Strangers	41 years	28 years

Source: National Homicide Monitoring Program, Australian Institute of Criminology.

age varies according to the relationship distance between the victim and the
offender. As the mean age of the offender decreases, so does the level of familiarity between the victim and the offender. Offenders tend to be older than
their victims in those femicides where the bond between them is strongest;
namely, in relationships involving intimate partners and other family members. However, offenders tend to be younger than their victims when the bond
between them is weaker (Smith & Stanko, 1999).

Racial Appearance

Racial appearance and victim–offender relationship were also associated with
differential homicide mortality. The percentage of Aboriginal/Torres Strait
Islander femicide victims who were killed by an intimate partner (75.4%)
was higher than the percentages for Caucasian (54.2%) and Asian (51%)
femicide victims. As previously noted, 57.6% of all femicide victims were
killed by an intimate partner.

Only 1.5% of Aboriginal/Torres Strait Islander victims were killed by
a stranger, whereas 17.2% of Caucasian victims and 16.3% of Asian victims were killed by a stranger. This difference may be explained in terms
of the structure of Aboriginal/Torres Strait Islander communities, where
people tend to live among immediate family and relatives in a close-knit
community. A stranger (who is most likely to be a displaced Aboriginal
from some other area) who enters such a community is more likely to be
noticed than in other settings and therefore has fewer opportunities to
commit femicide or homicide.

Femicides in Australia generally are committed by offenders who have
the same racial appearance as the victims, with only 5% being of an interracial nature. Furthermore, the interracial femicides were most likely to occur
between strangers. The locations of the femicide also tended to vary with

the racial appearance of both the victim and the offender. Femicides of Caucasian or Asian women were most likely to occur at a private residence. In contrast, Aboriginal/Torres Strait Islander women were most likely to be killed in a location other than a private residence.

One of the most significant differences between Caucasians and Aboriginal/Torres Strait Islanders was the overrepresentation of Aboriginal/Torres Strait Islanders as both victims and perpetrators of femicide. In 16% of the femicide cases, both the victim and the offender were of Aboriginal/Torres Strait Islander appearance. Overall, Aboriginal/Torres Strait Islander women accounted for approximately 15% of the femicide victims, even though they comprise only about 2% of the total female Australian population (Australian Bureau of Statistics [ABS], 1996).

Marital and Employment Status

A number of researchers have addressed the relationship between marital status and homicide victimization. Some argue that, for men, marriage is a form of social control that keeps them from engaging in the risky behavior that attends homicide victimization—frequenting bars, heavy drinking, staying out late, fighting, and so forth (Breault & Kposowa, 1997). Conversely, for women, marriage is more of a femicide risk than nonmarriage (Gartner & McCarthy, 1991). For example, Kposowa and Singh (1994) found that married women in the United States were twice as likely to be victims of femicide as married men were at risk of homicide.

The routine activities theory suggests that sociodemographic characteristics that are associated with individuals spending more time at home should also be associated with disproportionately high levels of femicide at or near the home in comparison with other locations (Messner & Tardiff, 1985). This theory further suggests that sociodemographic characteristics such as gender (female), employment status (not working), and marital status (married) are also associated with higher risks of femicide in the home (Carcach & James, 1998; Messner & Tardiff, 1985).

Our analysis shows that an increased likelihood of femicide was associated with four significant factors: (1) unemployed female victims; (2) unemployed male offenders; (3) victims and offenders being involved in intimate relationships; and (4) location in private residences. Furthermore, the lowest percentages of femicide among intimate partners or other family members were associated with the victims being employed. It may be that a woman's improved economic status reduces her exposure to femicide because she has fewer financial barriers to exiting violent relationships (Dugan, Nagin, & Rosenfeld, 1997).

Alcohol Use

Alcohol was not found to be a major factor associated with femicide involving Caucasian victims and offenders (only 12% of cases). However, in nearly 75% of the femicides involving Aboriginal/Torres Strait Islanders (where information was available), both the victims and the offenders were under the influence of alcohol.

Comparing Men and Women as Victim of Femicide and Homicide

Data in Table 14.3 provide a comparison between male homicide and female femicide victims on characteristics associated with the incident, victim and offender, and the victim–offender relationship. Following are some of the differences between femicides and homicides evident in this table:

- A woman is more likely than a man to be killed at home.
- A woman is more likely to be killed as a result of a domestic altercation, whereas a man is more likely to be killed as a result of an alcohol-related argument.
- A female victim is more likely to be younger than the male offender, whereas a male victim is more likely to be older than the offender.
- Females are less likely than males to be killed by females.
- Femicides are less likely than homicides to be of an interracial nature.
- Femicides are less likely than homicides to involve alcohol.
- A female is more likely to be killed by an intimate partner, whereas a male is more likely to be killed by a friend or acquaintance.

POLICY IMPLICATIONS

Our findings raise a number of policy implications:

- The need for women who are not working to have more access to resources and services that would protect them and allow them to protect themselves
- The need for subsidized counseling for couples who are both not working
- The need for comprehensive programs for the community of Aboriginal/ Torres Strait Islanders to treat and prevent alcohol and violence problems[1]
- The need for increased participation of women in the labor force in order to reduce their vulnerability to intimate partner femicide

Although violence between intimates exists across the economic spectrum, femicide and homicide between intimate partners tends to be concentrated at the lower end. Greater efforts are required to address the underlying causes of conflicts between intimate partners.

Table 14.3. A Comparison of Characteristics of Victims of Male Homicide and Femicide Aged 15 Years and Older, July 1, 1989–June 30, 1998

Characteristics	Femicide Victims (n = 875)	Male Victims (n = 1,574)
Incident Characteristics		
Incident occurred at private residence	*69.8%	54.7%
Incident occurred at other location	*30.2%	45.3%
ALLEGED MOTIVE OF INCIDENT		
Jealousy/desertion	*29.4%	7.1%
Domestic altercation	*43.7%	13.7%
Money/drugs	*7.3%	15.2%
Revenge	*2.6%	11.7%
Alcohol-related argument	*5.0%	24.1%
Other	*3.2%	19.4%
No apparent motive	8.8%	8.8%
MOST COMMON WEAPON USED TO KILL VICTIM		
Knife and other sharp instruments	33.1%	38.2%
Victim–Offender Characteristics		
AGE		
Mean age of victim	38 years	37 years
Mean age of offender	35 years	29 years
Median age of victim	35 years	34 years
Median age of offender	32 years	27 years
Victim younger than offender	*52.5%	31.0%
Victim same age as offender	7.4%	5.8%
Victim older than offender	*40.1%	63.2%
GENDER OF OFFENDER		
Male	*93.8%	85.8%
Female	*6.2%	14.2%
RACIAL APPEARANCE		
Victim and offender caucasian	75.3%	74.3%
Victim and offender Aboriginal/TSI	*15.5%	11.7%
Victim and offender of different race	*5.1%	9.6%
EMPLOYMENT STATUS		
Victim/offender working	10.9%	10.2%
Victim working/offender not working	*10.3%	22.6%
Victim not working/offender working	*16.5%	8.2%
Victim/offender not working	62.4%	59.0%
ALCOHOL CONSUMPTION		
Both victim and offender drinking	*20.7%	39.1%
Victim drinking but not offender	*2.5%	6.0%
Offender drinking but not victim	10.5%	8.3%
Neither victim/offender drinking	*66.3%	46.4%
Victim–Offender Relationship		
Intimates	*57.6%	11.1%
Family	11.8%	12.3%
Friends/acquaintances	*16.0%	44.9%
Strangers	*14.6%	31.8%

*p < .05

In addition, the overrepresentation of Aboriginal/Torres Strait Islander women as victims of femicide and the fact that the vast majority of both victims and offenders in this community were under the influence of alcohol at the time of the crime are also a major policy challenge.

The prevention of intimate, and often lethal, violence requires not only long-term changes in behavior but also cultural and social changes that would devalue violence as an appropriate way for men to resolve conflicts in intimate relationships.

Some offenders claim that violence directed at Aboriginal/Torres Strait Islander women is part of "traditional Aboriginal culture," while others disagree with this contention. However, indigenous women believe that violence is not acceptable in any form (Langton et al., 1991, cited in Saggers & Gray, 1998).

Identifying factors associated with the increased likelihood of femicide— as we have done here—and proposing and implementing sound policies based on these findings can be expected to contribute to the reduction of femicide in Australia.

NOTES

This is an edited version of Jenny Mouzos, "Femicide: An Overview of Major Findings," in *Trends & Issues in Crime and Criminal Justice*, 124, 1999, pp. 1–6, and a few passages from her long report *Femicide: The killing of women in Australia 1989–1998*. Canberra, Australia: Australian Institute of Criminology, 1999, pp. i–45.

1. For a comprehensive overview of ideas and strategies for managing alcohol in Aboriginal and Torres Strait Islander communities, see Brady (1998).

REFERENCES

Australian Bureau of Statistics (ABS). (1996). *Australian Population Census*. Canberra: Author.

Brady, Maggie. (1998). *The grog book: Strengthening indigenous community action on alcohol*. Canberra: Commonwealth Department of Health and Family Services.

Breault, K. D., & Augustine Kposowa. (1997). The effects of marital status on adult female homicides in the United States. *Journal of Quantitative Criminology*, 13, 217–230.

Carcach, Carlos, & Marianne James. (1998). Homicide between intimate partners in Australia. *Trends and Issues in Crime and Criminal Justice Series*, No. 90. Canberra: Australian Institute of Criminology.

Dugan, Laura, Daniel Nagin, & Richard Rosenfeld. (1997, April 28). *Explaining the decline of intimate partner homicide: The effect of changing domesticity, women's status, and domestic violence resources.* Unpublished Paper, H. John Heinz III School of Public Policy and Management, Carnegie Mellon University, Pittsburgh, PA.

Gartner, Rosemary, & Bill McCarthy. (1991). The social distribution of femicide in urban Canada, 1921–1988. *Law and Society Review, 25,* 287–311.

James, Marianne, & Carlos Carcach. (1998). Homicides in Australia: 1989–96. *Research and Public Policy Series,* No. 13. Canberra: Australian Institute of Criminology.

Kposowa, Arthur, & Gopal Singh. (1994). The effect of marriage on male and female homicides in the United States. *Sociological Focus, 27,* 343–362.

Messner, Steven, & Kenneth Tardiff. (1985). The social ecology of urban homicide: An application of the routine activities approach. *Criminology, 23,* 241–267.

Saggers, Sherry, & Dennis Gray. (1998). *Dealing with alcohol, indigenous usage in Australia, New Zealand and Canada.* Cambridge, UK: Cambridge University Press.

Smith, Jonathan, & Elizabeth Stanko. (1999). Women and lethal danger: The killing of and by women in England and Wales, 1986–1996. Unpublished Paper, ESRC Violence Research Program, Brunel University, Uxbridge, Middlesex, United Kingdom.

CONCLUSION

Femicide: Some Men's "Final Solution" for Women

Diana E. H. Russell

"Sex discrimination kills women daily."

—Bunch, 1990, p. 486

"Being a woman meant that you were murderable, and it was wrong of you so to be."

—Nicole Ward Jouve, 1986

"Week by week and month by month, women are kicked, beaten, jumped on until they are crushed, chopped, stabbed, seamed with vitriol, bitten, eviscerated with red-hot pokers and deliberately set on fire—and this sort of outrage, if the woman dies, is called 'manslaughter': if she lives, it is a common assault."

—Fenwick Miller, 1888

Most people believe that women have never had it better in Western Europe and North America. Some also believe that the situation of women is improving in other regions of the world. There are many sound reasons for this assessment. Yet in countries where women's power and status have risen due to successful feminist struggle and technological changes such as contraception, many men have reacted by escalating their already high levels of violence against women.

When those in power feel threatened or challenged by their subordinates, they typically feel entitled to use whatever force is necessary to maintain their power. Many people recognized this dynamic in South Africa during the apartheid era when the White supremacists became more violently repressive toward Black people in reaction to Black people's growing resistance and defiance of White rule. Yet most people fail to accept that the same dynamic is at work when men perceive women to be threatening their power and authority.

As many of the contributors to this volume have pointed out, the risk of women becoming victims of femicide by their male partners is much greater for those who initiate the ending of the relationship. Some men feel entitled to kill women they perceive as having disempowered or demasculinized them by defying male authority and superiority over females. Some men also feel entitled to kill any girl or woman they encounter because of real or imagined rejection or insult by *another* woman. For example, serial killer David Berkowitz stated: "I was determined and in full agreement with myself that I must slay a woman for revenge purposes and to get back on them for all the suffering they caused me."

Femicide, like rape, is a form of terrorism that functions to define gender lines, to enact and bolster male dominance, and to render all women chronically and profoundly unsafe. It stems from a misogynist culture as surely as lynching stems from a racist one. In 1976, Louise Merrill and I referred to all the femicides that were occurring at that time as "the twentieth century witchburnings" (Russell & Van de Ven, 1976, p. 144). Just over a decade later, Jane Caputi (1987) also argued that "we live in the midst of a period of intensified gynocide, equivalent in destruction to the European Witchcraze" (p. 117).

While many of the women who stepped out of line in early modern Europe were tortured and killed as witches—estimated by Anne Barstow (1994) to be 85,000 women—today such women are regarded as cunts or bitches (in the case of feminist women: femnazis, man haters, and lesbians) who deserve whatever horrors befall them, including femicide. "Why is it wrong to get rid of some fuckin' cunts?" Kenneth Bianchi, the so-called Hillside Strangler, demanded to know (Lindsey, 1984). "Kill Feminist Bitches!" is a revealing graffito found on the Western Ontario campus after the mass femicide of 14 female engineering students in Montreal by Marc Lépine (see Malette & Chalouh, 1991, for a Canadian feminist anthology on this anti-feminist massacre).

Despite the savagery of the mass femicide of "witches" in Europe during three centuries, the reality and the significance of that femicidal period continues to be distorted and diminished, if not erased. For example, the term *witchcraze*, which is often used to describe these institutionalized atrocities, even by notable feminist scholars (e.g., Barstow, 1994; Caputi, 1987), obscures the enormity of the misogynist brutalities in which men indulged.

The euphemism *witchcraze* also encourages people to consider these horrendous events as a historical curiosity (hence the making of Jack the Ripper into a hero and his transformation into a tourist attraction). Use of the word *witch*, and the belief, starting in the sixteenth century, that witches' alleged supernatural power came from the devil (Barstow, 1994), made *them* the evil ones rather than the males responsible for their torture and femicide. Hence, "although women committed far fewer crimes than men, the chief criminal stereotype of the period, that of the witch, was female" (Barstow, 1994, p. 25). This demonizing belief also justified the reign of terror against women, or what Barstow (1994) describes as the "intentional mass murder of women" (p. 26).

Just as the witch femicides are trivialized and depoliticized by the word *craze*, the femicides of today are trivialized and depoliticized by the claim that the perpetrators of femicide are mostly "crazy." As Caputi (1987) points out: "We are now expected to understand the contemporary terrorization of women, not in political terms, but as the aberrant behavior of mysterious sexual maniacs, preternatural monsters, or in psychological jargon, *psychopaths and sociopaths*" (p. 109; emphasis in original).

When women were burned, tortured, and murdered as witches, how many people recognized that the real reason for these femicidal acts was that men in power sought to terrorize women into mindless obedience by destroying those who stepped out of line? Women today are being slaughtered in large numbers, sometimes murdered after years of physical and mental torture by their husbands, lovers, or boyfriends; sometimes killed after excruciating suffering at the hands of unrelated perpetrators; sometimes abruptly eliminated by some man who considers killing a woman an insignificant act ("What's one less person on the face of the earth anyway?" commented Ted Bundy [Leyton, 1986, p. 67]; see other examples in Table C.1); sometimes massacred and dismembered by men who are sexually excited by such behavior.

Despite the sensational publicity given to selected femicides, most people are unable to recognize the femicidal nature of the period in which women are living—and dying—today. Some people might wonder if it is possible for global mass femicide to be unrecognized by the vast majority of people in the world. It is worth remembering that the reality of the Nazi holocaust was denied by most Germans while it was happening—including many Jews who realized too late the mortal danger they were in—not to mention the denial by the citizens and governments of the allied nations.

Most people are also unable to recognize that the nuclear family has functioned as a mini-concentration camp for millions of girls and women (see the incest survivor's story in Russell, 1997, Chapter 4). Although no barbed wire imprisons women in abusive marriages, their husbands often function as full-time guards who threaten to kill their wife-prisoners and/or their child(ren) and/or other members of their families if they attempt to escape

Table C.1. Quotes of Femicide Perpetrators

"The women I killed were filth-bastard prostitutes who were littering the streets. I was just cleaning up the place a bit."
    —Peter Sutcliffe, the Yorkshire Ripper (cited in Beattie, 1981, p. 133)

"I need to enslave a woman because I enjoy sex but am, in fact, a loner. I want to be able to use a woman however and whenever I want. And when I am tired, I simply want to put her away."
    —Leonard Lake, serial killer, whose tortures of women were documented on
       videotapes

"We sadists do not consider our victims to be genuinely human. Ted [Bundy] never thought of the women he killed as persons, but only as objects. I did the same and found it an excellent way to avoid any human feeling for them."
    —Gerard John Schaefer

"I didn't want to hurt them [women], I only wanted to kill them."
    —David Berkowitz

"Boy, it makes me feel powerful when I can make those girls do what I want—make them submit to me. I'm nothing in this life. . . . But I want to be something."
    —Albert DeSalvo, the Boston Strangler (cited in Leyton, 1986, p. 51)

"These girls weren't much more than children, I suppose, but I felt . . . that they were old enough to know better than to do the things they were doing . . . out there hitchhiking, when they had no reason or need to. They were flaunting in my face the fact that they could do any damn thing they wanted . . ."
    —Edmund Kemper (cited in Leyton, 1986, p. 51)

"I was thinking . . . I've killed two [women]. I might as well kill this one too."
    —Jeff (pseudonym), after raping a woman (cited in Ressler, Burgess, & Douglas,
       1988, p. 129)

---

or succeed in doing so. And all too often this threat is carried out (as has been documented by several authors in this volume).

Before providing more examples of the scope of femicide in the world today, I will focus on the extremity of some woman-hating femicides in the United States. The point of detailing such atrocities is not to horrify the reader, but to try to break through the resistance to recognizing that women are currently living during an era of extreme and increasingly brutal femicides, an era in which the myth persists among many privileged young college women that the feminist revolution has been achieved and that they have the same options and opportunities as men do.

THE EXTREMITY OF WOMAN-HATING FEMICIDES

Many law enforcement officers who see numerous murdered corpses have commented that increasing numbers of women are not just being killed, but are being subjected to excruciating torture, such as being slashed many times in their breasts, stomachs, and/or vaginas. These police officers have also noted that more of these vicious acts are being perpetrated on women *after* they have been murdered. These acts reveal an intense hatred of women, increase the trauma for the victims' loved ones, and, in general, serve to terrify the living.

Several of the following cases of femicide are drawn from the FBI's study of 36 convicted, incarcerated sexual femicide perpetuators conducted in 1982. Researchers Robert Ressler, Ann Burgess, and John Douglas (1988) believe this to be the largest sample of sexual killers ever to be interviewed for research purposes. All the femicide perpetuators were male, and most were White. Seven were convicted of killing one person, while the rest had killed multiple victims. Data were also gathered on 118 of these men's victims—most of whom were women.

These men were identified as sexual killers by

> evidence or observations that indicate that the murder was sexual in nature. These include: victim attire or lack of attire; exposure of the sexual parts of the victim's body; sexual positioning of the victim's body; insertion of foreign objects into the victim's body cavities; evidence of sexual intercourse (oral, anal, vaginal); and evidence of substitute sexual activity, interest, or sadistic fantasy. (Ressler et al., 1988, p. xiii)

Too many people believe sexual killers are simply "crazy" men who were probably brought up badly and traumatized in boyhood by neglectful or abusive mothers. As Caputi and I (1992) pointed out in our article on Lépine's mass femicide in Montreal, no one wastes time wondering whether individual lynchers or Nazi SS guards may have had some traumatic personal experiences with African Americans or Jews. Nor does anyone fret too much about whether the lynchers or SS guards were insane or psychopathic. People—at least now—generally accept that lynching and the torture of Nazi concentration camp inmates were forms of political violence, the goal of which was to preserve white supremacy and Aryan/Nazi supremacy, regardless of the individual psychopathology of the participants.

Nor does one have to argue that the preservation of male supremacy is an actual goal of the men committing femicides to see that it is, at the very least, one of the consequences of these crimes. What difference does it make for the *victims* of femicide or genocide if their killers are considered mentally ill or not? Being mentally ill does not free men from their misogyny or racism, so their illness is irrelevant to the contention that their femicidal or racist attacks are misogynistic or racist acts that serve to perpetuate misogyny or White supremacy. We have been so dazzled by the psychiatric approach to the causes of criminal behavior that we are often blind to the role of socio-cultural factors that contribute to the causation of criminal acts.

For example, Edmund Kemper, who murdered his grandparents, six female students, and his mother, reveals in his following statements how caught up he was in the notions of "appropriate" male sexuality to which most males in the United States subscribe.

> I couldn't follow through with the male end of the responsibility, so my fantasies became . . . if I killed them, you know, they couldn't reject me as a man. It was more or less making a doll out of a human being . . . and carrying out my fantasies with a doll, a living human doll.

> I had full intentions of killing them both [two women hitchhikers to whom he had offered a ride]. I would love to have raped them. But not having any experience at all in this area . . . this is one of the big problems I had.

> When they were being killed, there wasn't anything going on in my mind except that they were going to be mine. . . . That was the only way they could be mine. (cited in Leyton, 1986, p. 43)

Ressler and colleagues report that one-third of the 92 victims in their study for whom information was available showed evidence of having been tortured. Two examples follow.

Roy Norris of Los Angeles, California, pled guilty to torturing and killing five teenage girls together with Lawrence Bittaker in 1979. A 17-minute tape recording of one dying victim's screams was played at his trial. Shirley Ledford screamed for mercy as she was being raped and "mutilated with a pair of locking pliers, hit with a sledgehammer and jabbed in the ear with an icepick" ("Forty-five-year prison sentence," 1981, p. A19). According to a coroner's report, Ledford "had been strangled with a coat hanger and her face and body mutilated and cut" (Gillott, 1980, p. A1).

Jack King, a 65-year-old convicted child molester was found guilty of virtually destroying the face of 16-year-old Cheryl Bess by pouring acid on her head after he tried to rape her. He was convicted of "kidnapping, assault with intent to commit murder, attempted rape, forcible oral copulation, assault with a corrosive liquid, assault with a deadly weapon and mayhem" (*San Francisco Chronicle*, 1985, p. 54). Bess survived the attack, but she was permanently blinded, her hearing was severely damaged, and her face was totally disfigured (United Press, 1985, p. 22).

In the sexual femicides studied by Ressler and colleagues (1988), foreign objects were often inserted into "the vaginal and anal cavities of victims. This act is often combined with other acts of mutilation, such as slashing of the body, cutting of the breasts and buttocks, and biting of various parts of the body" (p. 55).

Some sexual killers also mutilate the dead woman's face and/or her genitals, cut off her breasts, amputate her limbs, disembowel her, vampirize her, and ejaculate into open stab wounds in her abdomen (Ressler et al., 1988).

These mutilations "often occur when the victim is already dead, a time when the killer has ultimate control over the victim." Some sex killers keep the dead woman's body in their homes. One man, for example, "killed two women and kept their body parts in his home for eight years. He made masks from their heads and drums and seat covers from their skins" (Ressler et al., 1988, p. 131).

One victim of the sex murderers studied by the FBI was found with her genitals mutilated and her breasts amputated. Her murderer had cut off her breasts when he returned to the crime scene 14 hours after killing her (Ressler et al., 1988). Returning to the crime scene is quite common for these killers. Six percent of them returned to have sex with the corpse, 8% to kill another victim, and 26% to relive their crime (Ressler et al., 1988).

Ressler and colleagues (1988) describe another femicide victim in this study who was found "with stab wounds in the vagina and groin and with her throat slashed. Her nipples had been removed and her face severely beaten, and her cut-off hair was found hanging from a nearby tree branch" (p. 56).

Another murderer in the sample of Ressler and colleagues was charged with the murder, robbery, and rape of a 24-year-old mother of two. Her corpse was found lying face up in a wooded area. Her left breast had been cut off and was missing. This man also abducted a 44-year-old woman at gunpoint, then shot her in the face, killing her. He returned the next day to mutilate her corpse, cutting her stomach and legs and cutting off her breasts, which he left lying between her legs (Ressler et al., 1988).

Another of the 36 murderers studied by these researchers had cut up the body of his victim and pulled out her fingernails.

In one case a woman who went outside to empty her garbage was shot in the head four times and

> thereafter disemboweled with a knife obtained in her home. No evidence of sexual assault or molestation was found, other than slash wounds to breasts and mutilation to internal reproductive organs. The victim was first slashed in the abdomen, and the assailant pulled her intestines out of the body cavity. The victim later had what was determined to be animal feces in her mouth. . . . A yogurt cup was found, and indications were that the murderer used the cup to collect blood from the victim, which he drank. (Ressler et al., 1988, p. 132)

A 27-year-old man severely slashed and mutilated a woman whom he also killed:

> She had been murdered in the bedroom where she was also disemboweled from the breastbone to the pelvic area. Internal organs, including spleen, kidneys, and reproductive organs, had been removed and mutilated. No attack was noted to external genitals. The murderer had attempted to remove an eye and had also inserted a knife in the anal canal, cutting the victim severely in this area. . . . A ring of blood was found on the floor, indicating that a bucket-type container was used for collecting blood. (Ressler et al., 1988, p. 132)

A young woman's nude corpse was found on the roof landing of the apartment building where she had resided.

> She had been badly beaten about the face and strangled with the strap of her purse. Her nipples had been cut off after death and placed on her chest. Scrawled in ink on the inside of her thigh was, "You can't stop me." The words "Fuck you" were scrawled on her abdomen. . . . An umbrella and ink pen had been forced into the [her] vagina. . . . There were postmortem bite marks on the victim's thigh, as well as contusions, hemorrhages, and lacerations of the [her] body. (Ressler et al., 1988, p. 146)

Ressler and colleagues describe some murderers as being exhilarated when they act out their murderous fantasies. One of them described his feeling afterwards as follows:

> I drive up to my apartment with two murdered girls in my car. The trunk is a mess, with one body stabbed to death. The other [body] is on the back seat. . . . I took the heads up to my room. I could sit there looking at the heads on an overstuffed chair, tripping on them on my bed, looking at them [when] one of them somehow becomes unsettled, comes rolling down the chair, very grisly. Tumbling down the chair, rolls across the cushion and hits the rug, bonk. The neighbor downstairs hates my guts. I'm always making noise late at night. He gets a broom and whacks on the ceiling. "Buddy," I say "I'm sorry for that, dropped my head, sorry." That helped to bring me out of the depression. (cited in Ressler et al., 1988, p. 53)

In 27% of the sexual homicides studied by Ressler and colleagues, the murderer kept a "souvenir" of his murder. "The value to the killer of these items as reminders of the murder outweighs the risk of being identified through the possession of such incriminating evidence. The souvenirs provide the killer with tangible proof that he was able to activate his fantasy," and also serves as with a catalyst for further fantasizing (p. 63). Examples of souvenirs include: "feet, breasts, and blood" (p. 63).

"These souvenirs have a special, sexual meaning," according to Ressler and colleagues (1988):

> Various articles of underwear are common fetish items saved by the killer. . . .
> In the case of the man who kept the feet of his victims in the freezer, the women's
> feet in high-heeled shoes provided him with sexual excitement. (p. 64)

Some offenders "keep personal items belonging to the victim as a type of trophy or prize commemorating a successful endeavor." For them, "the item is much like a mounted animal head is to the big game hunter—proof of his skill" (Ressler et al., 1988, p. 64).

Examples from sources other than the FBI study include the case of high school students Carol King and Robert Jensen, who were unfortunate enough to offer a ride to serial killer Charles Starkweather. Jensen was subsequently found shot six times. King was also murdered, with several stab wounds "directed at her groin, one of them extending through the wall of the cervix into the rectum" (Leyton, 1986, p. 206).

Forty-three-year-old Gary Heidnik, who is White, and 31-year-old Cyril "Tony" Brown, who is Black, were arrested and charged with rape, kidnap, and murder for the following femicides:

> When police raided the two-story house in the impoverished neighborhood, they
> were confronted by a chilling scene of death and human suffering. Three half
> naked, malnourished women were shackled to a sewer pipe in a basement that
> doubled as a secret torture chamber; and 24 pounds of human limbs were dis-
> covered stockpiled in a freezer as well as other body parts in an oven and a
> stewpot in the kitchen.
>
> The women captives, ranging in age from 18 to 26, told authorities grisly tales
> of rape, beatings and being forced to survive off dog food, bread and water.
> They also told of two women who died in captivity, one electrocuted in a watery
> pit underneath the cellar's concrete floor, the other killed in a fall. ("Black
> Women Report," 1987, p. 6)

Edmund Kemper, the previously quoted "coed Killer" of Santa Cruz, California, murdered six women students, usually picking them up when they were hitchhiking. He was a necrophiliac who sometimes had intercourse through the stab wounds in their bodies. He decapitated some of them, keeping their heads in his apartment. He also ate their flesh. Kemper ended his murder spree by killing, decapitating, and sexually violating the corpse of his mother (Cameron & Frazer, 1987).

Kemper explained what gave him sexual excitement as follows:

"You hear that little pop and pull their heads off and hold their heads up by the hair. Whipping their heads off, their body sitting there. That'd get me off." (Leyton, 1986, p. 42)

Kemper chuckled in front of his interviewer when he said: "With a girl, there's a lot left in the girl's body without a head. Of course, the personality is gone." Explaining why he ate the flesh of several of his victims, Kemper said: "I wanted them for my own, I wanted them to be a part of me—and now they are" (cited in Leyton, 1986, p. 43).

Although the annihilation of women has not been institutionalized in the United States, their annihilation in media portrayals *has* been. American males are increasingly saturated by femicidal images in the form of pornography and gorenography ("features, such as slasher films, that specialize in sensationalized and fetishized scenes of violence" [Caputi, 1992, p. 210]). Femicidal images are an integral part of the multibillion-dollar propaganda machine that effectively promotes misogynist attitudes and practices, including femicide (see Chapter 5). Sitting around a TV set or in a theater to watch movies of females being tortured and slaughtered is now a favorite leisure time activity for Americans, particularly teenagers.

A brochure advertising an R-rated movie "featuring selected clips from favorite gore movies," contained the following inducement:

> See bloodthirsty butchers, killer drillers, crazed cannibals, zonked zombies, hemoglobin horrors, plasmatic perverts and sadistic slayers slash, strangle, mangle, and mutilate bare breasted beauties in bondage. (cited in Goode, 1983, p. 4)

No wonder Ressler and colleagues (1988) found that:

> These men learn early that they can get away with violent behavior. In essence they see nothing wrong with what they are doing. Many of them emphasize that they are doing exactly what everyone else thinks of doing. (p. 40)

While the Nazi concentration camps were invented and implemented by the Nazi leadership, thereby qualifying as a clear-cut case of institutionalized genocide, femicide in most countries is practiced on a voluntary basis, without pay, by men of all classes and ethnic groups.

THE SCOPE OF FEMICIDE

Since the concept of femicide is still in its infancy, the focus to date, including in this book, has been on the most overt form of it—murder. However, as I pointed out in Chapter 2, femicide also includes covert forms of woman killing (social femicide), such as women being permitted to die because of misogynistic attitudes and/or sexist laws and social institutions. For example, there are many deaths in countries that have criminalized contraception and/or abortion. In 1976, the woman who testified about illegal abortions in Portugal reported that about 2,000 females died every year in that country as a result of unsafe abortions (Russell & Van de Ven, 1976, p. 9). I concluded the section on illegal abortions in the Tribunal book (I referred to this problem as compulsory motherhood) as follows:

> The number of women who actually die every year as a consequence [of the refusal of patriarchal societies to recognize our right to choose or reject motherhood] is not known, but it is probably as high as the number of casualties in the most lethal, patriarchal, geopolitical wars. However, the casualties of the war of men against women are hidden, and unrecognized for what they are. (Russell & Van de Ven, 1976, p. 26)

The massive number of women and girls described as "missing" constitutes further evidence of the hideous dimensions of femicide in certain regions of the world today. Amartya Sen (1990) concluded his scholarly article on this subject by asserting that "A great many more than a hundred million women are 'missing'" (p. 61). Sen arrived at this shocking estimate by calculating the "numbers of 'missing women' in relation to the numbers that could be expected if men and women received similar care in health, medicine, and nutrition" in large parts of Asia and Africa (p. 61). In China alone, he estimated on this basis that 50 million women were missing. Sen commented that "these numbers tell us, quietly, a terrible story of inequality and neglect leading to the excess mortality of women" (p. 61). He ended his article by saying that "we confront here what is clearly one of the more momentous and neglected problems facing the world today" (p. 66).

Unfortunately, patriarchal governments neglect many of the momentous problems that victimize women, even when they are blatant (such as intimate partner femicide). They typically do not even recognize the more covert forms of social femicide, such as the millions of cases in which sexist male behavior causes women and girls to die after contracting AIDS (see Chapter 9).

CONCLUSION

Hopefully, it is now clear to the reader why I began this chapter by comparing three centuries of mass femicide of witches in Europe with the global mass femicide that has been occurring in recent years. Indeed, my analysis makes it clear that there are many more femicides occurring today than occurred during the peak witch persecution period in Europe, from 1560 to 1760 (Barstow, 1994). In Chapter 9 I argued that millions of femicides are occurring as a result of the sexist attitudes (e.g., male entitlement) and behavior (e.g., promiscuity and predatory sexual acts) of men toward women and young girls in patriarchal societies.

My hope in citing a small sample of femicidal atrocities in this chapter, as well as in other chapters, is that they will rip away the many layers of denial and enable people to face the ubiquity of femicide, which is often combined with torture, maiming, desecration, and starvation of the bodies and psyches of women and girls throughout the world.

Once feminists in particular face the problem of femicide, we will presumably be able to tackle it as effectively as we have other, less lethal manifestations of violence against women. Although there is still an epidemic of nonlethal forms of violence against women and girls—such as rape, child sexual abuse, and woman battering—we *have* found ways to reform laws, social policies, and institutions relating to these crimes. We have also been able to help some of the survivors who have been willing to report their victimization, and we have placed the blame where it belongs—on the male perpetrators of these crimes—instead of on the female survivors. In addition, we have recognized the role of patriarchy in causing these woman-hating crimes.

The women's movement has an important and urgent task ahead. The first is to deal with our own desire to deny the enormity of many men's hatred of us, a hatred that is being increasingly manifested in femicide. The second is to confront others' denial. And, finally, our task is to embark on militant and multifaceted actions to combat and prevent femicide.

REFERENCES

Barstow, Anne L. (1994). *Witchcraze: A new history of the European witch hunts.* San Francisco: Pandora.

Beattie, John. (1981). *The Yorkshire Ripper story.* London: Quartet Books.

Black women report on sex, torture, murder at hands of White Philadelphia Bishop. (1987, April 13). *Jet*, pp. 6–8.

Bunch, Charlotte. (1990). Women's rights as human rights: Towards a re-vision of human rights. *Human Rights Quarterly, 12,* 486–498.

Cameron, Deborah, & Elizabeth Frazer. (1987). *The lust to kill: A feminist investigation of sexual murder.* New York: New York University Press.

Caputi, Jane. (1987). *The age of sex crime.* Bowling Green, OH: Bowling Green State University Popular Press.

Caputi, Jane. (1992). Advertising femicide: Lethal violence against women in pornography and gorenography. In Jill Radford & Diana E. H. Russell (Eds.), *Femicide: The politics of woman killing* (pp. 203–221). New York: Twayne/ Gale Group.

Forty-five-year prison sentence for "Torture Tape" killer. (1981, April 29). *San Francisco Chronicle, 1,* p. A19.

Gillott, Roger. (1980, February 15). Another L.A. shocker: Two men may have killed 30 to 40 girls. *Honolulu Star Bulletin, 1,* pp. A1, A4.

Goode, Erica. (1983, August 30). Study on violence, women. *San Francisco Chronicle,* p. 4.

Leyton, Elliott. (1986). *Hunting humans: Inside the minds of mass murderers.* New York: Pocket Books.

Lindsey, Robert. (1984, January 21). Officials cite rise in killers who roam U.S. for victims. *New York Times,* p. A1.

Malette, Louise, & Marie Chalouh. (Eds.). (1991). *The Montreal massacre* (Marlene Wildeman, Trans.). Charlottetown, Prince Edward Island, Canada: Gynergy Books.

Miller, Fenwick. (1888, October 2). Letter to the *Daily News. Pall Mall Gazette* (cited by Cameron & Frazer, 1987, p. 135).

Radford, Jill, & Diana E. H. Russell. (Eds.). (1992). *Femicide: The politics of woman killing.* New York: Twayne/Gale Group.

Ressler, Robert, Ann Burgess, & John Douglas. (1988). *Sexual homicide: Patterns and motives.* Lexington, MA: Lexington Books.

Russell, Diana E. H. (1997). *Behind closed doors in white South Africa: Incest survivors tell their stories.* New York: St. Martin's Press.

Russell, Diana E. H., & Nicole Van de Ven. (Eds.). (1976). *The proceedings of the International Tribunal on Crimes Against Women.* San Francisco, CA: Frog in the Well.

San Francisco Chronicle. (1985, August). p. 54.

Sen, Amartya. (1990, December 20). More than 100 million women are missing. *New York Review of Books,* pp. 61–66.

United Press. (1985, August 15). Man, 65, guilty of acid attack on girl's face. *San Francisco Chronicle,* p. 22.

Ward Jouve, Nicole. (1986). *The streetcleaner: The Yorkshire ripper case on trial.* London and New York: Marion Boyars.

Bibliography on Femicide

Almeida, Suely Souza de. (1998). *Femicidio: Algemas (in) visiveis do p'ublicio-privado.* [Femicide: (In)visible public and private handcuffs] Rio de Janeiro, Brazil: R. J. Revinter.

Amin, Razia Khan. (1983). An anatomy of femicide. In *Regional Seminar on "Femi-cide" in the Pacific Asian countries, Proceedings and findings of the regional seminar on "femicide" in the Pacific Asian countries* (pp. 52–56). Dhaka, Bangladesh: Bangladesh Jatiyo Mahila Ainjibi Samity.

Anonywomen. (1992). What can we do about femicide?: A proposal. In Jill Radford & Diana E. H. Russell (Eds.), *Femicide: The politics of woman killing* (pp. 346–347). New York: Twayne/Gale Group.

Avakame, Edem F. (1999, Fall). Females' labor force participation and intimate femi-cide: An empirical assessment of the backlash hypothesis. *Violence and Victims, 14*(3), 277–291.

Billy, Mary. (1993). *Femicide list: Facing the horror.* Squamish, British Columbia: M. Billy.

Billy, Mary. (1998, November). Why I keep a femicide list: Documenting violence against women. *Kinesis,* p. 16.

Bowker, Lee H. (1978). Femicide. In Lee H. Bowker, Meda Chesney-Lind, & Joycelyn Pollock, *Women, crime and the criminal justice system* (pp. 122–125). Lexington, MA: Lexington Books, D. C. Heath & Company.

Campbell, Jacquelyn C., Karen L. Soeken, Judith McFarlane, & Barbara Parker. (1998). Risk factors for femicide among pregnant and nonpregnant battered women. In Jacquelyn C. Campbell (Ed.), *Empowering survivors of abuse: Health care for battered women and their children* (pp. 90–97). Thousand Oaks, CA: Sage Publications.

Caputi, Jane. (1992). Advertising femicide: Lethal violence against women in por-nography and gorenography. In Jill Radford & Diana E. H. Russell (Eds.), *Femicide: The politics of woman killing* (pp. 203–221). New York: Twayne/Gale Group.

Caputi, Jane, & Diana E. H. Russell. (1990, September/October). Femicide: Speak-ing the unspeakable. *Ms., 1*(2), 34–37.

Caputi, Jane, & Diana E. H. Russell. (1992). Femicide: Sexist terrorism against women. In Jill Radford & Diana E. H. Russell (Eds.), *Femicide: The politics of woman killing* (pp. 13–21). New York: Twayne/Gale Group.

Christianson, Eleanor Sian Hudson. (1999). *Extortionate femicide in India: An in-vestigation into the socio-cultural history surrounding stridhan as the motive for dowry-related crime and suicide.* Unpublished master's thesis, Shippensburg University of Pennsylvania.

Cleary, Lynn. (1996). *Intimate femicide, the killing of females by their male partner: Factors, impacts and a model program design for domestic battery intervention.* Unpublished master's thesis, University of Nevada, Las Vegas.

Coleman, Michelle Ada. (1995). Intimate femicide: Masculinity, patriarchy and the sexual politics of murder. *Masters Abstract International, 34*(3), 1052.

Crawford, Maria, Rosemary Gartner, & Women We Honour Action Committee. (1992). *Woman killing: Intimate femicide in Ontario, 1974–1990: A report.* Toronto: Women We Honour Action Committee.

Dawson, Myrna, & Rosemary Gartner. (1998, November). Differences in the characteristics of intimate femicides: The role of relationship state and relationship status. *Homicide Studies, 2*(4), 378–399.

Dawson, Myrna, & Rosemary Gartner. (1999, April 14–15). *Femicide followed by suicide: The role of premeditation and proprietariness.* Paper presented at the 1999 Graduate Sociology Student Association Conference, University of Toronto, Toronto, Canada.

DeKeseredy, Walter S., & Linda MacLeod. (1997). *Woman abuse: A sociological story.* Toronto, Canada: Harcourt Brace.

Domingo, Chris. (1990, February 28). "We are more than fourteen": Montreal mass femicide. *Off Our Backs, 20*(2), 10.

Domingo, Chris. (1992, July). Femicide: An interview with Diana E. H. Russell. *Off Our Backs, 22*(7), 1–2.

Domingo, Chris. (1992). What the White man won't tell us: Report from the Berkeley Clearinghouse on Femicide. In Jill Radford & Diana E. H. Russell (Eds.), *Femicide: The politics of woman killing* (pp. 195–202). New York: Twayne/Gale Group.

Dube, Rube, Reena Dube, & Rashmi Bhatnagar. (1999, Spring/Summer). Women without choice: Female infanticide and the rhetoric of overpopulation in postcolonial India. *Women's Studies Quarterly, 27*(1–2), 73–86.

Ellis, Desmond, & Walter S. DeKeseredy. (1996). Homicide and femicide. In Desmond Ellis & Walter DeKeseredy, *The wrong stuff: An introduction to the sociological study of deviance* (pp. 68–103). Scarborough, Canada: Allyn & Bacon, Canada.

Ellis, Desmond, & Walter S. DeKeseredy. (1997, December). Rethinking estrangement, interventions, and intimate femicide. *Violence Against Women, 3*(6), 590–609.

Ellis, Desmond, & Gregory Kerry. (1994). *Life course and intimate femicide: An empirical study of the impact of social intervention.* Toronto, Canada: LaMarch Research Centre on Violence and Conflict Resolution.

Emang, Basadi. (1995). *A report on the proceedings of the national workshop on violence against women: Rape and femicide in Botswana.* Gaborone, Botswana: The Network and WiLDAF.

Faier, Elizabeth. (1999). *Honor killing, femicide, or cultural violence?: An examination of the Druze Murder in Israel.* Unpublished manuscript, Indiana University, Bloomington.

Farden, Deborah Helen. (1996). *Women killing: Intimate femicide in Saskatchewan 1988–1992.* Unpublished master's thesis, University of Saskatchewan, Saskatoon, Canada.

Gartner, Rosemary, Myrna Dawson, & Maria Crawford. (1998, Fall). Woman killing: Intimate femicide in Ontario, 1974–1994. *Resources for feminist research: RFR = Documentation sur la recherche Feministe, 26*(3–4), 151–173.

Gartner, Rosemary, & Bill McCarthy. (1991). The social distribution of femicide in urban Canada, 1921–1988. *Law and Society Review, 25*(2), 287–311.

Goin, Valerie Lynn. (1994). *Sex selection in China and India.* Unpublished master's thesis, University of Denver.

Helie-Lucas, Marieme. (1998). Fundamentalism and femicide. In *Asian Center for Women's Human Rights, Common Grounds: Violence against women in war and armed conflict situations. Papers presented at the International Conference on Violence Against Women in War and Armed Conflict Situations* (pp. 108–121). Quezon City, Philippines: Asian Center for Women's Human Rights.

Holmes, Helen B., & Betty Hoskins. (1987). Prenatal and preconception sex choice technologies: A path to femicide? In Gena Corea, Renate Duelli Klein, Jalna Hanmer, Helen B. Holmes, Betty Hoskins, Madhu Kishwar, Janice Raymond, Robyn Rowland, & Roberta Steinbacher (Eds.), *Man-made women: How new reproductive technologies affect women* (pp. 15–29). Bloomington: Indiana University Press.

Hom, Sharon K. (1992, Summer). Female infanticide in China: The human rights specter and thoughts towards (an)other vision. *Columbia Human Rights Law Reporter, 23*(2), 249–314.

Huq, Jahanara. (1983). The economics of femicide: The Bangladesh case. In *Regional seminar on "Femicide" in the Pacific Asian Countries, Proceedings and findings of the Regional Seminar on "Femicide" in the Pacific Asian Countries* (pp. 25–37). Dhaka, Bangladesh: Bangladesh Jatiyo Mahila Ainjibi Samity.

Jenkins, Philip. (1994). Everyman: Serial murder as "femicide." In *Using murder: The social construction of serial homicide* (pp. 139–157). Hawthorne NY: Aldine De Gruyter.

Khaleque, Selina. (1983). Femicide due to social, cultural and traditional norms and taboos. In *Regional Seminar on "Femicide" in the Pacific Asian Countries, Proceedings and findings of the Regional Seminar on "Femicide" in the Pacific Asian Countries* (pp. 41–48). Dhaka, Bangladesh: Bangladesh Jatiyo Mahila Ainjibi Samity.

Kumar, G. Stanley Jaya. (1994, January). Infanticide to femicide. *Asia Pacific Journal of Social Work, 4*(1), 39–45.

Landau, Simha F., & Rolef, Susan Hattis. (1998). Intimate femicide in Israel: Temporal, social, and motivational patterns. *European Journal on Criminal Policy and Research, 6*(1), 75–90.

Macdougall, Lorraine. (1999). *A qualitative study of intimate femicide: The perpetrator's perspective.* Unpublished master's thesis, Rhodes University, East London, South Africa.

MacNish, William. (1827). *The confessions of an unexecuted femicide* (3rd ed.). Glasgow: W.R. M'Phun, James Curll.

McFarlane, Judith M., Jacquelyn C. Campbell, Susan Wilt, Carolyn J. Sachs, Yvonne Ulrich, & Xiao Xu. (1999, November). Stalking and intimate partner femicide. *Homicide Studies, 3*(4), 300–316.

Meyers, Helene. (1991). *Femicidal fears in contemporary fiction: Feminist thought and the female gothic.* Unpublished doctoral dissertation, Indiana University, Bloomington.

Mills, Shereen. (1999, February 17). *Femicide and battered women who kill in South Africa.* Paper presented at the Center for African Studies, University of Illinois, Urbana.

Moracco, Kathryn E., Carol Runyan, & John Butts. (1998, November). Femicide in North Carolina, 1991–1993: A statewide study of patterns and precursors. *Homicide Studies, 2*(4), 422–446.

Mouzos, Jenny. (1999, August). Femicide: An overview of major findings. *Trends & Issues in Crime and Criminal Justice, 124,* 1–6.

Mouzos, Jenny. (1999). *Femicide: The killing of women in Australia 1989–1998.* Canberra, Australia: Australian Institute of Criminology.

Nenadic, Natalie. (1996). Femicide: A framework for understanding genocide. In Diana Bell & Renate Klein (Eds.), *Radically speaking: Feminism reclaimed* (pp. 456–464). Melbourne, Australia: Spinifex Press.

Palmeteer Pennee, Donna. (1994). Femicide in the critical construction of "the double hook": A case study in the interrelations of modernism, literary nationalism, and cultural maturity. Doctoral dissertation, McGill University, Canada.

Patel, Vibhuti. (1989). Sex-determination and sex pre-selection tests in India: Recent techniques in femicide. *Reproductive and Genetic Engineering, 2*(2), 111–119.

Patel, Vibhuti. (1989, January). Sex-determination and sex pre-selection test in India: Modern techniques for femicide. *Bulletin of Concerned Asian Scholars, 21*(1), 2–11.

Pocock, Chris. (Ed.). (1992–1994). *Memory and rage.* A quarterly newsletter on femicide.

Radford, Jill, & Diana E. H. Russell (Eds.). (1992). *Femicide: The politics of woman killing.* New York: Twayne/Gale Group.

Rahman, Hamida. (1983). Femicide due to religion and superstition. In *Regional Seminar on "Femicide" in the Pacific Asian Countries. Proceedings and findings of the Regional Seminar on "Femicide" in the Pacific Asian Countries* (pp. 60–69). Dhaka, Bangladesh: Bangladesh Jatiyo Mahila Ainjibi Samity.

Regional Seminar on "Femicide" in the Pacific Asian Countries. Proceedings and findings of the Regional Seminar on "Femicide" in the Pacific Asian Countries. (1983). Dhaka, Bangladesh: Bangladesh Jatiyo Mahila Ainjibi Samity.

Russell, Diana E. H. (1990). Femicide: The murder of wives. In Diana E. H. Russell, *Rape in marriage* (pp. 286–299). Bloomington: Indiana University Press.

Russell, Diana E. H. (1992). Femicidal lynching in the United States. In Jill Radford & Diana E. H. Russell (Eds.), *Femicide: The politics of woman killing* (pp. 53–61). New York: Twayne/Gale Group.

Russell, Diana E. H. (1992). Femicidal rapist targets Asian women. In Jill Radford & Diana E. H. Russell (Eds.), *Femicide: The politics of woman killing* (pp. 163–166). New York: Twayne/Gale Group.

Russell, Diana E. H. (1992). Slavery and femicide. In Jill Radford & Diana E. H. Russell (Eds.), *Femicide: The politics of woman killing* (pp. 167–169). New York: Twayne/Gale Group.

Russell, Diana E. H. (1998). Femicide. In Helen Tierney (Ed.), *Encyclopedia of women's studies* (2nd rev., exp. ed.) (pp. 469–471). Westport, CT: Greenwood Press.

Russell, Diana E. H., & Candida Ellis. (1992). Annihilation by murder and by the media: The other Atlanta femicides. In Jill Radford & Diana E. H. Russell (Eds.), *Femicide: The politics of woman killing* (pp. 161–162). New York: Twayne/Gale Group.

Scassa, Teresa. (1993, Spring). Sentencing intimate femicide: A comment on *R. v. Doyle* (1992). *Dalhousie Law Journal, 16*(1), 270–282.

Skilbeck, Rod. (1995). The shroud over Algeria: Femicide, Islamism and the hijab. *Journal of Arabic, Islamic and Middle Eastern Studies, 2*(2), 43–54.

Stout, Karen D. (1987). *Intimate femicide: Individual and state factors associated with the killing of women by men.* Unpublished doctoral dissertation, University of Texas, Austin.

Stout, Karen D. (1989, April). Intimate femicide: Effect of legislation and social services. *Affilia, 4*(2), 21–30.

Stout, Karen D. (1991, February). Intimate femicide: A national demographic overview. *Violence Update, 1*(6), 3, 9.

Stout, Karen D. (1993). Intimate femicide: A study of men who have killed their mates. *Journal of Offender Rehabilitation, 19*(3–4), 81–94.

Stout, Karen D., & Beverly McPhail. (1998). Battered women who kill and femicide: The final acts of violence against women. In Karen D. Stout & Beverly McPhail, *Confronting sexism and violence against women: A challenge for social work* (pp. 288–311). New York: Addison Wesley Longman.

Testimony on Femicide. (1976). In Diana E. H. Russell & Nicole Van de Ven (Eds.), *Crimes against women: Proceedings of the International Tribunal* (2nd ed.) (pp. 144–150). San Francisco: Frog in the Well.

Tshwaranang Legal Advocacy Centre. (1999). Femicide. In *The national legal manual for counsellors of rape and battered women* (pp. 421–438). Johannesburg, South Africa: Tshwaranang.

Vetten, Lisa. (1995). *"Man shoots wife": A pilot study detailing intimate femicide in Gauteng, South Africa.* Johannesburg, South Africa: People Opposing Woman Abuse.

Watts, Charlotte, Susanna Osam, & Everjoice Win. (1995). *The private is public: A study of violence against women in southern Africa.* Harare, Zimbabwe: Women in Law and Development in Africa.

Wilson, Margo, Martin Daly, & Joanna E. Scheib. (1997). Femicide: An evolutionary psychological perspective. In Patricia Adair Gowaty (Ed.), *Feminism and evolutionary biology: Boundaries, intersections, and frontiers* (pp. 431–465). New York: Chapman & Hall; International Thomson Publications.

Women We Honour Action Committee. (1990, December). *Final Report to the Ontario Women's Directorate: Research Project on Homicides Related to Domestic Violence Against Women.* Unpublished manuscript.

About the Editors
and Contributors

Diana E. H. Russell obtained a Postgraduate Diploma from the London School of Economics and Political Science (with Distinction) in 1961. She was the recipient of LSE's Mostyn Lloyd Memorial Prize, awarded to the best student studying for the Postgraduate Diploma. She subsequently received her Ph.D. from Harvard University in 1970.

Dr. Russell is Professor Emerita of Sociology at Mills College, Oakland, California, where she taught sociology and women's studies for 22 years. She is author, co-author, editor, or co-editor of 16 books. Her book *The Secret Trauma: Incest in the Lives of Girls and Women* was co-winner the 1986 C. Wright Mills Award for outstanding social science research that addresses an important social issue.

Dr. Russell, who lives in Berkeley, California, has lectured widely in the United States and abroad about the political situation in South Africa, rape, incest, child sexual abuse in general, pornography, femicide, and all forms of violence against women.

Roberta A. Harmes obtained her B.A. in Legal Studies at the University of California at Berkeley. Since 1995, she has been employed as the periodical coordinator at Colorado College. She has also been an independent feminist researcher for 10 years. Ms. Harmes has assisted Dr. Russell with several of her books, for example, *Making Violence Sexy: Feminist Views on Pornography*, *Dangerous Relationships: Pornography, Misogyny and Rape*, and *The Epidemic of Rape and Child Sexual Abuse*, by locating library materials, downloading materials from the Web, and obtaining hard-to-find statistics and numerous other types of information from all kinds of sources. Ms. Harmes has also co-published bibliographies on marital rape with Dr. Russell and Laura X.

Chrystos is a Two-Spirited Menominee activist, writer, and painter. She was born off the reservation in San Francisco on November 7, 1946. She is the author of *Not Vanishing*, *Dream On*, *In Her I Am*, *Fugitive Colors*, *Fire Power*, and *Wilder Reis*, as well as a contributor to numerous anthologies, most recently *Reinventing the Enemy's Language* and *My Home as I Remember*. She travels internationally, giving poetry performances and speeches. Her political activities include work against lesbian battering and other violence against women and on behalf of political prisoners, particularly Native women; literacy for youngsters of color; and land and treaty rights. Other areas of political activity include internalized racism workshops for women of color; ablism; and issues of environmental abuse. She is proud to have marched in another Take Back the Night in April 2000, as she has for more than 30 years. She is self-educated and lives alone in a small rental cabin in the Pacific Northwest.

Maria Crawford has a B.A. in sociology and an honors degree in social work. She has worked closely with assaulted women for more than 14 years. Her research interests include lethal violence in intimate partner relationships as well as designing alternative interventions aimed at reducing intimate femicide.

Myrna Dawson is a Ph.D. candidate in the department of sociology and a junior research fellow at the Centre of Criminology at the University of Toronto. Her research interests include criminal justice, violent victimization, and gender. Her current work examines the effect of victim–offender relationships on criminal justice decision making in cases of violent crime.

Rosemary Gartner is director of the Centre of Criminology and professor of sociology at the University of Toronto. She continues to do research into femicide and intimate femicide from a historical and comparative perspective, using data from the study described in this volume and from another study of four urban areas for the period 1900–1990. With Candace Kruttschnitt, she is also conducting a study of women's experiences of incarceration in two California prisons during the 1990s.

Sharon K. Hom is a professor of law at the City University of New York School of Law at Queens and a supervising attorney in the Immigrant and Refugee Rights Clinic. She was a Fulbright scholar in the People's Republic of China (1986–1988) and continues to be active in U.S.–China legal training exchanges and Chinese women's studies work. She sits on the boards of Human Rights Watch/Asia and Human Rights in China, and she also served as a judge for the Global Tribunal on Violence Against Women, convened for the Fourth World Conference on Women and the NGO Forum 95. She was a scholar in residence at the Rockefeller Foundation's Bellagio Center (summer 2000), working on a collaborative civil/human rights project.

Simha F. Landau is Mildred and Benjamin Professor of Criminology at the Hebrew University of Jerusalem, Israel. He received his Ph.D. in 1973 from the Hebrew University. His major field of research is violence and aggression, including violence in the family. He has published extensively on this and other topics in professional criminological and victimological journals and books. He is currently involved in an extensive study on femicide in Israel. He has held numerous visiting positions in universities and research institutions, among them the University of Pennsylvania, University of Illinois at Chicago, University of California, Berkeley, Home Office Research Unit in England, and the Max Planck Institute for International Criminal Law and Criminology in Freiburg, Germany.

Shereen Winifred Mills started her career as a public interest/human rights lawyer, working mostly with indigent people in South Africa. She is now involved in gender activism, doing research at the Gender Research Project of the University of the Witwatersrand in Johannesburg. Her work focuses on women's rights—particularly ensuring that women obtain substantive access to the right to equality. In 1998 she was awarded the Maria Pia Gratton Fellowship to the University of Illinois at Urbana–Champaign in the United States.

Jenny Mouzos, B.A., obtained a graduate diploma in criminology at the University of Melbourne, Australia. She has been employed at the Australian Institute of Criminology since July 1998. She is currently a research analyst at the institute, where she manages the National Homicide Monitoring Program and the National Firearms Monitoring Program. She has published a number of reports on issues relating to firearms and various types of homicide, including a study on femicide. She has just completed an extensive study examining 10-year trends and patterns of homicide and homicidal encounters in Australia.

Susanna Osam was a consultant for Women in Law and Development in Africa (WiLDAF).

Susan Hattis Rolef, Ph.D., was born in Haifa in 1943 to parents who came from Chicago in 1932. She obtained a B.Sc. in international relations at the London School of Economics and Political Science in 1965 and a Ph.D. at the University Institute for Higher International Studies in Geneva in 1970. She taught at the Hebrew University in Jerusalem from 1969 to 1975.

In addition to her academic work, Dr. Rolef worked for Yigal Allon and later for the Israel Labor party from 1977 to 1994. She has been working for the Knesset (Israeli parliament) as editor of the Knesset Web site since 1994. She has also assisted in setting up an information and research center in the Knesset. She is the author of many books and articles, including *The Political Dictionary of the State of Israel*, and wrote a weekly column in the *Jerusalem Post* from 1983 to 1998.

Rod Skilbeck obtained a B.A. (Hons.) from the University of Melbourne followed by an M.A. (Hons.) from Macquarie University. He has specialized since 1991 in the politics of the Middle East, concentrating on Algeria. His thesis ("Poles of Permissiveness: Power, Pop and God in Algeria") examined the historical roots of the contemporary civil conflict in Algeria and the spheres that the conflict has encompassed, including music, ethnicity, sexual politics, and urbanization. He has also published a chapter on Algerian music and its political effects in R. Kevin Lacey & Ralph M. Coury (Eds.), *The Arab-African and Islamic Worlds: Interdisciplinary Studies*. Peter Lang Publishing, October 2000. He currently manages a company that provides Internet-based academic simulations along with other applications.

Karen D. Stout is an associate professor of social work at the University of Houston, Graduate School of Social Work, where she is currently serving as chairperson of the political social work concentration. She lost her first therapy client to femicide before she was 23 years of age and remains forever committed to ending femicide and all forms of violence against women.

Charlotte Watts is a lecturer in epidemiology and health policy in the health policy unit of the department of public health and policy at the London School of Hygiene and Tropical Medicine in London, England. Between 1994 and 1997 she was transferred to the Musasa Project—an innovative rape prevention project in Zimbabwe—and the University of Zimbabwe. While at the university, she designed a comparative international study of femicide as well as conducting research on the prevalence of violence against women and the health implications of this problem.

Watts is the senior technical advisor to the World Health Organization's multicountry study on Women's Health and Domestic Violence Against Women. Her research interests include the international public health burden of violence against women, the linkages between violence against women and HIV/AIDS, and the development and evaluation of community interventions to address violence against women. She is currently teaching a course on Science, Politics, and Policy.

Everjoice Win is a Zimbabwean feminist. She has worked with various NGOs in Africa, including the Pan African Women in Law and Development in Africa (WiLDAF) and Akina Mama wa Afrika (AMWA). Her most recent assignment was with the Commonwealth Fund for Technical Cooperation, where she was an adviser to the Commission on Gender Equality in South Africa.

Index